Hiking
Waterfalls
Pennsylvania

Hiking
Waterfalls
Pennsylvania

A Guide to the State's Best Waterfall Hikes

Second Edition

Johnny Molloy

FALCON GUIDES

ESSEX, CONNECTICUT

FALCONGUIDES®

An imprint of The Globe Pequot Publishing Group, Inc.
64 South Main Street
Essex, CT 06426
www.globepequot.com

Falcon and FalconGuides are registered trademarks and Make Adventure
Your Story is a trademark of The Globe Pequot Publishing Group, Inc.

Distributed by NATIONAL BOOK NETWORK

British Library Cataloguing in Publication Information available

Library of Congress Cataloging-in-Publication Data available

ISBN 978-1-4930-7579-9 (paper: alk. paper)
ISBN 978-1-4930-7580-5 (electronic)

Printed in India

Contents

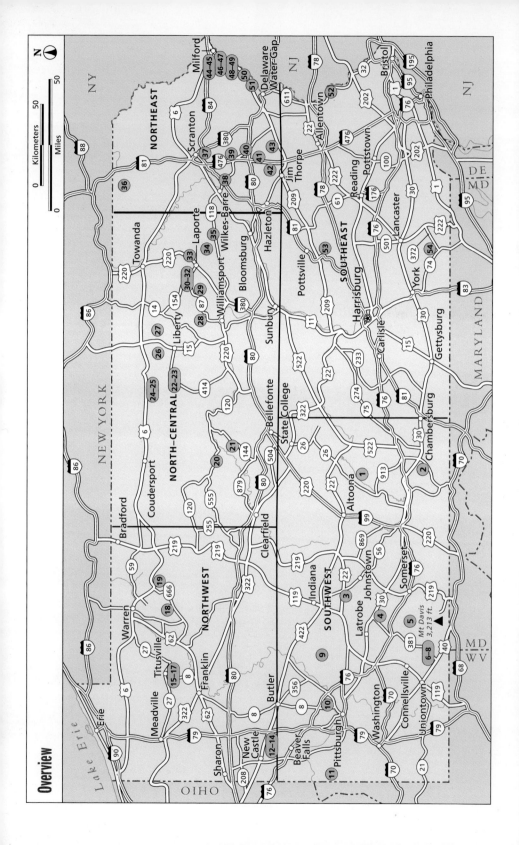

Overview

Acknowledgments

Thanks to all the people who build and maintain trails leading to Pennsylvania's myriad waterfalls. Thanks to Rusty Glessner for his love of Pennsylvania waterfalls and for taking the finest waterfall photos I have ever seen. Thanks to my wife, Keri Anne, for her support. Moreover, thank the Lord for creating waterfalls in the first place.

Waterfalls such as this one at Salt Springs State Park display myriad enchanting forms (hike 36).
RUSTY GLESSNER

The trail affords a side view of Alpha Falls (hike 14).

Introduction

Welcome to the completely updated second edition of *Hiking Waterfalls Pennsylvania*. What a pleasure it is to explore the waterfalls of Pennsylvania and to share them with you! Waterfalls are special—arguably the most enchanting spectacle in nature. At their most basic, they are simply falling water, yet after coming upon a waterfall, we are captivated and happily surprised at their transitory beauty.

Moreover, when combining waterfalls with hiking, you construct a superlative outdoor experience. Hiking to a waterfall adds a reward at the end of the trail for your efforts. Additionally, while hiking to waterfalls you will likely see other jewels in the sparking crown of nature.

Although simply moving water, waterfalls display a variety of characteristics—whether it is the wide, low tumble of Tobyhanna Falls near Blakeslee, the powerful roar of Ohiopyle Falls on the Youghiogheny River, or the delicate descent of Silverthread Falls in the Delaware Water Gap National Recreation Area. Perhaps the variety of cataracts found along Dingmans Creek comes to mind, or the geological fascination that is Hector Falls. Maybe you think of the oft-photographed spillers at Ricketts Glen State Park.

And there is more, for the hikes along the way to the waterfalls harbor additional rewards. Walk the giant hiker suspension bridge when visiting Boughton Falls, soak in the spectacular scenery of the Pine Creek Gorge en route to Bohen Run Falls, or walk the magnificently forested valley of Fall Brook at Salt Springs State Park. Each place is further enhanced by having both waterfalls and other superlative natural features we can enjoy on our hike.

Some of you may already have a favorite Pennsylvania waterfall, or maybe you are looking for new waterfalls to visit. In this guide, fifty-four hikes will lead you to over a hundred named waterfalls! Among these, even the most experienced Pennsylvania waterfaller will discover new destinations.

Additionally, anyone who has gone to a waterfall multiple times understands that waterfalls change with circumstances and seasons. This is a function of rain and time of year. For example, in spring you can see the white plunge of Jonathan Run Falls at Ohiopyle State Park, but that waterfall gushing in spring can slow to a trickle in autumn. However, a drenching summer thunderstorm may morph Frankfort Mineral Springs Falls into a brown roiling froth, and a frigid Arctic cold front can turn Dutchman Falls into a frozen ice sculpture. Of course, the changing seasons frame the waterfalls differently month to month. The muted tones of winter's leafless hardwoods or snowscape form a setting dissimilar to the colorful leaves of autumn or the shady forest of summer.

Using this guide you can explore over a hundred named waterfalls (plus other unnamed cataracts) stretched all across the Keystone State. The hikes range from quarter-mile jaunts to 10-mile treks, though most are on the shorter side.

Let's face it: In our rush-rush electronic universe we are hurriedly looking for an authority, "someone who knows," to help us pursue our goal of hiking to Pennsylvania's waterfalls. This is my approach: Imagine you and me relaxing around a campfire, and you ask about the best waterfall hikes in Pennsylvania. I tell you as one friend would tell another, rather than reading like a dry, dull textbook. Pennsylvania's waterfalls are too captivating for that! Yet this guide conveys concise, organized information to help busy people make the most of their limited and precious outdoor recreation time and provides an opportunity to experience the best waterfall hikes that can be had in the Keystone State.

While contemplating the waterfall hikes in this guide, the cataracts of the Delaware Water Gap National Recreation Area come to mind first. The popular Raymondskill Falls stands out, since it is Pennsylvania's highest cataract at 150 feet, as does the powerful push of Hackers Falls and the stair-step spillers of Hornbecks Creek. The three cataracts of Factory Falls, Fulmer Falls, and Deer Leap Falls and the incredible trail to see them display a concentration of highlights. Tumbling Waters drops off a stone shelf into an inviting glen before pushing onward off a cliff.

In addition, there are other waterfalls protected in Pennsylvania's state parks and state forests. Pioneer Falls creates a picturesque scene as it tumbles down a layered stone shelf into a mini-gorge plated with smooth, flat stone. At Beltzville State Park, Wild Creek Falls takes an unusual bumpy ride, while easily reached Rainbow Falls at Trough Creek State Park spills in stages, creating a variety of looks within one cataract. You can visit Buttermilk Falls and Lukes Falls at Lehigh Gorge State Park, or take the Double Run Nature Trail to see Cottonwood Falls at Worlds End State Park.

At McConnells Mill State Park, you start at a historic covered bridge then walk along renowned Slippery Rock Creek to visit misty Kildoo Falls. This preserve also harbors Hells Hollow Falls, where you can not only enjoy the pour-over but also an adjacent limekiln. Moreover, we have to mention what is arguably America's greatest waterfall hike at Ricketts Glen State Park, where over twenty cataracts can be admired on one trek!

Pennsylvania's state forests and game lands contain nearly 1.5 million acres and are not only repositories for human and natural history but also home to mountains, streams, wildlife, and waterfalls. Grab two cataracts on one hike when heading to Yost Run Falls and Kyler Fork Falls in Sproul State Forest. Angel Falls makes its dramatic drop along the Loyalsock Trail in Loyalsock State Forest, while feathery Cole Run Falls spills over its ledge at Forbes State Forest. Lesser-visited Jarrett Falls makes its pitch in state game land.

How fortunate we are to have these preserved lands laced with trails that lead to varied waterfalls! The foresight of creating parks, forests, and game lands that protect waterfalls and building trails within them benefits us greatly, lending opportunities to experience the aquatic splendor that runs through the Keystone State. These destinations also harbor the natural beauty for which Pennsylvania is known, from wilderness cataracts to waterfalls flowing through deep gorges to urban falls. May the

Rode Falls is pretty and delicate at a lower water level (hike 30).
RUSTY GLESSNER

hikes presented in this book help you appreciate the fantastic and varied waterfalls of Pennsylvania. Enjoy!

Helpful Hints for Photographing Waterfalls

Since all the hikes in this guide take us to waterfalls, it is only natural that many of us like to photograph these cascades, flumes, and cataracts of Pennsylvania. I photograph every waterfall I visit, preserving the collection on my computer and printing and framing some of my favorites. These are not all quality photographs—just snapshots to preserve a memory, as folks often do with their smartphones.

Not every photograph I take of a waterfall is great. Getting an excellent waterfall shot takes time, effort, and a little luck. For the best shots, you need a tripod, a digital camera with manual settings, and early morning or late afternoon light. Capturing the personality of a waterfall may mean several visits during different times of the year. Here are a few hints that may help you become a better waterfall photographer:

Tripod. You need a sturdy tripod because you cannot hold a camera sufficiently steady when using slow shutter speeds. Be sure the tripod is compact and light-weight so you will be willing to carry it with you no matter how long the water-fall hike. Set your camera and use a timer, reducing shake caused by pressing the shutter button.

ISO speed. The ISO setting on most modern digital cameras is designed to approximate the ISO speed of a chosen film and corresponding camera setting used in a traditional film camera. The lowest ISO number you will find on a digital camera, usually 80 but sometimes lower, is generally the preferred setting for shooting waterfalls. This number will yield the greatest detail, sharpness, effects, and color accuracy.

Shutter speed. Slow shutter speeds give a sense of movement. The movement of flowing water is completely stopped at 1/2000 second. The fastest water will soften starting at 1/60 second. At 1/15 second, water movement will be clearly seen, but not be completely blurred. Most waterfall photographs are shot at 1/8 second or slower to produce a soft quality. After a while you will find the shutter speed you like most, although the flow rate and speed of the waterfall will dictate your shutter speed.

Time of day. Midday sun creates harsh lighting and shadows. Visit a waterfall at daybreak or an hour before sunset, and use the wonderful quality of the light. Cloudy days afford additional photo opportunities.

Exposure. The white water of a falls will often cause underexposure of your shot, making the water gray and the foliage slightly dark. The beauty of digital cameras is being able to see what you just shot and adjust aperture, shutter speed, or ISO setting.

Perspective. Waterfall photographs need a reference to indicate their size. To give a feeling of depth and space, use foreground elements such as trees, rocks, and people. Try to frame the waterfall.

Position. Shoot from the top, bottom, or side of the falls. Treat the waterfall like a piece of architecture. Be creative while shooting the waterfall from different perspectives.

People. The high reflectance of water tends to underexpose people in a waterfall photograph. Position people considering proper lighting for both them and the waterfall.

Rainbows. If you are lucky enough to find a rainbow at the end of a waterfall, take as many pictures as you can. Shoot at different settings, then delete the least worthy pictures back at home on your computer.

Watch the horizon. Horizon lines should be level and in general not placed in the center of the composition. In the image area, look for wasted space, light and dark areas, and distracting elements.

The above tips will increase your chances for a spectacular waterfall photograph, making a lasting memory of your Pennsylvania waterfall hike.

The upper drop of Tumbling Waters (hike 50)

How to Use This Guide

Take a close enough look, and you will find that this guide contains just about everything you will ever need to choose, plan for, enjoy, and survive a waterfall hike in Pennsylvania. Stuffed with useful area information, *Hiking Waterfalls Pennsylvania* features fifty-four mapped and cued hikes leading to over a hundred named waterfalls, grouped together geographically. Following is an outline of the book's major components.

Each hike starts with a short **summary** of the hike's highlights. These quick overviews give you a taste of the hiking adventure and the waterfall(s) to be visited. You'll learn about the trail terrain and what surprises each route has to offer.

Following the overview, you will find the **hike specs**—quick, nitty-gritty details of not only the waterfall but also the hike to it:

Waterfall height: This is how far the waterfall drops from top to bottom.

Waterfall beauty: This is a 1 to 5 number, 5 being the most beautiful waterfall.

Distance: The total distance of the recommended route—one-way for loop hikes or the round-trip on an out-and-back or lollipop hike. Options are additional.

Difficulty: Each hike has been assigned a level of difficulty—easy, moderate, or difficult. The rating system was developed from several sources and personal experience. These levels are meant to be a guideline only and may prove easier or harder for different people depending on ability and physical fitness. An easy waterfall hike will generally cover 3 miles or less total trip distance, with minimal elevation gain and a paved or smooth-surfaced dirt trail. A moderate waterfall hike will cover up to 7 miles total trip distance in one day, with moderate elevation gain and potentially rough terrain. A difficult hike may cover more than 10 miles total trip distance in one day, have strenuous elevation gains, and/or have rough or rocky terrain.

Hiking time: The average time it will take to cover the route. It is based on the total distance, elevation gain, and condition and difficulty of the trail. Your fitness level will also affect your time.

Trail surface: General information about what to expect underfoot.

Other trail users: Such as horseback riders, mountain bikers, inline skaters, etc.

Canine compatibility: Know the trail regulations before you take your dog hiking with you. Dogs are not allowed on several waterfall hikes in this book.

Land status: City park, state park or forest, national park or forest, etc.

Fees and permits: Whether you need to carry any money with you for park entrance fees and permits.

Maps: This is a list of other maps to supplement the maps in this book. USGS maps are the best source for accurate topographical information, but the local park map may show trails that are more recent. Use both.

Trail contact: This is the phone number and website for the local land manager in charge of all the trails within the selected hike. Get trail access information before you head out, or contact the land manager after your visit if you see problems with trail erosion, damage, or misuse.

The **Finding the trailhead** section gives you dependable driving directions to where you'll want to park. This also includes GPS trailhead coordinates, which you can plug into your device and then navigate to the trailhead. **The Hike** is the meat of the chapter. Detailed and honest, it is a carefully researched impression of the waterfall, the hike, and interesting things you may see along the way, both natural and human. Under **Miles and Directions**, mileage cues identify all turns and trail name changes, as well as points of interest.

How to Use the Maps

Overview map: This map shows the location of each hike in the area by hike number.

Route map: This is your primary guide to each hike. It shows the waterfalls, all of the accessible roads and trails, points of interest, water, landmarks, and geographical features. It also distinguishes trails from roads and paved roads from unpaved roads. The selected route is highlighted, and directional arrows point the way.

Trail Finder

Hike #	Hike Name	Best Hikes to Tall Waterfalls	Best Hikes to Secluded Waterfalls	Best Waterfall Hikes for Swimming	Best Waterfall Hikes for Children	Best Waterfall Hikes for Nature Lovers	Best Waterfall Hikes for Backpackers
1	Rainbow Falls				●	●	
2	Jarrett Falls		●				
3	Buttermilk Falls of Indiana County	●					
4	Adams Falls				●		
5	Cole Run Falls		●		●		
6	Ohiopyle Falls, The Slides, Cascades Waterfall				●	●	
7	Fechter Run Falls, Upper Jonathan Run Falls, Jonathan Run Falls, Sugar Run Falls	●				●	
8	Cucumber Falls	●				●	
9	Jackson Falls					●	
10	Fall Run Falls	●			●		
11	Frankfort Mineral Springs Falls				●	●	
12	Hells Hollow Falls		●			●	
13	Kildoo Falls					●	

Hike #	Hike Name	Best Hikes to Tall Waterfalls	Best Hikes to Secluded Waterfalls	Best Waterfall Hikes for Swimming	Best Waterfall Hikes for Children	Best Waterfall Hikes for Nature Lovers	Best Waterfall Hikes for Backpackers
14	Alpha Falls	●			●		
15	Pioneer Falls	●				●	
16	Plum Dungeon Falls	●	●				
17	Boughton Falls, Miller Falls, Lower Miller Falls		●				
18	Logan Falls		●		●		●
19	Hector Falls		●		●	●	●
20	Round Island Run Falls		●			●	●
21	Yost Run Falls, Kyler Fork Falls		●		●	●	●
22	Stone Quarry Run Falls, Water Tank Run Falls	●			●		
23	Jerry Run Falls, Bohen Run Falls	●				●	
24	Falls of the Turkey Path at Colton Point State Park	●					
25	Falls of the Turkey Path at Leonard Harrison State Park	●			●	●	

Hike #	Hike Name	Best Hikes to Tall Waterfalls	Best Hikes to Secluded Waterfalls	Best Waterfall Hikes for Swimming	Best Waterfall Hikes for Children	Best Waterfall Hikes for Nature Lovers	Best Waterfall Hikes for Backpackers
26	Sand Run Falls	●	●	●		●	●
27	Fall Brook Falls		●			●	
28	Jacoby Falls	●					
29	Angel Falls, Gipson Falls	●				●	
30	Rode Falls		●				●
31	Cottonwood Falls				●	●	
32	Alpine Falls		●				●
33	Dutchman Falls			●	●		
34	Sullivan Falls	●		●	●		
35	Falls of Ricketts Glen	●			●	●	
36	Falls of Salt Springs State Park				●	●	
37	Nay Aug Falls				●	●	
38	Seven Tubs			●	●	●	
39	Choke Creek Falls		●	●			●
40	Tobyhanna Falls				●	●	

Hike #	Hike Name	Best Hikes to Tall Waterfalls	Best Hikes to Secluded Waterfalls	Best Waterfall Hikes for Swimming	Best Waterfall Hikes for Children	Best Waterfall Hikes for Nature Lovers	Best Waterfall Hikes for Backpackers
41	Hawk Falls			•	•		
42	Buttermilk Falls, Lukes Falls	•			•		
43	Wild Creek Falls		•		•		
44	Hackers Falls				•	•	
45	Raymondskill Falls	•					
46	Factory Falls, Fulmer Falls, Deer Leap Falls				•	•	
47	Dingmans Falls, Silverthread Falls	•			•	•	
48	Lower Hornbecks Falls	•	•		•	•	
49	Upper Hornbecks Falls	•				•	
50	Tumbling Waters	•	•			•	
51	Bushkill Falls				•	•	
52	High Falls at Ringing Rocks Park				•		
53	Sweet Arrow Lake Falls				•		
54	Mill Creek Falls of York County				•	•	

Map Legend

Municipal

≡⟨81⟩≡ Interstate Highway

≡⟨209⟩≡ US Highway

≡⟨381⟩≡ State Road

━━━━ Local/County Road

= = = = Unpaved Road

┝━━┥ Railroad

•—•—• Power Line

·· — ·· — State Boundary

Trails

------ Featured Trail

------ Trail

Water Features

Body of Water

Marsh

River/Creek

Intermittent Stream

Waterfall

Rapids

Spring

Land Management

National Recreation Area

State/County Park/Forest

Game Lands/Natural Area

Symbols

▲ Backcountry Campsite

▥ Boardwalk/Steps

🛥 Boat Launch

≍ Bridge

■ Building/Point of Interest

Ⱥ Campground

† Cemetery

▬ Dam

Ⱦ Gate

🅿 Parking

▲ Peak/Elevation

🛉 Picnic Area

👥 Ranger Station/Park Office

🚻 Restroom

◈ Scenic View

○ Town

⟨20⟩ Trailhead

❓ Visitor/Information Center

♿ Wheelchair Accessible

Waterfall Hikes of
Southwest Pennsylvania

Cole Run Falls has a historically low flow in autumn (hike 5).

1 Rainbow Falls

This waterfall walk at Trough Creek State Park presents a layered cataract plus geological and other aquatic scenery, mainly in the form of Balanced Rock and Great Trough Creek. Leave the trailhead in deep riparian forest around Great Trough Creek, then cross a cool suspension bridge over the waterway. From there walk to the base of layered, stair-stepping Rainbow Falls, where Abbot Run tumbles into Great Trough Creek. Next, make the short climb along Rainbow Falls to Balanced Rock, hanging on the edge of the gorge above Great Trough Creek.

Waterfall height: 30 feet
Waterfall beauty: 4
Distance: 0.6-mile out-and-back
Difficulty: Easy
Hiking time: About ½ hour
Trail surface: Natural
Other trail users: None

Canine compatibility: Leashed pets allowed
Land status: State park
Fees and permits: None
Maps: Trough Creek State Park; USGS Entriken
Trail contact: Trough Creek State Park, (814) 658-3847, www.dcnr.state.pa.us/stateparks

Finding the trailhead: From the town of Saxton, take PA 913 north for 2.2 miles to Little Valley Road. Turn left and follow Little Valley Road for 6.4 miles to the intersection of Old Plank Road. Keep straight on Little Valley Road for 1.8 more miles to reach an intersection and the Trough Creek State Park Ranger Station. Turn left here on Trough Creek Drive and follow it for 1.8 miles to the Suspension Bridge / Rainbow Falls / Balanced Rock trailhead. GPS: 40.322238, -78.129847

The Hike

Trough Creek State Park not only features Rainbow Falls, but also has many other attractions that can enhance your visit. Geological highlights include Raven Rock, Copperas Rock, and Balanced Rock, the last of which you can see during your walk to Rainbow Falls. Historically speaking, the preserve features a historic furnace, forge site, dam, and cemetery. Almost all these sites are connected by a trail network coursing through the Great Trough Creek valley. The state park also has fine facilities, including a lodge, campground, and picnic areas. I suggest expanding your range of activities while visiting this fine Pennsylvania state park.

Nevertheless, being waterfall lovers, we want to see the aquatic attraction that is Rainbow Falls. The walk to the angled spiller starts off in fun fashion as you take the swinging bridge over Great Trough Creek, an alluring waterway in its own right. You then follow the stream amid wooded, everywhere-you-look state-park-level scenery to reach the confluence of Abbot Run and Great Trough Creek.

Here you find Rainbow Falls, so named for the occasional occurrence of refracted light through the lowermost curtain drop of around 10 feet at the base of the cataract.

Winter finds Rainbow Falls running full amid scattered snow.
RUSTY GLESSNER

You will see that Rainbow Falls is such an angled cascade that it is hard to pin down the exact height of the waterfall. The final drops of Abbot Run stairstep down in differing gradients before meeting Great Trough Creek. Waterfall visitors do agree that Rainbow Falls has two primary drops of around 10 feet each, one the aforementioned base of the falls and the other upstream a bit. See for yourself and calculate your height of the falls.

While at Rainbow Falls, go ahead and make the short climb to Balanced Rock. You will hike along the falls then turn away and reach a bluff upon which stands a large angled boulder precariously perched well above Great Trough Creek. Try to get here early because after seeing these two physical features, you will likely want to visit more of Trough Creek State Park.

Miles and Directions

0.0   From the trailhead, take a wide gravel track toward Great Trough Creek.

0.1   Reach the suspension bridge over Great Trough Creek. Cross the span, admiring the fine scenery up and down the stream. Come to a trail intersection immediately after crossing

Balanced Rock teeters on its precarious perch.

the bridge. The Rhododendron Trail heads left, but you turn right on the Abbot Run Trail under a canopy of yellow birch, black birch, and rhododendron. Admire the mossy boulder field above you.

0.2 Cross the bridge over Abbot Run at the base of Rainbow Falls. The lowermost segment of Rainbow Falls creates a curtain drop in front of you, while stair-step cascades rise above. Note the other curtain drop upstream. Follow the steps along the right side of the falls and climb along the cataract. Just ahead, curve right toward Balanced Rock, ascending along the base of a cliff line above Abbot Run.

0.3 Reach Balanced Rock and a wide stone ledge. Look down toward Rainbow Falls and Great Trough Creek. Admire the perched boulder from different angles. Backtrack to the trailhead.

0.6 Arrive back at the trailhead, completing the waterfall walk.

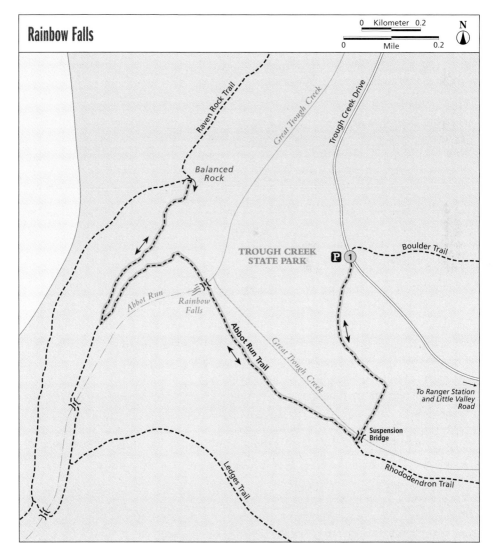

Rainbow Falls

2 Jarrett Falls

The hike to Jarrett Falls starts below the dam of Meadow Grounds Lake. Below the dam you will follow Roaring Run as the changing valley cuts between parallel ridges. The trail and stream crisscross and you then reach Jarrett Falls, a stair-step spiller at the end of the line.

Waterfall height: 11 feet
Waterfall beauty: 4
Distance: 3.4-mile out-and-back
Difficulty: Moderate, does have creek crossings
Hiking time: About 2 hours
Trail surface: Natural
Other trail users: None

Canine compatibility: Leashed pets allowed
Land status: State game lands
Fees and permits: None
Maps: State Game Lands 053; USGS Meadow Grounds
Trail contact: Pennsylvania Game Commission, Southcentral Region,(833) 742-4868, www .pgc.pa.gov

Finding the trailhead: From the intersection of US 522 and Lincoln Way in downtown McConnellsburg, take Lincoln Way west for 1 mile to Back Run Road. Turn left and follow Back Run Road for 1 mile, then turn right onto Meadow Ground Road, which you follow for 1.6 miles, surmounting Meadow Mountain. The road turns to gravel. Continue for just 0.1 mile after descending from the mountain crest and veer left on gravel Mountain Drive. Follow it southwest to come alongside what was the lake, then make a final right turn to reach the dam parking area after 0.9 mile. The hike starts at the east end of the dam. GPS: 39.904917, -78.057733

The Hike

Lying between Meadow Mountain and Scrub Mountain in south-central Pennsylvania, not far from the Maryland border, State Game Lands No. 53 is dominated by Meadow Grounds Lake, slowing the water of Roaring Run. State Game Lands No. 53 covers a little over 5,000 acres among the nearly 1.5 million acres managed by the Pennsylvania Game Commission.

Back in 1965, Roaring Run was impounded, becoming Meadow Grounds Lake, and became a popular fishing venue for Fulton County and adjacent communities. Decades later, the dam was deemed unsafe and the lake was drained during 2013. However, in 2021 the 200-acre impoundment was refilled after the spillway was enlarged. Once again anglers are fishing from piers or from their boats, and the waters of Roaring Run drain the valley between Meadow Mountain and Scrub Mountain, rushing south from the dam outflow.

Meadow Grounds Lake affects Jarrett Falls in terms of flow release from the dam. Generally speaking, waterfalls below dams have a more constant flow of water, making them good choices during the dry times of late summer and autumn.

Jarrett Falls displays its multifaceted look.

The dam is even more intriguing for waterfall hikers heading to Jarrett Falls, for the hike starts at the east side of the dam and crosses over to its west end. Here you will see a sign indicating the Jarrett Trail, named for long-serving state game warden Carl E. Jarrett, who patrolled Fulton County from 1954 to 1978. The hike then turns down the Roaring Run valley, spanning the dam outflow on a bridge. The path settles down as a singletrack trail, winding alongside Roaring Run, both southbound. Roaring Run flows gently to your left. Pines, mountain laurel, and oaks reflect the dry nature of the upper valley.

Feeder streams enter Roaring Run, adding to its flow. Ahead, you cross over to the left bank of Roaring Run at a power line clearing. This is a potentially confusing area, with user-created trails heading down both banks in the clearing, leading waterfall hikers astray. The now-deeper valley begins to show birch and surviving hemlock. The creek picks up a little more steam here, increasing in shoals and rapids.

A hiker bridge puts you on the right bank. Big boulders clog the valley in places. Expect to step over some fallen hemlock as the valley transitions away from this evergreen. The stream and the trail drop at a faster rate and Roaring Run continues to demonstrate this with more drops, including some minor warm-up cascades.

You then come to Jarrett Falls. Heading downstream, you will first see an enormous overhanging cliff line to the right of the trail at the brink of the falls. This is a

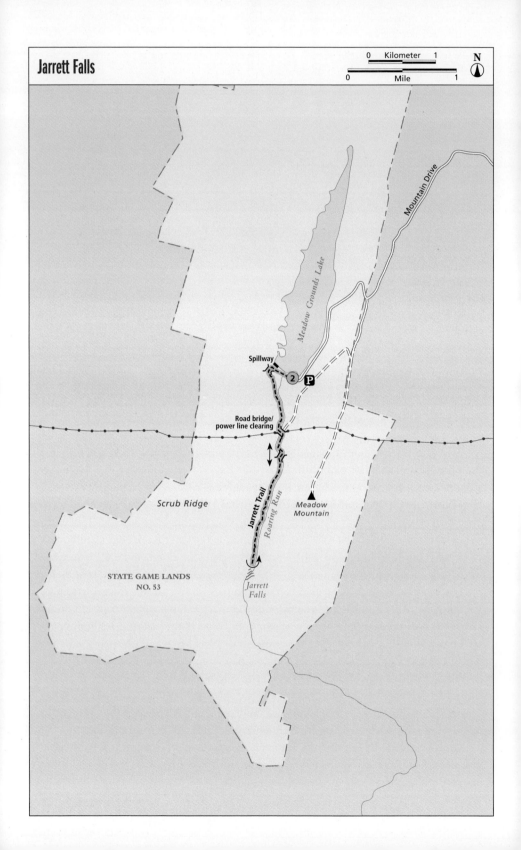

Jarrett Falls

0   Kilometer   1

0   Mile   1

N

Mountain Drive

Meadow Grounds Lake

Spillway

2 P

Road bridge/
power line clearing

Scrub Ridge

Jarrett Trail

Roaring Run

Meadow
Mountain

STATE GAME LANDS
NO. 53

Jarrett
Falls

fine top-down observation area. However, to reach the base of the cataract, cross over to the left bank then get below the irregular horseshoe-shaped yet tiered spiller, dropping 11 feet. This is one of those changeling falls. It delivers a different appearance at differing flows, making it a good target for each season.

Despite the lake being restored, the trail continues to have a reputation as being a bit overgrown in the warm season and has more blowdowns than we like. Nevertheless, the hike here adds one more piece to the mosaic that is the Pennsylvania waterfall hiking experience.

Miles and Directions

0.0 Leave the parking area and walk west atop grassy Meadow Grounds Lake dam.

0.1 Reach the far end of the dam and turn left on the Jarrett Trail, angling down to a trail bridge crossing the outflow of the lake.

0.2 Step over a stream entering on your right.

0.6 Step over another tributary, then reach a power line clearing and power line maintenance road. Turn left here, bridging Roaring Run on the power line maintenance road, then continue downstream in woods on the left bank after passing through the clearing.

0.8 Stay on the left bank, rising on a rocky bluff. Soon return to the creek on a rocky, rooty track.

0.9 Cross over to the right-hand bank of Roaring Run on a hiker bridge.

1.2 You are well above the creek, staying above the fallen hemlocks.

1.5 Cross over to the left bank without benefit of footbridge. You may have to ford here.

1.6 The trail seems to dead-end at a big boulder, but descend to the water and cross over to the right bank. There is no bridge; however, cables have been installed to aid your crossing. Ahead, walk near a two-tier low cascade.

1.7 Reach another cable-aided stream crossing and Jarrett Falls. You can keep on the right bank and view the falls from their brink, but it is an unfavorable photography angle. To reach the base of the falls, cross over to the left bank then work your way to the base of Jarrett Falls. Backtrack to the trailhead.

3.4 Arrive back at the trailhead, completing the waterfall hike.

3 Buttermilk Falls of Indiana County

This short yet rewarding waterfall trek starts at a former private retreat turned small park and designated natural area and works its way to a cascading 45-foot spiller you can view from an overlook. A picnic area enhances this little gem of a preserve.

Waterfall height: 45 feet
Waterfall beauty: 4
Distance: 0.4-mile out-and-back
Difficulty: Easy
Hiking time: About ½ hour
Trail surface: Gravel
Other trail users: None

Canine compatibility: Leashed pets allowed
Land status: County park
Fees and permits: None
Maps: Buttermilk Falls Natural Area; USGS New Florence
Trail Contact: Indiana County Parks & Trails, (724) 463-8636, www.indianacountyparks.org

Finding the trailhead: From the intersection of US 22 and US 219 near Ebensburg, take US 22 west for 18 miles to Clay Pike Road. Turn left and follow Clay Pike Road for 1.8 miles to Southwell Road. Turn left and follow Southwell Road for 0.2 mile, then turn right onto Valley Brook Road and follow it for 0.2 mile to dead-end at the parking area. Official park address is 570 Valley Brook Rd., New Florence. GPS: 40.419170, -79.067675

The Hike

What do the grandfather of Fred Rogers, aka Mr. Rogers of children's public television fame, and waterfall hiking in Pennsylvania have in common? Answer: Buttermilk Falls, of course. The land through which Buttermilk Falls tumbles in Indiana County was once owned by Mr. Rogers's grandfather Fred McFeely, himself a well-heeled businessman from Latrobe.

Starting in 1930, Fred McFeely developed his retreat within earshot of Buttermilk Falls. During this time McFeely's grandson Fred capered among the nearby woods, doubtlessly visiting Buttermilk Falls regularly. Fred the younger later became a Presbyterian minister and created the public television children's show *Mr. Rogers' Neighborhood*, which promoted family values. The show lasted from 1968 to 2001, making famous the sweaters and sneakers worn by Fred Rogers as well as his personal kindness. One cannot help but wonder if the beauty of Buttermilk Falls had an effect on Mr. Rogers's philosophy. This is but one stop on the Fred Rogers Trail, which tours ten sites that were a part of the influential man's life.

In 1956 Fred McFeely sold the property, which was eventually donated to Indiana County in 1996. The 45-acre tract was proclaimed a natural area by the county, whereupon trails, restrooms, and a picnic ground were developed, making the falls accessible to inspire us all.

Buttermilk Falls as seen from the official overlook

Hikers can admire Buttermilk Falls from its base.
RUSTY GLESSNER

The walk is an easy one. It leaves the parking area, where you can see the foundations and retaining walls from McFeely's retreat as well as hear Buttermilk Falls in the hollow below. The wide trail curves past the picnic area and into woods pocked with trees young and old. The walk ends at a wooden deck where you can admire Buttermilk Falls as it free-falls over a ledge, splashes onto an outcrop, then makes a second much longer drop, spreading its white flow into a shallow plunge pool below.

The wooden deck is clearly the safest place to view Buttermilk Falls, as the walls of the gorge become nearly sheer around and below the cataract. However, a path does circle above the falls and to the other side of the stream, where adventurous

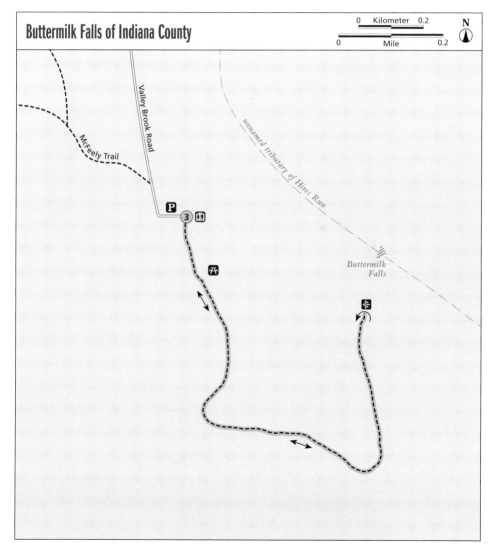

Buttermilk Falls of Indiana County

0   Kilometer   0.2

0   Mile   0.2

N

Valley Brook Road

McFeely Trail

unnamed tributary of Hires Run

Buttermilk Falls

3

photographers and admirers can get a bottom-up view of the falls. Exercise caution if taking this unofficial trail to the base of the cataract.

Miles and Directions

0.0 From the parking area, follow a concrete track past restrooms then join a wide gravel track, passing a picnic area with several tables.

0.2 Reach the Buttermilk Falls viewing deck. You can view the cataract as it pours through a gap and spreads while tumbling 45 feet. Backtrack to the trailhead.

0.4 Arrive back at the trailhead, completing the walk.

4 Adams Falls

This waterfall is located at Linn Run State Park. Here a tributary of Linn Run reaches an overhanging rock shelf, then pours over a cleft in the overhang, creating a veil of descending water before splattering onto an angled slope, splashingly reverberating from the small rock house formed by the overhang. The walk there is short and pleasant. After bridging the tributary forming Adams Falls, circle around for a head-on view of the cataract.

Waterfall height: 16 feet
Waterfall beauty: 4
Distance: 0.4-mile out-and-back
Difficulty: Easy
Hiking time: About ¾ hour
Trail surface: Natural
Other trail users: None

Canine compatibility: Leashed pets allowed
Land status: State park
Fees and permits: None
Maps: Linn Run State Park; USGS Ligonier
Trail contact: Linn Run State Park, (724) 238-6623, www.dcnr.state.pa.us/stateparks

Finding the trailhead: From the intersection of PA 711 and US 30 in Ligonier, take US 30 east for 2 miles, then turn right onto PA 381 south. Follow PA 381 south for 3 miles, then turn left on Linn Run Road. Follow Linn Run Road for 1.9 miles to enter the park. Take the first left on the first road crossing the bridge over Linn Run, near the picnic area, to climb a hill and immediately reach the trailhead on your right. GPS: 40.168897, -79.232802

The Hike

Linn Run State Park is situated in the Laurel Highlands, bordering larger Forbes State Forest, and lies close to both Laurel Highlands State Park and Laurel Ridge State Park. The preserve was originally developed by the Civilian Conservation Corps in the 1930s, and its rustic cabins built during that era remain a draw, as does Adams Falls. The numerous picnic areas strung along Linn Run are favored by visitors as well. A picnic area is located at the trailhead for the walk to Adams Falls, including a picnic shelter in case of inclement weather. Restrooms and a playground for kids complete the picture.

The walk to popular Adams Falls is short and doable by most everyone. A large sign points you toward the falls, and a pleasant stroll leads to an unnamed tributary of Linn Run. Here stands an arched bridge, spanning the tributary. Just below, the tributary flows over the edge, forming Adams Falls. A fence prevents waterfall visitors from working to the base of the falls from this side of the stream; therefore, continue over the bridge then curve right to finally enjoy an elevated view of the 16-foot spiller as it forms a curtain of white cutting through a stone cleft. The rock house below the falls is easily visible from this vantage.

If you want to extend your walk, simply follow the Adams Falls Trail. It makes a 1-mile loop amid boulders and evergreens in conjunction with the Iscrupe Trail.

Adams Falls makes its dive from a rock cleft into a rock house. RUSTY GLESSNER

Miles and Directions

0.0 From the picnic area trailhead, join the wide Adams Falls Trail, fronted by a pair of vehicle-blocking boulders. Linn Run flows below amid greenery and hardwoods. Maples and oaks shade the trail.

0.2 Reach the intersection with the Iscrupe Trail, which heads left and makes a loop with the Adams Falls Trail. Keep straight and soon span the bridge over the tributary forming Adams Falls. Continue just a bit, then turn downstream and reach a fine elevated overlook of Adams Falls. Backtrack to the trailhead.

0.4 Arrive back at the trailhead, completing the short waterfall walk.

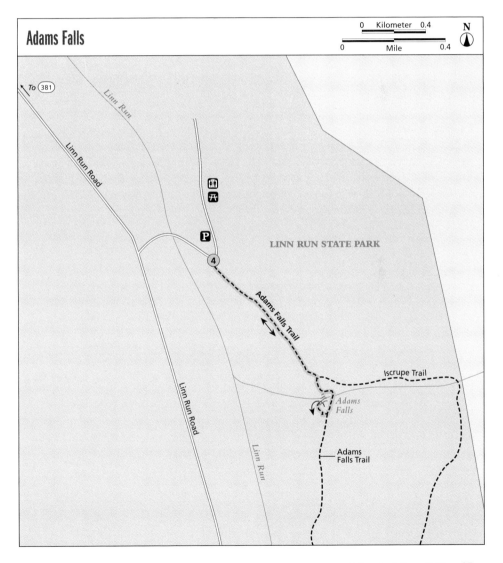

5 Cole Run Falls

Cole Run Falls is situated on an attractive tract of Forbes State Forest, deep in the Laurel Highlands. The waterfall itself matches the beauty of the forest, creating a white veil as smallish Cole Run fashions a vertical descent over an overhanging shelf of stone, behind which lies a small rock house. Though the waterfall is on a trail, the distance from the trailhead to Cole Run Falls is short, barely qualifying it as a waterfall hike. All the same, the mountain spiller is worth the drive and short walk to see it.

Waterfall height: 16 feet
Waterfall beauty: 4
Distance: 0.2-mile out-and-back
Difficulty: Easy
Hiking time: About ½ hour
Trail surface: Natural
Other trail users: None
Canine compatibility: Leashed pets allowed
Land status: State forest
Fees and permits: None
Maps: Forbes State Forest–Blue Hole Trail Map; USGS Kingwood
Trail contact: Forbes State Forest, (724) 238-1200, www.dcnr.state.pa.us/forestry

Finding the trailhead: From the intersection of PA 281 and PA 653 in New Centerville, take PA 653 west for 4.8 miles, then turn right onto Ream Road. Follow Ream Road for 1 mile, staying right on Ream Road a short distance more, then turn left on Fall Run Road. Follow Fall Run Road for 0.9 mile, then turn right onto Gary Road. Follow Gary Road for 0.9 mile, then turn left on Cole Run Road. Follow Cole Run Road for 0.3 mile to bridge Cole Run and reach the trailhead on your left. GPS: 39.972783, -79.284050

The Hike

Forbes State Forest consists of several tracts of land in the Laurel Highlands of southwest Pennsylvania. The Blue Hole Tract, on the east side of Laurel Ridge, contains several streams, namely Fall Creek, Blue Hole Creek, and Garys Run. Cole Run is a tributary of Blue Hole Creek. Emerging from Patterson Spring, Cole Run drains wooded ridges of the state forest, gently gurgling downward until it crosses under Cole Run Road. Here the stream dives off a plateau, increasing its gradient. Cole Run Falls is found where Cole Run begins its steep dive into the gorge created by Blue Hole Creek.

Time, water, ice, and gravity have undercut the rock ledge from which Cole Run drops, adding to the allure of this 16-foot spiller. The fallen relics of the rock cleft lie scattered at the base of the falls, bordering a shallow pool. Beyond the pool, Cole Run curves down and out of sight, on its steep journey to meet Blue Hole Creek.

The walk from the trailhead to the falls is a simple matter. It is just a few hundred feet on the Cole Run Trail before the spur path leads down to the base of Cole Run Falls. If the distance is too short, just continue on the 2-mile Cole Run Trail. It turns back to Cole Run Road after heading down Cole Run Creek then along Blue Hole

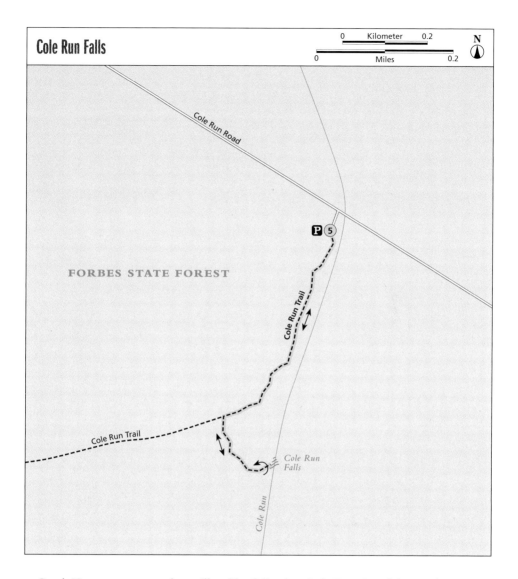

Cole Run Falls

FORBES STATE FOREST

Cole Run Road

Cole Run Trail

Cole Run Trail

Cole Run Falls

Cole Run

Creek. You can return to the trailhead by following Cole Run Road for a mile, creating a 3-mile loop.

Miles and Directions

0.0 Leave the small Cole Run Trail parking area on a singletrack path. Rhododendron-choked Cole Run flows to your left. Ahead, the Cole Run Trail leaves right, while a user-created path drops to the base of Cole Run Falls.

0.1 Reach the base of Cole Run Falls. Here Cole Run pours over an overhung ledge, splattering 16 feet below into a pool. Backtrack to the trailhead.

0.2 Arrive back at the trailhead, completing the short waterfall walk.

An arching tree trunk frames Cole Run Falls.
RUSTY GLESSNER

Cole Run Falls is clothed in winter splendor.
RUSTY GLESSNER

6 Ohiopyle Falls, The Slides, Cascades Waterfall

On this trek you can bag three very different waterfalls in one swoop at a fine Pennsylvania state park. Ohiopyle Falls is a powerful rumbler on the Youghiogheny River, while the other two cataracts are on a tributary named Meadow Run. The Slides is a long channel flowing over bare rock. Cascades Waterfall (also known as Meadow Run Cascades) makes a wide track ending in a vertical drop. Linking these three spillers fashions a truly fun trek.

Waterfall height: In order, 30 feet, 25 feet, 18 feet
Waterfall beauty: 5
Distance: 3.8-mile out-and-back
Difficulty: Easy
Hiking time: About 1¾ hours
Trail surface: Mostly natural
Other trail users: None
Canine compatibility: Leashed pets allowed
Land status: State park
Fees and permits: None
Maps: Ohiopyle State Park; USGS Ohiopyle
Trail contact: Ohiopyle State Park, (724) 329-8591, www.dcnr.state.pa.us/stateparks

Finding the trailhead: The hike starts at the Ohiopyle State Park visitor center just across PA 381 from the village of Ohiopyle. GPS: 39.866233, -79.494400

The Hike

The hamlet of Ohiopyle owes its existence to the falls on the Youghiogheny River. Back in the 1860s, loggers saw the forests of the Laurel Highlands as ripe for cutting, and the cataract on the Youghiogheny River could provide power to operate saws to cut the timber into manageable sizes. Thus the town of Falls City came to be. Here massive sawn trees were turned into wood products and shipped off to market via the railroad that came to town in 1871. While the rail line sent products from Falls City, tourists from Pittsburgh came to Falls City to see the reason for the city's name.

In 1891 Falls City became Ohiopyle, the name given to the cataract on the Youghiogheny. By this time the falls were turning turbines, bringing electricity to Ohiopyle. And with the conveniences brought by electricity and the rail line, this area became a full-fledged tourist destination.

Ohiopyle Falls is still a tourist destination for outdoor lovers who come to enjoy not only the waterfalls of Ohiopyle State Park but also its hiking trails, campgrounds, and other attractions. The Youghiogheny River lures in rafters, kayakers, and anglers. Today you can follow in the footsteps of the 19th-century tourists, starting your adventure at Ohiopyle Falls then making your way to Meadow Run, a tributary

Ohiopyle Falls, The Slides, Cascades Waterfall

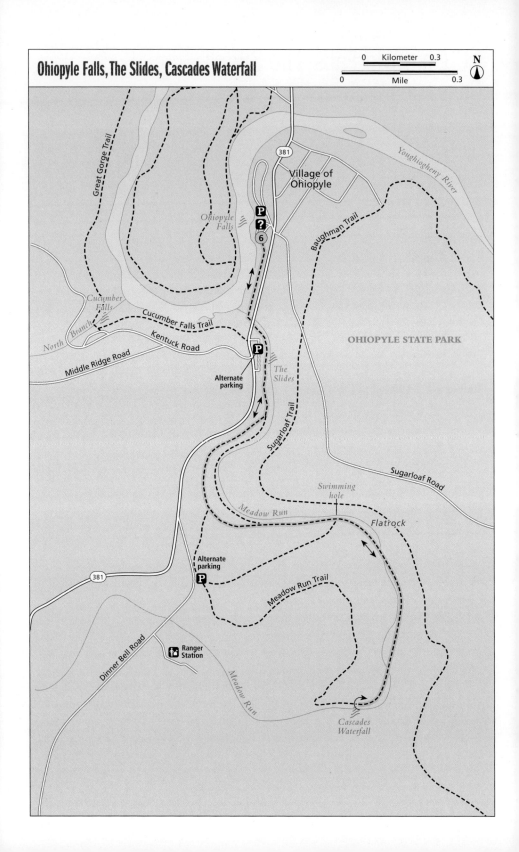

Kilometer 0 0.3

Mile 0 0.3

N

381

Village of Ohiopyle

Youghiogheny River

Great Gorge Trail

Ohiopyle Falls

P

?

6

Baughman Trail

Cucumber Falls

North Branch

Cucumber Falls Trail

Kentuck Road

Middle Ridge Road

P

Alternate parking

The Slides

OHIOPYLE STATE PARK

Sugarloaf Trail

Sugarloaf Road

Swimming hole

Meadow Run

Flatrock

381

Alternate parking

P

Meadow Run Trail

Dinner Bell Road

Ranger Station

Meadow Run

Cascades Waterfall

of the Youghiogheny River, and to The Slides, a grooved channel of moving water forming a sloped cataract that wild-water enthusiasts slide down.

Continue walking along and above the gorge of Meadow Run, passing rock houses, bluffs, and lesser cataracts to reach Cascades Waterfall, also known as Meadow Run Cascades. The spiller drops over a short ledge then makes a wide-angled descent before executing a final drop. This waterfall will cap off your Ohiopyle State Park triple crown of cataracts, each one offering its own unique character.

Miles and Directions

0.0 From the parking area at the Ohiopyle State Park visitor center, walk toward the center, stopping to see Ohiopyle Falls on the Youghiogheny River. The 30-foot river-wide spiller thunders over a ledge mixed with a few large boulders. A mill was once stationed here, using the power of the falling water. Twin viewing platforms deliver superior vantages of the brawny white tide. Continue toward the visitor center, then pick up a trail that soon leads to a sidewalk along PA 381.

Ohiopyle Falls is a Pennsylvania waterfall icon.
RUSTY GLESSNER

A portion of Cascades Waterfall makes its wide descent.
RUSTY GLESSNER

0.3 Cross the road bridge over Meadow Run, then pick up a trail traveling beneath the bluffs.

0.4 The spur from the parking area on PA 381 comes in on your right. Here, reach the base of The Slides, a grooved channel in a wide, flat base of layered rock, sliding about 25 feet over a long distance. Continue hiking past The Slides and stay along the bank. Ahead, bridge a little tributary of Meadow Run. The trail morphs into a natural-surface singletrack pathway.

0.6 Reach a trail split. Here the official trail leads right and uphill, while a rough manway continues along the stream, ultimately to fight past a bluff and rock house. Avoid the manway. Instead, climb the official trail to make a break in the cliff line, joining the top of the bluff and continuing upstream amid oaks, maples, and other hardwoods. Look for a view from the bluff's edge down to Meadow Run below.

0.9 Come to an intersection. Here a path leaves right for an alternate parking area on Dinner Bell Road. Stay left, curving along a bend of Meadow Run.

1.2 Reach another trail intersection. At this point a path leads right, also to the alternate parking on Dinner Bell Road. Another short path leads left to a big swimming hole on Meadow Run. Stay straight with the trail as it continues curving around a bend.

1.3 Come to Flatrock. This is a large, open, slightly angled rock slab above another deep swimming hole. Keep up along Meadow Run, among rhododendron and mossy boulders.

1.8 Return to river level after rising over a bluff. Keep straight on a now-wider path as a user-created trail cuts sharply left to reach Meadow Run.

1.9 Reach the short spur leading left to Cascades Waterfall. Here you emerge at a gravel bar at the wide cascades base. The 18-or-so-foot pour-over drops over a short ledge, then makes an angled descent among rocks and boulders before making a second and final short vertical drop. Backtrack to the visitor center parking area.

3.8 Arrive back at the visitor center parking area.

The upper part of Cascades Waterfall spills over in dramatic fashion.
RUSTY GLESSNER

7 Fechter Run Falls, Upper Jonathan Run Falls, Jonathan Run Falls, Sugar Run Falls

Make a scenic and rewarding hike to two major and two minor cataracts within the bounds of Ohiopyle State Park. Start in a quiet area of the park, then descend Jonathan Run amid regal forest. Find warm-up Fechter Run Falls, then Upper Jonathan Run Falls. Next, meet angled Jonathan Run Falls, deep in the valley. The hike then meets the Youghiogheny River and the GAP Trail. Briefly trace the rail trail then turn up Sugar Run, where you find Sugar Run Falls, a narrow, tall waterfall stairstepping down layered stone. The four cataracts give you a reason to savor the superlative scenery of this trek.

Waterfall height: In order, 14 feet, 10 feet, 12 feet, 34 feet
Waterfall beauty: 4
Distance: 4.4-mile out-and-back
Difficulty: Moderate
Hiking time: About 2½ hours
Trail surface: Natural, pea gravel on GAP Trail
Other trail users: Bicyclers

Canine compatibility: Leashed pets allowed
Land status: State park
Fees and permits: None
Maps: Ohiopyle State Park; USGS South Connellsville, Mill Run
Trail Contact: Ohiopyle State Park, (724) 329-8591, www.dcnr.state.pa.us/stateparks

Finding the trailhead: From the Ohiopyle State Park visitor center in Ohiopyle, take PA 381 south for 0.3 mile, then turn right on Kentuck Road. Follow Kentuck Road for 1 mile to a four-way intersection. Keep straight here, now following Holland Hill Road. Stay with it for 1.5 miles to reach the Jonathan Run trailhead on your right. GPS: 39.891467, -79.507100

The Hike

Jonathan Run and Sugar Run, both tributaries of the Youghiogheny River, flow within the protected confines of Ohiopyle State Park. Jonathan Run has a bigger watershed, thus more volume, and flows year-round, whereas Sugar Run can run dry in autumn during below-average rainfall years. Fechter Run is a smallish tributary of Jonathan Run and also tends to run low in autumn. Nevertheless, when issuing, all three streams put on an impressive show, not only with their waterfalls but also with natural beauty to be expected at a Pennsylvania state park.

This area is a lesser-visited parcel of Ohiopyle State Park and offers more solitude than other waterfall destinations here. The four primary waterfalls are also worthy destinations, although the two falls along Jonathan Run and along Fechter Run do require a bit of scrambling. Interestingly, although they are not visible from the trail,

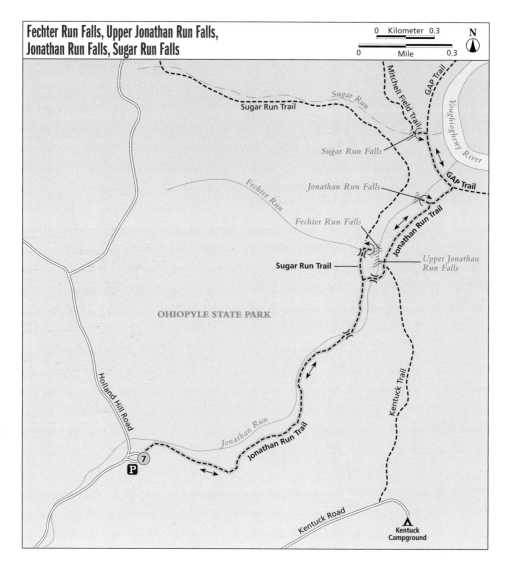

0   Kilometer 0.3   N

0   Mile   0.3

Sugar Run Trail

Sugar Run

Sugar Run Falls

Mitchell Field Trail

GAP Trail

Youghiogheny River

Fechter Run

Jonathan Run Falls

GAP Trail

Fechter Run Falls

Sugar Run Trail

Jonathan Run Trail

*Upper Jonathan
Run Falls*

OHIOPYLE STATE PARK

Kentuck Trail

Holland Hill Road

Jonathan Run

Jonathan Run Trail

7

P

Kentuck Road

Kentuck
Campground

you will hear the two cataracts spilling over their respective ledges on Jonathan Run.
Contrastingly, the hike leads directly to Sugar Run Falls—you can't miss it.

The hike starts by leading down Jonathan Run, an attractive vale thickly populated with trees shading the dashing, stony watercourse. The trail wanders off and on
the creek bottom before bridging Jonathan Run. At the second bridge crossing you
make a little detour on the Sugar Run Trail, then come to the bridge over Fechter
Run, your cue to follow Fechter Run downstream to Fechter Run Falls. Here Fechter Run tumbles in stages, its biggest curtain drop at the end.

Now to the falls on Jonathan Run. Backtrack and rejoin the Jonathan Run Trail,
bridging Jonathan Run. You will then come to Upper Jonathan Run Falls. This spiller

makes a straight drop over a rock shelf, contrasting with the atypical Jonathan Run Falls, located downstream. There Jonathan Run pours over an angled ledge, giving it an asymmetrical appearance. Big boulders and rocks border this harder-to-reach cataract.

Beyond that point, make your way to the Youghiogheny River and the GAP Trail. The level rail trail leads you over Jonathan Run and Sugar Run. Next, the Mitchell Field Trail makes a serpentine singletrack way to the base of 34-foot Sugar Run Falls. With ample water, it is the most impressive of the four falls. Sugar Run Falls spills and slaloms in stages over ever-widening layered ledges, flanked in rhododendron.

Not a bad hiking adventure, bagging four waterfalls on one hike. Just make sure the creeks are flowing before you hit the trail.

Rock layers form stairsteps in scenic Sugar Run Falls, a 34-foot spiller framed in rhododendron.
RUSTY GLESSNER

Miles and Directions

0.0 Leave the parking area on the Jonathan Run Trail. Descend a singletrack path into woods of cherry, yellow birch, and beech, with an understory of ferns. Tulip trees and oaks find their places. Soon saddle alongside Jonathan Run, to your left. Watch for a closing clearing and leveled-off spots that indicate a former homesite on your right.

0.2 Bridge a little tributary of Jonathan Run. Leave the stream flats and work along a slope of the valley.

1.0 A hiker bridge carries you across Jonathan Run. Continue downstream, now on the left bank.

1.2 Reach a trail intersection. Here the Sugar Run Trail heads straight and uphill. Head left on the Sugar Run Falls Trail, making a little detour to Fechter Run Falls.

1.3 Come to the bridge over Fechter Run. Turn downstream, scrambling toward Fechter Run Falls, about 50 yards distant. You have to work around the ledges to get a face-on view of the 14-foot staged spiller. Backtrack to the Jonathan Run Trail.

1.6 Return to the Jonathan Run Trail and continue downstream after crossing the bridge over Jonathan Run, now on the right-hand bank.

1.8 Meet the Kentuck Trail, coming in on your right from the state park campground. Here a user-created trail leads left down to Jonathan Run and Upper Jonathan Run Falls. This pour-over tumbles about 10 feet over a ledge into a shallow pool. Return to the now-wider official trail.

2.0 Come to a very steep user-created spur leading to Jonathan Run Falls. Work your way through rhododendron down to the falls, an angled ledge with a vertical drop of about 12 feet, spilling among a few fallen rocks into a moist vale pocked with big boulders. Return to the main trail, continuing downstream.

2.1 Reach the wide gravel GAP Trail. The Youghiogheny River crashes in its own rapids well below. Head left here on the GAP Trail, gently curving to the right as the "Yough" curves.

2.3 Head left on the Mitchell Field Trail, a rocky singletrack winding toward Sugar Run in thick woods.

2.4 Emerge at the base of 34-foot Sugar Run Falls. This layered cataract widens from the top over layers of rock. The falls photograph well, and a timed shot can capture the stair-stepping water spilling down the individual ledges before reaching a pool. Backtrack to the trailhead.

4.4 Arrive back at the trailhead, completing the four-pronged waterfall hike.

Fechter Run Falls descends in multiple drops in late spring.
RUSTY GLESSNER

Low light and a long exposure make Upper Jonathan Run Falls stand out against autumn glory. RUSTY GLESSNER

Differing heights and speeds of Upper Jonathan Run Falls create a compelling waterfall.
RUSTY GLESSNER

8 Cucumber Falls

It is but a short walk to this classically formed cataract at waterfall-wealthy Ohiopyle State Park. First, you will be eye level with the hanging spiller, looking down into a dark vale into which it falls. Next, go to the fall's base along the edge of the small canyon, then boulder hop to get a bottom-up look at the ledge over which Cucumber Falls makes its drop. A longer hike option to Cucumber Falls can be made if starting at the Ohiopyle State Park visitor center.

Waterfall height: 32 feet
Waterfall beauty: 5
Distance: 0.2-mile out-and-back
Difficulty: Easy
Hiking time: About ½ hour
Trail surface: Natural
Other trail users: None

Canine compatibility: Leashed pets allowed
Land status: State park
Fees and permits: None
Maps: Ohiopyle State Park; USGS Fort Necessity
Trail contact: Ohiopyle State Park, (724) 329-8591, www.dcnr.state.pa.us/stateparks

Finding the trailhead: From the visitor center in the hamlet of Ohiopyle, take PA 381 south for 0.3 mile, then turn right on Kentuck Road. Follow Kentuck Road for 0.5 mile to the trailhead on your right. GPS: 39.862800, -79.502833

The Hike

Ohiopyle State Park is known for its waterfalls, of which Cucumber Falls is one. And this curtain-type cataract more than holds its own. The reason for the wealth of waterfalls at this park is the aquatic centerpiece of the preserve—the Youghiogheny River. This difficult-to-spell yet superlatively beautiful waterway cuts a gorge through the park, creating vertical variation whereby its tributaries—such as North Branch—fall steeply, creating waterfalls. Affectionately known as the "Yough," the river draws not only waterfall fans but also rafters, kayakers, and anglers to Ohiopyle State Park and beyond. The Great Allegheny Passage, also known as the GAP Trail, follows a former railroad grade along the Youghiogheny River.

The Youghiogheny has rapids and even a waterfall of its own—Ohiopyle Falls. That cataract is located near the park visitor center, just across from the small hamlet of Ohiopyle. The town serves the needs of state park visitors, such as rafters, kayakers, and waterfall enthusiasts like you and me.

It is less than a mile walk from the visitor center to Cucumber Falls if you wish to take a longer route. Unfortunately, the initial part of the walk travels along the shoulder of PA 381 and thus is less appealing. However, after crossing the Meadow

Moving water and still ice combine to create a winter scene at Cucumber Falls.
RUSTY GLESSNER

Run bridge on PA 381, hikers can follow the Cucumber Falls Trail that travels along the bank of the Youghiogheny then reaches North Branch and travels up the creek just a short distance before reaching the base of Cucumber Falls.

However, most park visitors take the top-down approach to reach Cucumber Falls. Here a path leads from the parking area on Kentuck Road, traveling just a short distance to reach an overlook of the falls as it dives off a sturdy overhanging sandstone ledge then spills a little over 30 feet into a semicircular amphitheater, where the falling noise echoes off the cave-like overhang. Boulders and trees complement the geological scenery.

For an additional view of Cucumber Falls, take the trail switchbacking down to North Branch via stone steps. A little rock hopping will lead upstream to the base of the falls. Admire the rock house formed on either side of the falls. The wide base as well as elevated boulders afford photographers multiple angles from which to shoot the falls. Photographers also take note that Cucumber Falls retains its attraction at low water levels as well as higher flows and in subfreezing conditions.

This autumn morning finds Cucumber Falls just a trickle.

A winter thaw reveals yet another face of Cucumber Falls.
RUSTY GLESSNER

Miles and Directions

0.0 Join a gravel path leading to the right from the Cucumber Falls parking area. Immediately turn right and join the connector path heading east for Cucumber Falls and the Ohiopyle State Park visitor center (to the left you would join the Great Gorge Trail). Shortly reach an overlook of Cucumber Falls as North Branch spills over an overhanging sandstone ledge into a rock cathedral below. After viewing the falls from here, continue down steps leading into the gorge below.

0.1 Come to the base of Cucumber Falls after switchbacking down the side of the gorge and rock hopping upstream. Backtrack to the trailhead.

0.2 Arrive back at the trailhead.

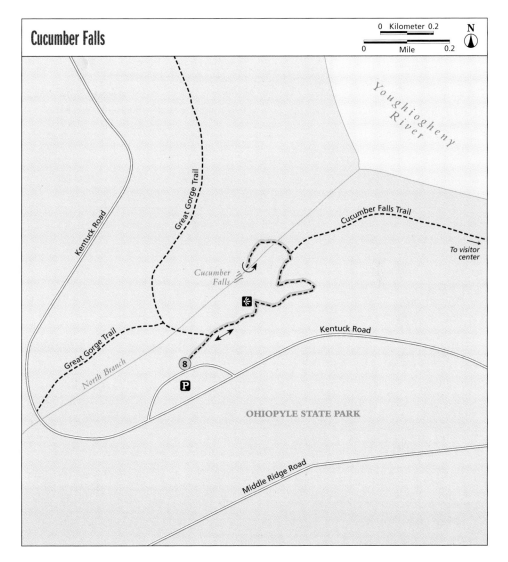

9 Jackson Falls

View a trio of fine waterfalls following an improved rail trail most of the route. The walk takes place in the reclaimed Roaring Run watershed, a tributary of the Kiskiminetas River east of Pittsburgh, near the town of Apollo. The walk is easy and you can view not only Lower Jackson Falls and Jackson Falls but also a tributary waterfall when the streams are up. Finally, the access trail network continues beyond the falls and connects to other features in the Roaring Run watershed, a privately owned but publicly open tract.

Waterfall height: In order, 20 feet, 10 feet, 12 feet
Waterfall beauty: 4
Distance: 1.4-mile out-and-back
Difficulty: Easy, does have a little scrambling at end
Hiking time: About ¾ hour
Trail surface: Gravel, natural
Other trail users: Bicyclers
Canine compatibility: Leashed pets allowed
Land status: Privately owned land conservancy, open to public
Fees and permits: None
Maps: Roaring Run Watershed; USGS Vandergrift
Trail contacts: Roaring Run Watershed Association, www.roaringrunapollo.org

Finding the trailhead: From downtown Apollo just northeast of the Kiskiminetas River, take First Street (PA 56) east for 2.1 miles to Kings Road. Turn right and follow Kings Road for 1.1 miles, then veer left onto Brownstown Road. Follow it for 0.8 mile to the official Rock Furnace trailhead, where you make an acute right turn into the parking lot. Do not park anywhere other than the official trailhead, which has room for about 10 cars. GPS: 40.564812, -79.517987

The Hike

The Roaring Run Watershed Association has transformed a formerly mined but scenic valley and a defunct rail line into an attractive hiking and bicycling venue. In 1983 the organization was formed and former area coal-mining rail lines were converted into rail trails that form the heart of a pathway system that also includes hiking and biking paths traversing 653 acres of land and waters along the Roaring Run valley. More land continues to be acquired, and the natural beauty once again shines for us to enjoy.

Of course they have waterfalls too. Jackson Falls is the aquatic star of the show here. Located on a tributary of Roaring Run known as Rattling Run, Jackson Falls is actually two notable cataracts located within a short distance of one another. The uppermost fall can be considered *the* Jackson Falls. It rashly dives 20 feet over a naked stone lip into an overhung semicircular stone amphitheater where a large plunge pool fans outward, a classic waterfall in multiple regards.

Lower Jackson Falls makes a shorter ledge drop and is much less dramatic, as it is partially obscured by fallen boulders. Nor does it have the overhung stone cliffs and sizable plunge pool. However, it does provide contrast, displaying how one stream can produce two distinct cataracts in a short span.

The lowermost fall is on a tributary of Rattling Run, itself providing a curtain-type drop over layered rock. Its flow can change the spiller from a gleaming sheet of splashing aqua to dribbling disappointment. However, the three cascades—along with the walk to them—will be worth your time and effort no matter the season.

The Rock Furnace Trail makes for an inviting pathway.

Jackson Falls in springtime

You can access this trio of spillers via the Rock Furnace Trail, descending from the signed parking area. After cruising along Roaring Run, take the well-walked spur up Rattling Run, first passing the tributary fall, Lower Jackson Falls, then Jackson Falls itself.

If you wish, you can continue on the Rock Furnace Trail to access other paths and view highlights such as Camel Rock and the ruins of the Biddle Iron Furnace, in operation from 1825 to 1850.

Note: In the past, people have walked directly from Brownstown Road through private property to Jackson Falls. The landowner has placed large No Trespassing signs to discourage this. Do not go this way. Honor private property rights. Even taking the official Rock Furnace Trail, note that private property runs close along Rattling Run in places. Stay apprised of property boundaries.

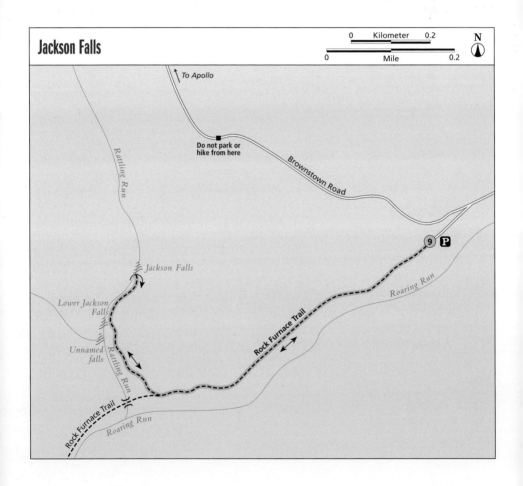

Miles and Directions

0.0 From the Rock Furnace trailhead off Brownstown Road, take the Rock Furnace Trail south-west. Roaring Run flows below to your left. The walking on the wide gravel rail trail is easy. A youngish hardwood forest rises overhead.

0.2 Climb a little hill well above the creek. Wooden fences border the trail in places.

0.5 Split right up Rattling Run on a user-created waterfall access trail. Ahead, the Rock Furnace Trail keeps straight, bridging Rattling Run, and continues toward the Kiskiminetas River and the rail trail along it connecting the communities of Apollo and Edmon. Squeeze up along Rattling Run.

0.6 Pass an unnamed tributary fall spilling over a ledge on the far side of Rattling Run, then come to Lower Jackson Falls, a 10-foot spiller that tumbles over a ledge then splashes amid boulders haphazardly strewn in Rattling Run. Continue upstream to Jackson Falls, squeezing up the hollow.

0.7 Reach unmistakable Jackson Falls. It free-falls from an overhung stone lip into a cavern-ous stone amphitheater with a large circular pool, ceaselessly reverberating with the waves from the cataract's drop. Backtrack to the trailhead.

1.4 Arrive back at the trailhead, completing the walk.

10 Fall Run Falls

Nestled in the heart of urban Pittsburgh, Fall Run provides a surprisingly scenic waterfall hike. Most Steel City residents are completely unaware of 95-acre Fall Run Park, tucked away amid neighborhoods in Shaler Township. Start at the upper end of the park's developed facilities then work your way up the creek, crisscrossing the stream and passing warm-up cascades. The hike culminates in a shocking nearly 30-foot spiller—the largest cataract in the greater Pittsburgh area. Turn around at the upper end of the preserve, backtracking to enjoy the cascades of Fall Run one more time.

Waterfall height: 28 feet
Waterfall beauty: 3
Distance: 1.6-mile out-and-back
Difficulty: Easy
Hiking time: About 1 hour
Trail surface: Natural
Other trail users: None

Canine compatibility: Leashed pets allowed
Land status: Township park
Fees and permits: None
Map: USGS Glenshaw
Trail contact: Shaler Township, (412) 486-9700, www.shaler.org

Finding the trailhead: From the intersection of PA 28 and PA 8 on the north side of the Allegheny River just a little north of downtown Pittsburgh, take exit 5 on PA 28 onto PA 8 north. Drive for 2.6 miles to a traffic light and turn right on Fall Run Road (across from Three Rivers Harley Davidson). Follow Fall Run Road for 0.1 mile, then split left into Fall Run Park. Follow the main park road to dead-end at the trailhead, near the park shelter. GPS: 40.530467, -79.947867

The Hike

Commonly accorded a height of 30 feet, Fall Run Falls may be a little shy of that, but I bet you will be so surprised at the continuous beauty of this little linear park amid 21st-century urban Pittsburgh that you won't be at all disappointed. Back in the last century, the lower part of what is Fall Run Park was state game land, where hunters pursued deer and other wild animals. Time marched on and suburbia crept out from the banks of the Monongahela, Allegheny, and Ohio Rivers until the state game commission declared the tract off-limits to hunting. Therefore, the base of what became Fall Run Park was preserved. The upper part of Fall Run was then acquired, and Fall Run Park as we see it came to be.

The park is set in the deep hollow of Fall Run. The lower part of the park is equipped with a picnic pavilion, ball fields, swing sets, and other assets to be expected at an urban preserve, then you get to the end of the park road and a parking area.

The scene changes from there—and you enter the declivitous Fall Run vale, where wooded hillsides rise green and proud and lush. Fall Run dashes clear over

This vantage point gives the hiker a top-down view of Fall Run Falls.

rocks, making little rapids divided by pools. You will note a sewer line has been run up the vale (a sacrifice of urbanity), but all you see are the occasional manhole covers. The natural area is named for Judge D. M. Miller, and you will observe much of nature here in the form of rock outcroppings, thick vegetation, and, of course, moving water. And that moving water not only comes from Fall Run but also little tributaries contributing their aqua to the mix, flowing over layered limestone beside rising sycamores.

The sides of the hollow rise steep as you bridge the stream, continuing up the valley. Unfortunately, since Fall Run does drain an urban area, the post-storm runoff is higher and faster than in backcountry areas, resulting in occasional flooding that damages the multiple trail bridges. However, when the flow is up, these tributaries form falls of their own, from slides over wide stone slabs to curtain-type cataracts raining over ledges.

Bluffs and boulders add geological wonderment to the hike. Unfortunately, some visitors see the rocks as tableaus for graffiti, but do not let it deter you from admiring the works of nature here. Fall Run Falls will not disappoint. The waterfall shoots off a rock shelf, then makes a 10-foot sheer curtain-type drop over layered rock. It then splashes onto a curved stone slab, making a moving sheet of white as it descends another 18 or so feet, depending on the flow rate. A shallow pool bordered by a well-visited gravel bar collects Fall Run Falls then pushes it onward.

The hike pushes upward, though the main waterfall highlight has been visited. Here the now-flatter vale is veined with more tributaries. The trail works its way among them using additional bridges in places before curving around a distinctive layered bluff, ending at a small parking area off Ledgeview Drive. Houses are in sight. Nevertheless, Fall Run Fall and the bordering valley remain a vital natural wonder for Pennsylvania waterfallers.

Spring is the best time to visit Fall Run Falls, for not only maximum water but also wildflowers. You will be surprised at the variety of blooms you will see here—from foamflowers to trillium to mayapples. By autumn, many of the tributaries will be nothing but trickles. In winter, north-facing Fall Run Falls can become a white ice sculpture.

Miles and Directions

0.0 From the trailhead, pick up a well-used trail, entering the wooded valley of Fall Run and leaving urbanity behind. Fall Run flows to your left.

0.1 Cross over to the left bank on a hiker bridge. Ahead, bridge Fall Run again.

0.2 Span a bridge over to the left bank. Admire a rising bluff across the stream. Ahead, pass a slide cascade coming in from across the stream as well as a 6-foot fall spilling just upstream of it on Fall Run. Bridge the stream again.

0.3 Bridge again to the left bank, still heading upstream. Appreciate the bluffs rising above.

0.4 Bridge over to the right-hand bank, then pass a big boulder.

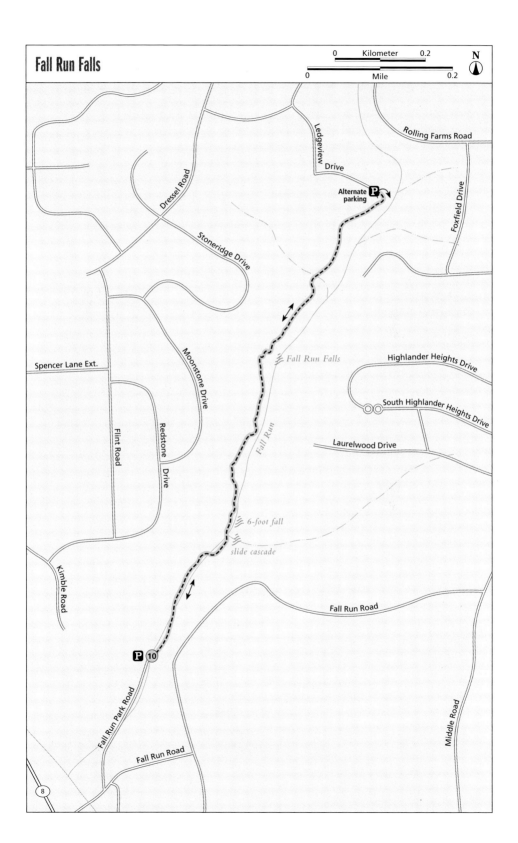

Fall Run Falls

0   Kilometer   0.2

0   Mile   0.2

N

Rolling Farms Road

Ledgeview Drive

Foxfield Drive

Alternate parking

Dressel Road

Stoneridge Drive

Highlander Heights Drive

Fall Run Falls

Spencer Lane Ext.

Moonstone Drive

South Highlander Heights Drive

Laurelwood Drive

Fall Run

Flint Road

Redstone Drive

6-foot fall

slide cascade

Kimble Road

Fall Run Road

Fall Run Park Road

Fall Run Road

Middle Road

8

0.5 Bridge the stream yet again; you are on the left-hand bank. Ahead, come to Fall Run Falls in an open area. Here steps lead to the top of the 28-foot spiller. Fall Run slips past a narrow cleft in the rock then follows gravity's orders, splashing into a shallow pool. Ascend the steps, checking out the falls from the top down. Continue up Fall Run.

0.8 Emerge at the upper parking area after passing more bridges and around a distinctive ledge above Fall Run. Backtrack to the trailhead.

1.6 Arrive back at the trailhead, completing the waterfall hike.

Fall Run spills first over a ledge then morphs into an angled slide.

11 Frankfort Mineral Springs Falls

This waterfall hike at Raccoon Creek State Park west of Pittsburgh delivers a scenic cataract amid rich wildflowers. Here you will enter a trail network in the Frankfort Mineral Springs area, where a resort once cultivated guests who consumed its purportedly healing waters. When the lands were acquired as a Pennsylvania state park, the springs and the nearby falls were targets for trails. Today we can use those trails to visit this low-flow but picturesque flume spilling into an oversize cave-like rock grotto. Ruins of the old mineral springs resort are located nearby.

Waterfall height: 14 feet
Waterfall beauty: 5
Distance: 0.4-mile loop
Difficulty: Easy
Hiking time: About ½ hour
Trail surface: Natural
Other trail users: None

Canine compatibility: Leashed pets allowed
Land status: State park
Fees and permits: None
Maps: Raccoon Creek State Park; USGS Burgettstown
Trail contact: Raccoon Creek State Park, (724) 899-2200, www.dcnr.state.pa.us/stateparks

Finding the trailhead: From Pittsburgh, take US 22 west to the last exit in Pennsylvania, joining PA 18. Take PA 18 north for 5.3 miles to reach the Frankfort Mineral Springs trailhead on your left. GPS: 40.497890, -80.427980

The Hike

Being close to Pittsburgh can be a very good thing, for that is part of how Raccoon Creek State Park came to be. Back in the Great Depression of the 1930s, the works program that was the Civilian Conservation Corps (CCC) was commissioned to develop a series of parks within proximity of major metropolitan areas, including Pittsburgh. The CCC was to rehabilitate marginalized subsistence farmlands and then develop park facilities, from trails to campgrounds to fishing lakes. The Raccoon Creek valley west of Pittsburgh was chosen, and 7,572-acre Raccoon Creek State Park came to be and is a major recreation destination for metro Pittsburgh to this day.

As charged, the park includes camping with 172 sites from developed to primitive and a 101-acre lake for swimming, fishing, and self-propelled boating. The park features a whopping 44 miles of hiking and backpacking trails, 17 miles of mountain biking trails, and 16 miles of equestrian trails. A lodge, cabins, interpretive programs, and more round out the offerings at this jewel of a Pennsylvania state park.

What became Raccoon Creek State Park wasn't all worn-out farmland. It also included Frankfort Mineral Springs, around which a resort was established in the mid-1850s. The water of the springs was the centerpiece of what became a summer

Frankfort Mineral Springs Falls spills 14 feet into a large, wet rock grotto.

Trillium graces the flats near Frankfort Mineral Springs Falls.

retreat for the wealthy escaping the heat and haze of Pittsburgh in the summertime. By the 1880s the resort was going gangbusters, housing 200 guests at a time, who enjoyed twirling in the dance hall and dashing about the tennis courts as well as partaking of the mineral spring, located in the grotto of the waterfall we visit on this hike.

Back in the late 1800s, spring-centered resorts were the rage among the wealthy throughout our land. This western Pittsburgh resort enjoyed two decades of success then went into decline, becoming a boardinghouse and traveler's hotel, especially after mass use of the private automobile altered vacationing patterns. As with many other large wooden structures of its day, the main resort building eventually succumbed to fire.

It was not until the 1960s that Frankfort Mineral Springs was purchased and added to Raccoon Creek State Park. Some trails here follow old roads and others are newly built trails connected to the greater park pathway network.

We can now see the waterfall, the springs, and ruins of a stone building at the resort site. While hiking here, imagine visitors a century and a half ago, relaxing in the countryside, sipping mineral water on the resort porch, and checking out the waterfall after a summer thunderstorm. Before that, imagine Levi Dungan staking claim to this land in 1772, farming the soil around the mineral springs. And before that, imagine aboriginal Pennsylvanians returning to the springs time and again, also seeking the upwelling for medicinal value. Today the grotto is more revered for the water falling from its lip than the springs from under its rim, yet we can enjoy them both on this walk.

After leaving the PA 18 trailhead, you head up the south side of the creek valley, the waterway being an unnamed tributary of Raccoon Creek. Wildflowers, especially trillium, grow in staggering numbers in spring. (There is also a designated wildflower reserve in another area of the park.) The valley closes and you are soon at the grotto. A short hiker bridge spans the creek, landing you at the base of Frankfort Mineral Springs Falls. The stream slices through an overhanging lip, splattering onto mossy rocks at the base of a cave-like shelter of a size far outstripping the size of the stream. In fact, the stream forming the falls can dry up in autumn while the springs themselves continue to flow.

From the falls, sturdy stone steps lead you up and away, linking to the Heritage Trail and the broken blocks of a former building. Here you join the Heritage Trail, an old road, and follow it back downhill to PA 18 and the trailhead. Consider expanding your hike or engaging in other activities at this fine Pennsylvania state park, designed for the enjoyment of greater Pittsburgh and beyond.

Miles and Directions

0.0 From the trailhead parking lot, cross a little hiker bridge then reach a three-way trail intersection. Head left on the Mineral Springs Loop Trail, which also leaves right. Your return route is the Heritage Trail, a wide track going straight ahead. The singletrack Mineral

Springs Loop Trail winds through a flowery flat, then saddles alongside a rising hill to the left and the stream to the right.

0.1 Cross the unnamed stream first by bridge then by rock hopping. Cross the stream a third time. Hikers will be pleasantly shocked by the sheer number of trillium blooming here in late April.

0.2 Span a hiker bridge, then reach Frankfort Mineral Springs Falls and Frankfort Mineral Springs. The waterfall drops about 14 feet into the large, wet grotto. The mineral springs drip/run into a stone trough to the right of the falls as you face them. Walk past the mineral springs and take the stairs to reach the stone rubble of a building and intersection with the Heritage Trail. Turn right on the Heritage Trail, descending an old road.

0.4 Arrive back at the trailhead, completing the walk.

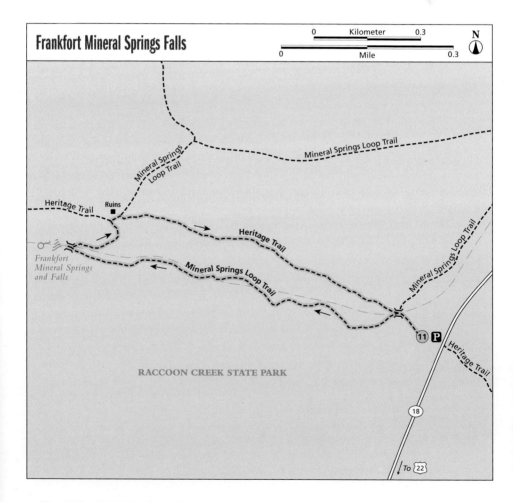

Frankfort Mineral Springs Falls

Waterfall Hikes of Northwest Pennsylvania

The Gerard Trail provides a full view of Pioneer Falls (hike 15).

12 Hells Hollow Falls

This waterfall with the eye-catching name at McConnells Mill State Park not only offers a scenic cataract to visit, but you can also enjoy viewing the geologically fascinating "channels" through which the stream runs. Furthermore, a historic limekiln will be discovered at the site of this 18-foot cataract, with more cascades above the primary drop. The walk is fun and easy, resulting in the rewards of the hike being far more than the effort required.

Waterfall height: 18 feet
Waterfall beauty: 4
Distance: 1.2-mile out-and-back
Difficulty: Easy
Hiking time: About ¾ hour
Trail surface: Natural
Other trail users: None
Canine compatibility: Leashed pets allowed

Land status: State park
Fees and permits: None
Maps: McConnells Mill State Park; USGS Portersville
Trail contact: McConnells Mill State Park, (724) 368-8811, www.dcnr.state.pa.us /stateparks

Finding the trailhead: From exit 96, Portersville, on I-79 north of Pittsburgh, take PA 488 west for 0.5 mile to US 19. Turn right onto US 19 north and follow it for 0.2 mile then turn left, staying with PA 488 west/Portersville Road. Follow Portersville Road for 1.9 miles, then turn right on Mountville Road and follow it for 2.9 miles to Heinz Camp Road. Turn right and follow Heinz Camp Road for 1.9 miles, then turn right on Shaffer Road and follow it for 0.2 mile to reach the trailhead on your right. GPS: 40.931067, -80.239867

The Hike

A name like Hells Hollow conjures up images of challenging terrain, rugged dense growth, and a generally difficult place. In actuality, the hike to Hells Hollow Falls is not only easy but also interesting and scenic.

Part of the greater Slippery Rock Creek Gorge at McConnells Mill State Park, Hells Hollow is an example of the fascinating geology to be found at this Pennsylvania preserve. Furthermore, you will see that the geology of Hells Hollow has been appreciated not only by waterfall hikers like us, but also for its industrial value. The layered limestone you will view in this valley was regarded as a potential source of lime, and a kiln was built here in the 1850s, right next to Hells Hollow Falls. At this kiln, limestone-rich rock was placed into a fire-heated brick-lined furnace built directly into the hillside. After the rock was heated and the slag removed, a usable form of lime was then collected. That was how lime was made back in the 19th century, and for thousands of years before then. Today we can see the limestone kiln from

Hells Hollow Falls

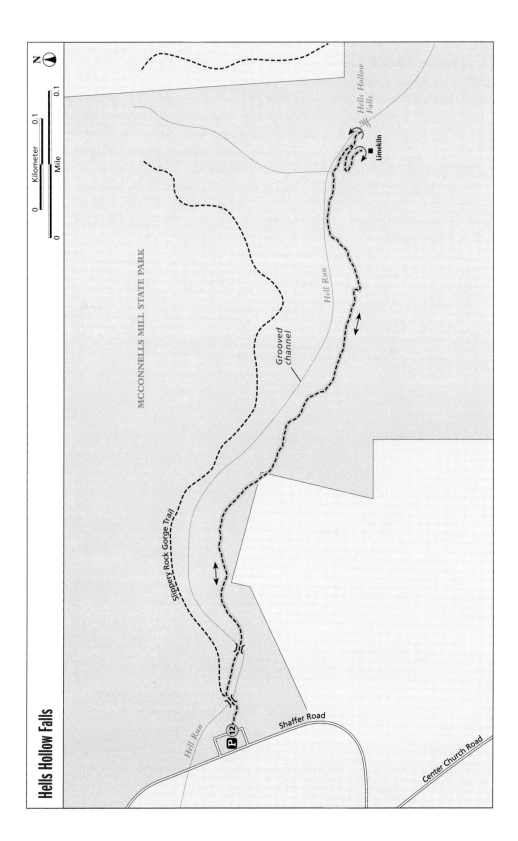

N

Kilometer
0   0.1   0.1

0   0.1
Mile

MCCONNELLS MILL STATE PARK

Hells Hollow Falls

Limekiln

Hell Run

Grooved channel

Slippery Rock Gorge Trail

Hell Run

P 12

Shaffer Road

Center Church Road

two angles—from the bottom looking in, where we can actually get down and crawl into the furnace, as well as from the top down.

Among other uses, lime is mixed with mortar for construction; it is also a fertilizer component. Limekilns have been operated by men for thousands of years and come in myriad forms. The kiln at Hells Hollow has the two basic elements common to all kilns—an opening at the base and at the top. The reason the kiln was located exactly where it is has nothing to do with the waterfall, but rather the spot offers easy access to the top of the kiln where the limestone was dropped in, along with alternating layers of fuel, which could be either very dry wood or charcoal. The whole thing was then lit and maintained at a certain temperature over a period of days. If all went well, lime was the result.

Making lime was a rough, dirty, and even hellish business. Perhaps this is where the vale got its name, though one legend states a military officer was lost late at night and stumbled toward the eerie glow of the burning limekiln and briefly believed he was entering hell itself. Contrastingly, Hells Hollow waterfall is a delight. You will

A full face-on view of Hells Hollow Falls is augmented by the frozen cataract to the right.
RUSTY GLESSNER

The limekiln next to Hells Hollow Falls was used to process limestone into usable lime.

first walk an open valley alongside Hell Run, a place rich with wildflowers and rising trees, then pass a former homesite or perhaps a building site for the limekiln operation. Next you will view a strangely grooved section of stream bank, where Hell Run has carved a slender channel through the layered limestone, a remarkable sight. Take the time to explore this little area, also looking for sinkholes in the woods around Hell Run, an additional result of eroding limestone.

The stream then starts cutting a gorge, and Hells Hollow Falls is the result. Suddenly you descend and then are at the falls and the kiln. Wooden steps lead to the base of the falls. Hells Hollow Falls spills in a few warm-up cascades over a flat stone surface before making its primary drop over a slightly angled and irregular surface to then slow in a shallow stony pool. Getting a head-on view without getting your feet wet could be especially troublesome in winter with high water and low temperatures. However, in summertime or when the water is low, waterfallers can scramble wet-footed for a direct look at the spiller.

Miles and Directions

0.0 From the trailhead, join the Hells Hollow Trail and immediately cross Hell Run on a hiker bridge.

0.1 Just ahead the trail splits. Stay right with the Hells Hollow Trail while the Slippery Rock Gorge Trail continues its journey down to Slippery Rock Creek and McConnells Mill. Cross back over to the right-hand bank, descending a gorgeous wide valley.

0.2 Pass a homesite or building site to the right of the trail. The foundation is apparent. A tributary comes in from the right. Phlox, trillium, and mayapple rise in spring. The Slippery Rock Gorge Trail continues to be visible across Hell Run.

0.3 Look left on Hell Run for the noteworthy slender grooved channel through which the creek flows. The stream begins to cut a bit into the landscape.

0.6 Reach Hells Hollow Falls and the limestone kiln after dropping into a steep vale. Walk directly past the base of the kiln, then descend steps to reach the bottom of the falls. Here you can see the 18-foot pour-over as it makes an initial stream-wide drop followed by the primary fall. Make sure to walk to the top of the kiln, peering down inside. Backtrack to the trailhead.

1.2 Arrive back at the trailhead, completing the waterfall hike.

13 Kildoo Falls

Kildoo Falls is located at the bottom of the Slippery Rock Creek Gorge near historic McConnells Mill, part of McConnells Mill State Park. The dense concentration of highlights at this locale also includes a picturesque covered bridge. And of course there is the walk to Kildoo Falls, where you cruise along beautiful Slippery Rock Creek then turn up Kildoo Run. A little scrambling along Kildoo Run leads up to the 16-foot curtain-type cataract. While here, take time to check out the historic mill and covered bridge, and perhaps have a meal at the convenient picnic area at the trailhead.

Waterfall height: 16 feet
Waterfall beauty: 3
Distance: 0.6-mile out-and-back
Difficulty: Easy, does have some scrambling at the end
Hiking time: About ½ hour
Trail surface: Asphalt, natural
Other trail users: None

Canine compatibility: Leashed pets allowed
Land status: State park
Fees and permits: None
Maps: McConnells Mill State Park; USGS Portersville
Trail contact: McConnells Mill State Park (724) 368-8811, www.dcnr.state.pa.us /stateparks

Finding the trailhead: From exit 99 on I-79 north of Pittsburgh, take US 422 west for 1.7 miles to McConnells Mill Road. Turn left and follow McConnells Mill Road for 1.2 miles to reach the upper McConnells Mill parking area on your right. A few parking spots exist down by the mill but are quickly snatched up. However, additional parking can be reached by continuing on McConnells Mill Road just a bit farther to Kildoo Road. Turn right on Kildoo Road and go 0.1 mile, then turn right on Kennedy Road and find the small parking area by the covered bridge. GPS: 40.952988, -80.170026

The Hike

You will find a lot of cool stuff packed into one small area down here at the bottom of the Slippery Rock Creek Gorge—not only Kildoo Falls but also the historic Mc-Connells Mill (1868) and the McConnells Mill covered bridge (1874), a National Historic Landmark. Then you add in the 930-acre Slippery Rock Gorge Natural Area, a National Natural Landmark featuring the gorgeous waterway as well as outstanding flora and geology. That is a lot of superlatives in one spot! Therefore, even though the waterfall hike is short, there is plenty to see.

The park's namesake stands tall and proud above the rocks and rapids of Slippery Rock Creek. A dam used to provide a constant water supply and divert water stands just upstream of McConnells Mill. In the old days, moving water provided power to operate water turbines that in turn turned grinding stones transforming wheat, corn, and oats into flour. Despite the rugged nature of the area, local residents flocked to the mill to have their crops ground. Thus McConnells Mill became a natural gathering point for the general community. This explains the erection of the covered bridge just downstream from the mill—that way residents on the other side of Slippery Rock Creek could access the mill.

However, times and technology change, and in 1928 the mill closed for good. In the 1940s owner Thomas Hartman conferred the mill and adjacent lands to the Commonwealth of Pennsylvania, and McConnells Mill State Park came to be in 1957. Since that time the preserve has been a draw for visitors including climbers, whitewater boaters, and anglers. (By the way, swimming is not allowed in aptly named Slippery Rock Creek.) Nevertheless, the hiking trails are the primary draw here. Hikers can visit multiple waterfalls and trek along the gorge in incredible surroundings where rock bluffs overhang the trails, rapids dash among massive boulders, and vegetation grows thick in the canyon depths.

You will get a taste of this en route to Kildoo Falls. Pick up the Kildoo Trail on the east bank of Slippery Rock Creek, the same side where McConnells Mill stands. Begin walking south, entering a rich, lush world of green contrasting with the pale gray rock found in the gorge. The trail travels directly alongside the stream, allowing favorable aquatic views. Massive mossy boulders lie in silent repose beside the path, while Slippery Rock Creek sings downstream. A steep hillside rises to your left. It isn't long before you are at Kildoo Run and a bridge spanning this tributary of Slippery Rock Creek. Work your way up bouldery Kildoo Run and reach Kildoo Falls spilling off a naked ledge, behind which lies a rock house. Kildoo Bridge stands above it, complicating waterfall photography. Visitors often walk behind the falls for fun.

At this point you can return to the trailhead three ways: Simply backtrack the way you came; backtrack down Kildoo Run, then continue on the Kildoo Trail and make a 2-mile loop circling around both sides of Slippery Rock Creek; or scramble up above Kildoo Falls, then walk Kennedy Road back to McConnells Mill. I recommend making the 2-mile loop on the Kildoo Trail to better understand why the Slippery Rock Creek Gorge was designated a National Natural Landmark. Furthermore, for best waterfall viewing I recommend coming here from winter through spring, as Kildoo Falls can nearly dry up in summer and fall. Also, when Slippery Rock Creek is running high, whitewater kayakers will be out in force, intrepidly plying the stream's rapids.

Kildoo Falls pours forth white onto a stone-littered base.

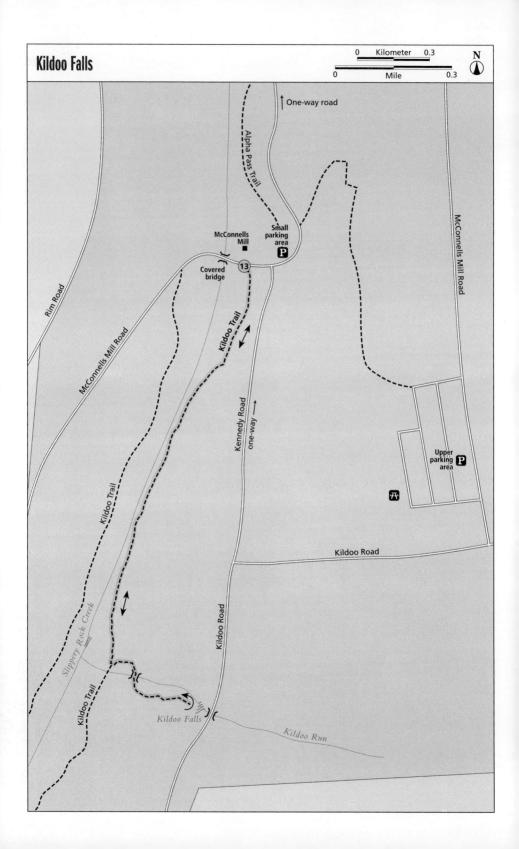

Miles and Directions

0.0 From the trailhead on the east side of Slippery Rock Creek near the covered bridge, pick up the asphalt Kildoo Trail and head down the gorge, following the stream downriver.

0.2 Pass a notable rapid on Slippery Rock Creek. Just after that, come to a bridge crossing Kildoo Run. Look up then join the user-created path working up the left bank of Kildoo Run. While clambering up, cross over to the right-hand bank of Kildoo Run as the watercourse slaloms among big boulders.

0.3 Reach Kildoo Falls as it dives off a protruding rock rim above a stone-littered base. From here you can backtrack, make the 2-mile Kildoo Trail loop, or climb up to Kennedy Road and walk back that way.

0.6 If backtracking, arrive back at the trailhead, completing the waterfall hike.

This historic covered bridge can be found at the trailhead.

14 Alpha Falls

Also known as Spillway Falls, this cataract makes a slender, delicate drop over a vertical ledge en route to the depths of the Slippery Rock Creek Gorge at McConnells Mill State Park. It is an easy and short walk from McConnells Mill Road, working down to the base of a cliff line. You then cruise along the cliff line to reach the base of this 34-foot splashing faucet of white.

Waterfall height: 34 feet
Waterfall beauty: 4
Distance: 0.2-mile out-and-back
Difficulty: Easy
Hiking time: About ½ hour
Trail surface: Natural
Other trail users: None
Canine compatibility: Leashed pets allowed

Land status: State park
Fees and permits: None
Maps: McConnells Mill State Park; USGS Portersville
Trail contact: McConnells Mill State Park, (724) 368-8811, www.dcnr.state.pa.us /stateparks

Finding the trailhead: From exit 99 on I-79 north of Pittsburgh, take US 422 west for 1.7 miles to McConnells Mill Road. Turn left and follow McConnells Mill Road for 0.6 mile to reach the Alpha Pass trailhead parking area on your right. There is room here for about 4 cars. GPS: 40.960040, -80.168828

The Hike

The only disappointment about the Alpha Falls experience is that the hike is a bit short, but fear not, for the scenery is good and you can visit two other waterfalls—Hells Hollow Falls and Kildoo Falls—that are also located at McConnells Mill State Park and detailed in this guide. By the way, note the driving directions—this waterfall is located just a few miles off I-79, so you could always make a quick detour to Alpha Falls, a flume spiller dashing off the upper gorge of Slippery Rock Creek.

Though currently called Alpha Falls, the name Spillway Falls seems more appropriate, as it makes a tapered dive from the edge of the canyon rim. The walk uses the Alpha Pass Trail, which is also part of the long-distance North Country Trail. Therefore, though your hike is short, you will be walking a portion of one of the country's longest long-distance trails (more about that below). But first you can take a stroll to an observation point at the top of Alpha Falls. It is reached via a short spur that crosses the stream above the falls then comes to a little cleared observation area fronted by a wooden fence. The view is steep here, and gaining a proper perception of the falls can be difficult. That is why we next walk to the base of the falls for an improved bottom-up vista.

Alpha Falls widens on its 34-foot descent.

The walk joins the Alpha Pass Trail/North Country Trail, descending off the rim. Angle down using steps under forest, reaching a spur trail. This path meanders toward Alpha Falls at the foot of a steep cliff line, where mosses and vegetation cling to crevices in the crag. You then reach the base of Alpha Falls. Here the unnamed tributary makes its white tumble, splashing its way down from the cliff before collecting then pushing beyond your viewing spot.

If you want to extend the walk, rejoin the Alpha Pass/North Country Trail. The North Country Trail traverses about 4,600 miles, covering seven states, of which Pennsylvania is one. By the way, this falls can run low and slow by midsummer; therefore, late winter through spring is the best time to visit.

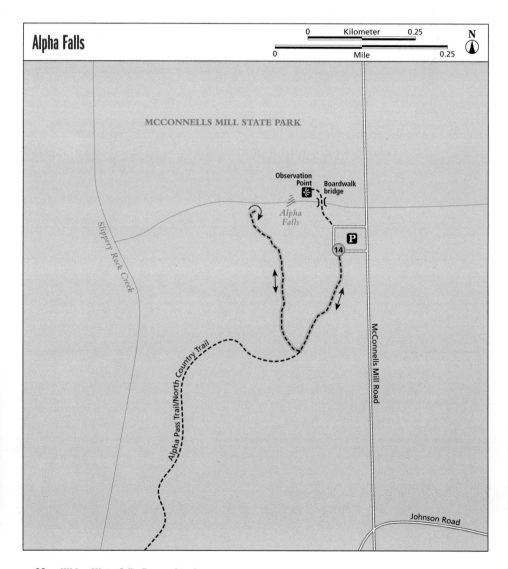

Alpha Falls

MCCONNELLS MILL STATE PARK

Observation Point

Boardwalk bridge

Alpha Falls

Slippery Rock Creek

Alpha Pass Trail/North Country Trail

McConnells Mill Road

Johnson Road

Miles and Directions

0.0 Leave the Alpha Pass trailhead, descending on the Alpha Pass Trail/North Country Trail. After 200 feet, take the official spur trail leaving right toward Alpha Falls.

0.1 Reach Alpha Falls after working the base of a vertical cliff line. The 34-foot flume spills narrowly from the rock rim above, then stays slim as it escapes over layered rock before splashing onto a lower ledge and then off a large boulder. The waterway then regroups and drives downhill in lesser drops and pools toward Slippery Rock Creek. Backtrack to the trailhead.

0.2 Arrive back at the trailhead, completing the waterfall walk.

ABOUT THE NORTH COUNTRY SCENIC TRAIL

Part of the Alpha Falls hike uses the North Country National Scenic Trail (NCT), a 4,600-mile multistate long-distance path that runs in conjunction with several trails, as it does with the Alpha Pass Trail here. Light blue blazes indicate the NCT, which traverses the northwest corner of Pennsylvania. The trail's slogan is "Exploring America's Northwoods." It is not anywhere near complete, but disconnected sections aspire to link New York state to Pennsylvania onward to Ohio, Michigan, Wisconsin, Minnesota, and South Dakota, ending in North Dakota.

Born of 1968's National Trails System Act, the North Country National Scenic Trail was birthed as the Appalachian Trail and Pacific Crest Trail were being officially recognized and protected. The idea of a North Country Trail was explored more in depth, and by 1980 the North Country National Scenic Trail was officially authorized by Congress.

Most of the Pennsylvania portion of the NCT—almost 100 miles—travels through the Allegheny National Forest. This hike's particular segment runs through McConnells Mill State Park, cutting through the Slippery Rock Creek Gorge, yet one more scenic swath of the Keystone State.

15 Pioneer Falls

This hike at Oil Creek State Park takes you to Pioneer Run, a tributary of Great Western Run and Oil Creek. Pioneer Run cuts a 500-foot-deep valley during its short flow. Part of this descent appears as Pioneer Falls, an attractive ledge drop also known as Greg Falls. En route to the cataract, the hike passes vestiges of the oil industry, for it was born here in this dazzling preserve that has made a natural recovery of epic proportions since the birth of the world's first oil boom—and bust.

Waterfall height: 18 feet
Waterfall beauty: 5
Distance: 1.6-mile out-and-back
Difficulty: Easy
Hiking time: About 1 hour
Trail surface: Natural
Other trail users: None

Canine compatibility: Leashed pets allowed
Land status: State park
Fees and permits: None
Maps: Oil Creek State Park; USGS Titusville South
Trail contact: Oil Creek State Park, (814) 676-5915, www.dcnr.state.pa.us/stateparks

Finding the trailhead: From Oil City, take PA 8 north for 9 miles to Petroleum Center Road. Turn right and follow Petroleum Center Road for 1.2 miles to Pioneer Road. Turn left and follow Pioneer Road, a dirt road, for 2.1 miles to dead-end at the Pioneer trailhead, which is also a lesser-used access to the park's Bicycle Trail. (Do not stop at the Gerard Trail parking area reached at 1.7 miles.) GPS: 41.531233, -79.665333

The Hike

This waterfall hike starts at the former community of Pioneer, once a bucolic farmed flat at the bottom of the Oil Creek Gorge. (Oil Creek was named for the naturally occurring oil seeps that are in its valley.) Then in August of 1859, an oil well met with success 69 feet below the surface and a "black gold" rush ensued. Men and supplies descended on the area. Roads and infrastructure were built, and oil wells were haphazardly dug. The once-natural tree-covered slopes and occasional cleared flats of farmland were instantaneously turned into quagmires of oil, water, and soil, a hideous mixture that left the once-unspoiled Oil Creek valley a black, soupy mess. Photos from that era show nearly denuded hillsides from which wooden oil derricks rose mixed with pipes, barrels, and an array of infrastructure, along with buildings and roads.

The oil boom was over by 1870 and the valley was left behind, though smaller drilling operations continued through the years. Today, though metal and some wooden relics of that era survive, the valley has recovered impressively. The trees have returned in grandeur, the soil has stabilized, Oil Creek and its feeder streams have cleared, and the quagmire is long gone. The historical importance of the world's first commercial oil well and the returned beauty of the Oil Creek valley rightly convinced the Commonwealth of Pennsylvania to establish a state park here.

They did a fine job, creating hiking and bicycling trails, paddler put-ins and take-outs, and picnic areas. Perhaps more importantly, the park established a number of historical tableaus, partly re-creating locales using the left-behind infrastructure to convey the historical time line of Oil Creek. In my personal opinion, this is one of the single best state parks not only in Pennsylvania but in all the East. The combination of human and natural history overlain on a superlative landscape and layered with multiple outdoor recreation opportunities make this preserve special and a mandatory Keystone State experience.

Pioneer Falls, aka Greg Falls, adds to this extraordinary legacy. Though a low-flow cascade best appreciated from late winter through mid-spring, the walk is a good one. Starting at the remote Pioneer trailhead, you will make your way up the steep vale away from Oil Creek and quickly spot oil-era relics, quickening your pulse (the climb

Pioneer Falls makes its initial drop then moves on over sheets of limestone.

up the stream valley does that a little too). And then you arrive at Pioneer Falls. Here, as the trail curves around the hollow, the stream spills over a stone lip then widens, making its way down a layered rock face, splashing outward as another lip below juts out. The water then curtains from this second rim before splashing over an angled rockslide to finally settle, skittering over flat rock slabs toward Oil Creek.

Photography opportunities are numerous despite the steep slope around Pioneer Falls. Pick the right time and your efforts will be well rewarded. While here, explore the rest of the park possibilities, from bicycling to historical interpretation to paddling and fishing—and other waterfalls!

The tiered stone strata over which Pioneer Falls drops create a menagerie of white water.

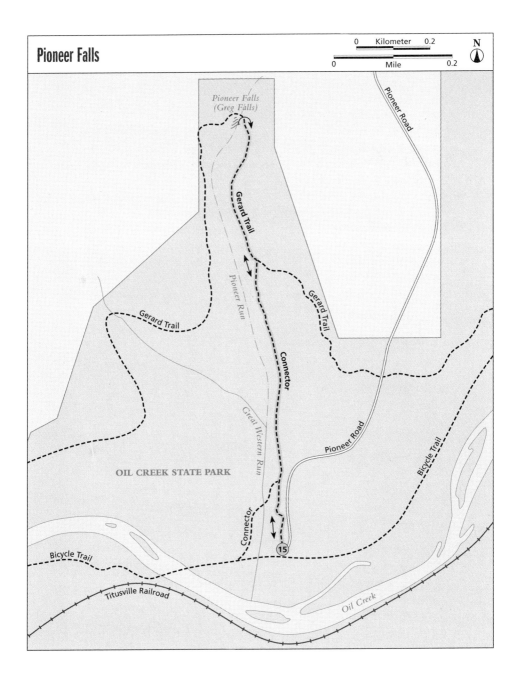

Pioneer Falls

Miles and Directions

0.0 With your back to Oil Creek and the Bicycle Trail, join a white-blazed singletrack connector path heading north into hardwoods. Pass a partly embedded concrete structure, your first relic of the oil boom. Come to a trail intersection after 300 feet. Another connector trail leads left and downhill to cross Great Western Run and then meet the Bicycle Trail. Our waterfall hike keeps straight, still on the original connector trail heading into Pioneer Run.

0.2 Pass upright wood-and-metal barrels as well as metal pipes, remainders of a century and a half back. Continue up Pioneer Run, sometimes passing water seeps on the steep hillside.

0.5 Intersect and join the Gerard Trail, the park's 36-mile backpacking path that makes a big loop through the preserve. Stay left here, cutting deeper into the hollow after passing under a transmission line.

0.8 Reach Pioneer Falls, also called Greg Falls. It drops a little under 20 feet over layered strata then slides downward to Great Western Run and Oil Creek. Photographers can approach the falls from multiple angles. Backtrack to the trailhead.

1.6 Arrive back at the trailhead, completing the walk.

16 Plum Dungeon Falls

On the top five list of all-time Pennsylvania waterfall names, Plum Dungeon Falls is one of those cataracts that is easier to view from afar than to reach and photograph. However, other more accessible spillers can be seen (and reached) here in this lesser-visited parcel of historic and eye-appealing Oil Creek State Park. This trek, using a segment of the park's long-distance Gerard Trail, takes you not only to Plum Dungeon Falls but also to a couple of other falls, enhancing the waterfall hike. Bring a long-range lens if you wish to photograph Plum Dungeon Falls, or prepare to do a little off-trail scrambling to capture the cataracts along this unnamed multipronged tributary of Oil Creek.

Waterfall height: In order, 40 feet, 25 feet, 15 feet
Waterfall beauty: 4
Distance: 1.8-mile out-and-back
Difficulty: Easy, but prepare to scramble if photographing waterfalls.
Hiking time: About 1 hour
Trail surface: Natural

Other trail users: None
Canine compatibility: Leashed pets allowed
Land status: State park
Fees and permits: None
Maps: Oil Creek State Park; USGS Titusville South
Trail contact: Oil Creek State Park, (814) 676-5915, www.dcnr.state.pa.us/stateparks

Finding the trailhead: From Oil City, take PA 8 north for 13 miles to Black Road. Turn right and follow Black Road for 0.7 mile to Dutch Hill Road. Turn right and follow Dutch Hill Road for 3.2 miles (it turns to Miller Farm Road along the way), bridging Oil Creek at 3 miles. Continue beyond the bridge for 0.2 mile and reach the parking area on your left. GPS: 41.564667, -79.651700

The Hike

To me, the name Plum Dungeon Falls conjures up images of crashing waters sheeting into a deep, dark, and foreboding gorge. And that image isn't far off. The creative waterfaller who named the falls and the reason for naming the cataract thus has been lost to time, but the moniker made me eager to jump on Oil Creek State Park's master path—the Gerard Trail—and see this spiller for myself. I was not disappointed, especially when considering you get a couple of bonus cataracts in the bargain.

The singletrack Gerard Trail leaves this little-used trailhead and climbs the side slope of a hillside angling toward Oil Creek, with nary a drop of stream around, much less a waterfall. Oak, cherry, and beech rise overhead. The Gerard Trail climbs to the edge of the Oil Creek Gorge, cresting a wooded hill then turning into the stream responsible for Plum Dungeon Falls. However, at this point the waterway is gently gurgling along, giving waterfall hikers no hint that this is the stream they are seeking. (Following the stream downhill from this point is a fool's game and much too steep and dangerous for sane hikers.) Continuing on, you cross a larger steam in an evergreen copse, expecting this to be the stream of Plum Dungeon Falls. It isn't, but the creek forms an angled cataract that is the most accessible of the falls on this hike.

The Gerard Trail leaves the water, but soon you come to a signed spur trail, which leads to a tantalizing signed overlook of 40-foot Plum Dungeon Falls. Here the narrow flume pours forth then widens over a wet rock face, reaching the base of the gorge and flowing on.

If you are tempted to view the falls, just backtrack to the last creek crossing then enter the canyon from there, picking your way downstream. You will also see the angled cataract of that unnamed stream. Below that fall, you will observe a sheet cascade coming in before finding Plum Dungeon Falls. However, if you visit in late summer, autumn, or during dry periods, you will not see much water at all, so save this waterfall hike for a rainy day or wetter time of the year.

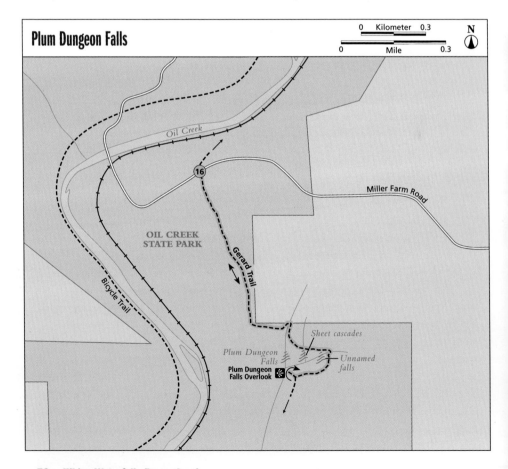

Miles and Directions

0.0   Leave the Miller Farm Road trailhead on the Gerard Trail, southbound. Ascend a steady, steep side slope, angling upward through the forest.

0.4   Come very near the state park boundary.

0.5   Level off, then pass through a ferny flat.

0.6   Dip into an evergreen copse and step over the innocuous-looking streamlet that is to be Plum Dungeon Falls, then step over smaller rock spring branches.

0.8   Hop over the largest stream yet in an evergreen copse, just before it drops into the 500-foot-deep canyon leading to Oil Creek. Circle around to view the most accessible falls of the hike as well as a low-flow sheet cascade.

0.9   Reach the signed spur trail to Plum Dungeon Falls. Follow the spur 50 yards to an overlook across a developing gorge. Here you can see the cataract spilling over a wide rock face framed in evergreens, though a complete view is not possible. Backtrack to the trailhead.

1.8   Arrive back at the trailhead, completing the waterfall hike.

This unnamed falls previews what is to come when you reach Plum Dungeon Falls.

17 Boughton Falls, Miller Falls, Lower Miller Falls

This trek presents an opportunity to make a foot tour of remarkable Oil Creek State Park, one of Pennsylvania's finest preserves. Start at the bottom of the Oil Creek Gorge, then make your way along the east side of the canyon, crossing tributaries and hilltops displaying the park's everywhere-you-look beauty. Finally reach Boughton Run, with Boughton Falls dashing over a stone face in a deep, evergreen-rich hollow. The hike passes a gorge-top vista before crossing Oil Creek on a huge suspension bridge. Climb to the north rim of the gorge, then visit Miller Falls. Finally, descend to view Lower Miller Falls with its dramatic spill as well as machinery left over from the world's first oil boom. Be prepared for a long day full of highlights.

Waterfall height: In order, 28 feet, 8 feet, 17 feet
Waterfall beauty: 5
Distance: 10.2-mile loop
Difficulty: Difficult due to distance and elevation changes
Hiking time: About 6½ hours
Trail surface: Natural

Other trail users: None
Canine compatibility: Leashed pets allowed
Land status: State park
Fees and permits: None
Maps: Oil Creek State Park; USGS Titusville South
Trail contact: Oil Creek State Park, (814) 676-5915, www.dcnr.state.pa.us/stateparks

Finding the trailhead: From Oil City, take PA 8 north for 13 miles to Black Road. Turn right and follow Black Road for 0.7 mile to Dutch Hill Road. Turn right and follow Dutch Hill Road for 3.2 miles (it turns to Miller Farm Road along the way), bridging Oil Creek at 3 miles. Park in the lot on the right just after crossing the bridge, between the bridge and the railroad tracks. GPS: 41.565008, -79.656563

The Hike

This is more than a waterfall hike—it is an adventure. And not only is it a great opportunity to view waterfalls at Oil Creek State Park, but you can also learn about the history of this "gorge-ous" destination. The hike is a long one, so come well prepared, then let the scenery unfurl before you. After finishing you will come away with not only an appreciation for the falling waters of this area but also a concrete vision of Pennsylvania beauty and splendor.

Oil Creek State Park encompasses over 6,250 acres of land bordering Oil Creek and the canyon lands that rise above it. Within the park you can enjoy over 52 miles of trails, including a rail trail and the 36-mile Gerard Trail, a hiker-only loop path that much of this particular waterfall hike uses. Other connector trails enable you to make shorter circuits using a portion of the Gerard Trail. Backpackers can enjoy overnighting at two hike-in shelters here, both conveniently located near the trail. (The Gerard Trail is named for Dan Gerard, who developed and maintained the trail for sixteen years before passing away in 1997.) Anglers vie for bass and rainbow trout in Oil Creek. Brook trout can be found in some of the tributaries.

Oil Creek makes for a fine spring-through-early-summer paddling destination, presenting easy rapids for beginner paddlers, and a float is a fantastic way to enjoy the gorge. Other park visitors revel in the gorge via the Oil Creek & Titusville Railroad excursion train. It makes a 26-mile round-trip during the warm season, departing from Titusville. Cap off your adventure with a visit to the Drake Well Museum, where you can learn all about the world's first oil boom, which took place within this park.

Although our primary reason for visiting Oil Creek State Park is waterfalls, you cannot escape history in this gorge—the first part of the walk passes along a former 19th-century pipeline route and a cemetery before coming to some simple cascades on an unnamed creek. Work your way along Jones Run, then through the Toy Run valley. Rise to a flat and once-settled area, where the Gerard Trail wanders off, and on old roads before reaching Boughton Run and 28-foot Boughton Falls, nestled at the depth of the canyon, shaded by pines and other evergreens. It is not easy to reach the fall's base, but it can be done. You are better off trying to reach the base of Boughton Falls from the north side of the creek, where the Gerard Trail soon takes you.

Beyond Barton Run you come to a bench and cleared overlook. Here hikers are rewarded with an up-canyon panorama. The large swinging bridge that you use to span Oil Creek is clearly visible hundreds of feet below. You continue along a side slope before reaching a spur that leads down to the suspension bridge, using many switchbacks. Enjoy inspiring views from the bridge itself before turning downstream in lush bottomland.

Then up you go, climbing steadily into an unnamed watershed to reach the west rim of the Oil Creek Gorge. The trail meanders along the upper mountain slope before reaching a trail intersection. Take a side trip here to Miller Falls, an 8-foot curtain drop, then backtrack, taking an official "shortcut" trail dropping into the heart of Miller Run.

After navigating your way down the lower Miller Run gorge, you come to an area rich with silent, rusted machinery—an outdoor living museum of this valley's petroleum past. Here a short side trail leads to Lower Miller Falls, a stair-step cascade that tumbles well below, where you can see more relics of Oil Creek's industrial glory days. Lower Miller Falls is definitely the more dramatic of the two falls along Miller Run, as it makes a 17-foot angled drop followed by a series of irregular tumbles that could be called cascades before splashingly curving out of sight. Rejoin the Gerard Trail as it surmounts the ridge dividing Miller Run from Wolfkiel Run.

The hike makes one last dash along Wolfkiel Run, crossing an unusual A-frame bridge before reaching a picnic area and the Bicycle Trail. Here it is but a short walk

Boughton Falls makes its majestic angled drop.

to the Miller Farm Road Bridge that takes you across Oil Creek and back to the trailhead, completing the waterfall hike and tour de force of Oil Creek State Park.

Miles and Directions

0.0 Leave the Miller Farm Road Bridge trailhead on a white-blazed path climbing steps, walking east, from the far side of the railroad track. Immediately climb a steep hillside rising above Oil Creek. Come to a graveyard with some stones upright, others askew, and still others flat on the ground. Join the route of an 1865 oil pipeline. Note the dug holes beside the trail/pipeline route.

0.4 Meet the Gerard Trail. Turn left toward Drake Well. Ahead, angle into an unnamed stream, bridging it just above a 12-foot cascade with lesser falls nearby. Leave the hollow and continue up the canyon. Steps and boardwalks aid your passage.

1.3 Bridge Jones Run, then turn up the flowery vale. Go on and off an old roadbed.

1.6 Cut through the divide separating Jones Run from Toy Run. Surprisingly, climb instead of dropping to Toy Run.

1.8 Cross a tributary of Toy Run, then another tributary of Toy Run. Turn up along Toy Run amid yellow birch, beech, and fern.

2.3 Cross Toy Run on a footbridge.

2.4 Pass the foundations of an old homesite. Stay with the blazes and ignore unmarked pre-park roads and trails.

2.7 Step over a tributary of Boughton Run. Descend.

3.1 Reach Boughton Falls at an overlook. The 28-foot cascade lies below in evergreens. The cataract pours from a stone tongue then makes an angled descent over stratified rock, widening before making a short curtain drop at its base. The hike continues, crossing Boughton Run and another tributary before leaving the stream for good.

3.8 Reach a bench and cleared vista. Enjoy an upstream prospect of the Oil Creek Gorge. The hiker suspension bridge looks small in the distance. You will be crossing that bridge ahead. Look around for evidence of the oil industry.

4.5 Turn left at a signed intersection. Descend into the gorge via switchbacks, going on and off old roads. Stepping stones and boardwalks aid your passage.

5.0 Reach the swinging bridge and the Oil Creek & Titusville Railroad line. A shaded picnic table makes a good resting spot, especially since it is located roughly halfway on the hike. After resting, cross the suspension bridge, soaking in views of the creek and the rising hillsides. Once across the creek, turn left and cruise waterside flats rich with trees and brush. Avoid user-created spurs shortcutting right to the Bicycle Trail. Look for ruins of the former community of Broughton.

Miller Falls shines on a dark day.
RUSTY GLESSNER

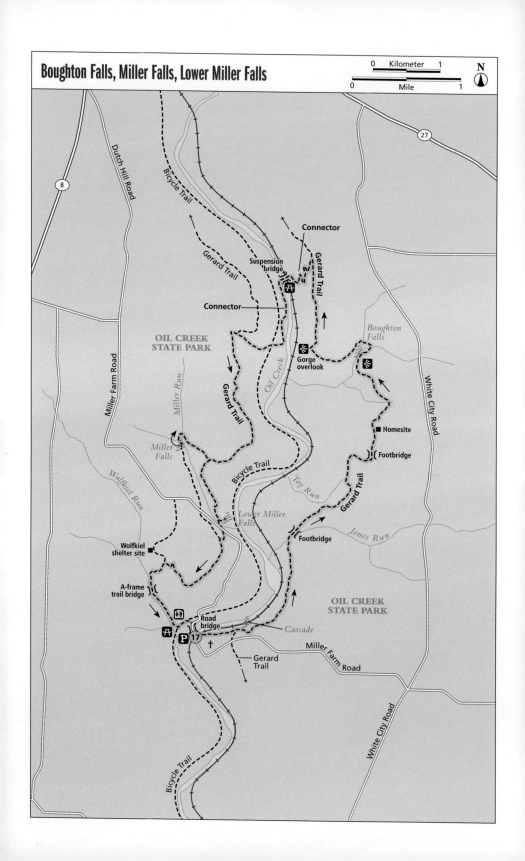

Boughton Falls, Miller Falls, Lower Miller Falls

0 — Kilometer — 1
0 — Mile — 1

N

27

8

Dutch Hill Road

Bicycle Trail

Gerard Trail

Suspension bridge

Connector

Gerard Trail

Connector

OIL CREEK STATE PARK

Miller Run

Gerard Trail

Oil Creek

Gorge overlook

Boughton Falls

White City Road

■ Homesite

)|(Footbridge

Miller Farm Road

Miller Falls

Bicycle Trail

Toy Run

Gerard Trail

Wolfkiel Run

Lower Miller Falls

)|(Footbridge

Jones Run

Wolfkiel shelter site ■

A-frame trail bridge

Road bridge

P 17

Cascade

OIL CREEK STATE PARK

†

Gerard Trail

Miller Farm Road

White City Road

Bicycle Trail

Gerard Trail

5.6 Officially cross the Bicycle Trail after turning away from Oil Creek. Ahead, pass a scarred clearing from the oil days. Climb into woods and work up a steep draw.

5.9 Rejoin the Gerard Trail and head left toward Wolfkiel Run. Continue climbing and curve around the hollow, bridging the hollow's stream. Keep ascending, passing old oil barrels and other relics. Level off and cruise along the rim of the canyon.

7.1 Come to a trail intersection. For the moment, stay right with the Gerard Trail and head toward Miller Falls. Pass through hardwoods, looking for old stone fences from farming days, then enter a hemlock copse.

7.4 Hop over Miller Run, then curve to another stream, bridging this second stream.

7.5 Reach Miller Falls, to the left of the trail. The spiller drops about 8 feet over a stone ledge then flows on, the least impressive of the falls here at Oil Creek State Park. Backtrack to the last intersection.

7.9 Join the connector trail pushing deep into Miller Run. The trail then crisscrosses the stream in a steep-sided section of the gorge without benefit of bridges. The exact route changes with the levels of the stream. You will see many old oil relics down here.

8.4 Reach the signed spur trail to Lower Miller Falls amid some large pieces of machinery, a metal museum. Take the spur trail to reach 17-foot Lower Miller Falls, a classic angled cascade dropping into a plunge pool followed by lesser tumbles before flowing out of eyeshot.

8.5 Cross Miller Farm Road. If you are exhausted, you can simply follow Miller Farm Road downhill to the bridge over Oil Creek and the trailhead on the far side of the bridge. The hike described here stays with the connector then climbs.

8.7 Rejoin the Gerard Trail again. Head left for Wolfkiel Run.

9.4 Reach the signed spur trail leading right to the Wolfkiel Run shelter site. Stay left, descending toward Wolfkiel Run.

9.4 Come to Wolfkiel Run. Turn left, heading downstream in woods.

9.7 Cross Wolfkiel Run on a distinctive A-frame trail bridge, labeled "Alfred's Bent Nail Bridge."

9.9 Emerge at a picnic area beside the Bicycle Trail. Head down to the Bicycle Trail and cross Wolfkiel Run via a bridge. A restroom stands nearby. Walk northeast on the Bicycle Trail.

10.0 Split right on a white-blazed connector trail, then quickly meet Miller Farm Road. Head right on Miller Farm Road.

10.2 Cross Oil Creek on the Miller Farm Road Bridge, then come to the parking area, completing the waterfall hike and tour of Oil Creek State Park.

Hikers executing this loop walk this suspension bridge over Oil Creek.

18 Logan Falls

Located in the heart of the Allegheny National Forest in northwest Pennsylvania, Logan Falls presents an opportunity to visit a remote section of Pennsylvania's only national forest. Located on Logan Run, a simple track leads down to this 10-foot tumbler in a deep wooded setting.

Waterfall height: 10 feet
Waterfall beauty: 4
Distance: 0.6-mile out-and-back
Difficulty: Easy
Hiking time: About 1½ hour
Trail surface: Natural
Other trail users: None

Canine compatibility: Leashed pets allowed
Land status: National forest
Fees and permits: None
Maps: Allegheny National Forest; USGS Mayburg
Trail contact: Allegheny National Forest, (814) 927-6628, www.fs.usda.gov/allegheny

Finding the trailhead: From East Hickory, take PA 666 east for 25 miles to Lynch. Cross the bridge over Tionesta Creek, joining Blue Jay Road. Follow Blue Jay Road south for 1.1 miles, then take an acute right onto FR 128/Job Corps Road. Drive FR 128 for 5.2 miles to reach Deadmans Corners, an intersection of 5 forest roads. Angle right onto FR 180 and follow it for 2.5 miles to find a rectangular parking area on the right. Look for the "LF" spray-painted on a tree beside the parking area for 3 or 4 cars. The parking area also has a big boulder to the right of it as you look at it from the road. GPS: 41.584675, -79.159518

The Hike

Logan Falls is one of those cataracts that Pennsylvania waterfallers always mean to visit but never seem to make it happen. It is not close to anywhere. However, enough visitors come to this remote tract of the Allegheny National Forest to keep the trail well beaten down, despite the fact it is not recognized as a marked and maintained trail by the Forest Service. I cannot understand why they do not make this an official trail then sign and maintain it, especially since the Allegheny National Forest has very few waterfalls within its 517,000 acres.

Nonetheless, hikers have been visiting Logan Falls for decades. Located in the Tionesta Creek watershed between Sheffield and Marienville, Logan Falls makes for an easy walk through northern hardwoods, where boulders flank the path. As you descend into the Logan Run watershed, its sonorous rapids reach your ears. Suddenly you are astride Logan Falls as the stream makes an S-curve through rich woods. The two-pronged spiller first drops as a vertical curtain then makes a widely angled descent before slowing in a plunge pool.

Both the bottom and the top of the falls are easy to reach. When the water is at normal levels, you can keep your feet dry while searching for the prime photography

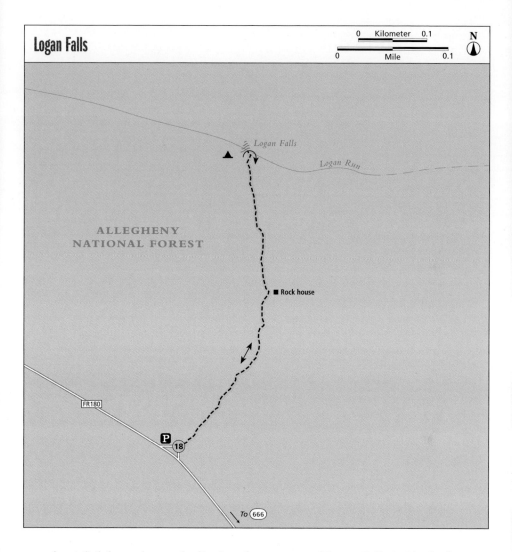

Logan Falls

Logan Run

ALLEGHENY
NATIONAL FOREST

■ Rock house

FR180

P
18

To 666

angles. A lightly used campsite lies just downstream of Logan Falls, inside the lower part of the stream curve. The trail dies out beyond the camp, adding to the remoteness of this parcel of Pennsylvania.

Miles and Directions

0.0   From the trailhead, leave the parking area, descending on a singletrack path. Large boulders flank the trail. A notable boulder garden rises to your left. Overhead, a youngish northern hardwood forest shades the trail.

0.1   Pass a small rock house beside the trail.

0.3   Come to Logan Falls and Logan Run amid birches. The two-tiered cataract spills into a shallow pool then cascades downstream. Backtrack to the trailhead.

0.6   Arrive back at the trailhead, completing the walk.

The waters of Logan Falls make their drop.

19 Hector Falls

Upon seeing Hector Falls, you will agree that this is one of the—if not the—most unusual waterfalls in the state of Pennsylvania. This low flow but high drama cataract in the Allegheny National Forest pours over a pointed stone lip then runs down vertical blocklike walls, splattering into a gloomy mini-gorge of other blocklike boulders. You can stare at this waterfall from behind it, from a high level straight on, and at the bottom of the rock gorge. Do not miss this one!

Waterfall height: 22 feet
Waterfall beauty: 5
Distance: 2.0-mile out-and-back
Difficulty: Easy
Hiking time: About 1 hour
Trail surface: Natural
Other trail users: None

Canine compatibility: Leashed pets allowed
Land status: National forest
Fees and permits: None
Maps: Allegheny National Forest; USGS Ludlow
Trail contact: Allegheny National Forest, (814) 927-6628, www.fs.usda.gov/allegheny

Finding the trailhead: From the intersection of PA 666 and US 6 in Sheffield, head east on US 6 for 6.2 miles, then turn right onto South Hillside (you will see a sign for Tionesta Scenic Area). Follow Hillside a short distance, then turn left on Water Street. Follow it a short distance, then turn right on Scenic Drive. Cross railroad tracks and Scenic Drive becomes FR 133. Follow FR 133 for 0.7 mile, then turn right onto FR 258 and follow it for 2.1 miles to a parking area and gated FR 330 on your left. Look for "HF" spray-painted on a tree. Do not block the forest road gate at the trailhead. GPS: 41.695738, -78.980710

The Hike

This is another waterfall—one of the few in the massive Allegheny National Forest— that should be a showcase natural feature for the national forest. It is perplexing that Hector Falls is not developed as a recreational resource, for not only does it stand tall in its own right, but it is a showstopper of a cataract when compared to all the other spillers in the Keystone State.

The unusual geological configuration is the reason for Hector Falls' specialness. It appears like a giant boy dropped his toy blocks where the unnamed stream tumbles. The squared-off characteristics of these boulders make it stand out. It almost looks man-made, but no human could re-create this work of God.

Hector Falls' stream flows along, minding its own business, then reaches the precipice. Normally such ledges run straight across, or may be inverted from erosion, but instead Hector Falls makes its drop over a flat block that is pointed outward in the middle, forcing the falls to pour over ledges perpendicular to one another. The water

Hector Falls executes its most unusual descent.

then runs down the perpendicularly pointed block 22 feet, dashing onto rocks and debris that have tumbled over the edge in times past.

The base of the falls is bordered by more of these squared-off blocks, creating a strange and dusky vale overhung with evergreens and yellow birch. The stream shallowly gurgles down and out of the odd basin and resumes more "normal" characteristics en route to its mother stream, East Branch Tionesta Creek.

Save your visit for when the water is flowing, the more the better. To get an idea of how Hector Falls is running, simply check online the USGS gauge at Brokenstraw Creek at Youngsville, PA. If this relatively close stream is at or above normal flow, then go, but only during winter through spring. Summer flows—thunderstorms excepted—will be too low to show off the spectacle of this fall. Do not bother during autumn.

The hike leaves the trailhead and works down gated FR 330. It rambles south, dropping off a ridge, then angles down to the stream of Hector Falls and a gas well clearing, bordered in boulders on its downstream side. To reach the falls, simply trace the foot trail leaving south from the boulders. The waterway will be to your left. You are getting close when you enter a dark copse of evergreens. Here you can safely approach the falls from the top and look into the hemmed-in outflow of the falls. Curve around to the right and get a top-down face-to-face look at Hector Falls. This is my favorite viewpoint. Finally, work down to the right of the blocks, cross the stream, and get a bottom-up look at the falls.

After viewing this spiller from all three angles, I bet you will reach the same conclusion as I: Hector Falls is the *most* unusual waterfall in Pennsylvania.

Miles and Directions

0.0 From the parking area, walk around the pole gate and descend on FR 330. The walking is easy.

0.2 Briefly level off then resume descending. Pass a wildlife clearing on your right.

0.6 The road splits. A gated road keeps straight. Instead, head left and continue descending.

0.8 Reach the gas well clearing and the end of the road, coming alongside a creek to your left. Continue descending beyond the boulders on a foot trail.

1.0 Reach the top of Hector Falls. Curve right to explore the cataract from multiple vantages. Backtrack to the trailhead.

2.0 Arrive back at the trailhead, completing the hike to the unusual waterfall.

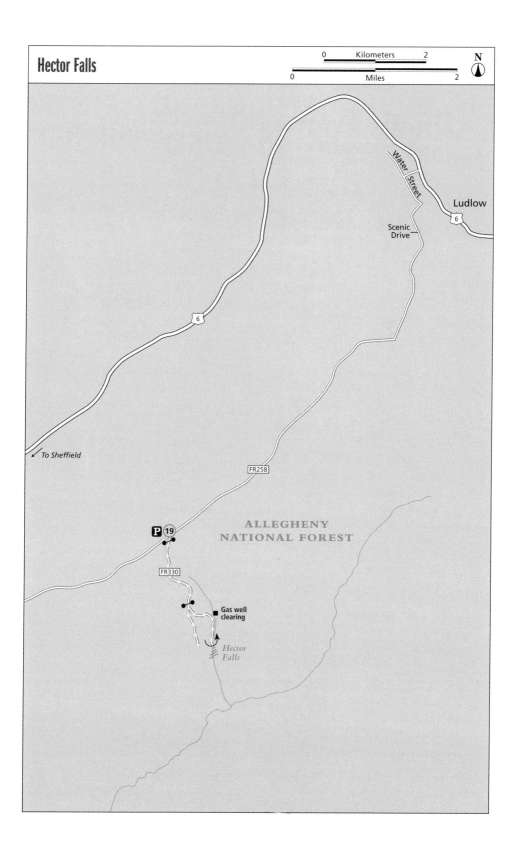

Hector Falls

0 Kilometers 2
0 Miles 2

N

Water Street

Ludlow

6

Scenic
Drive

6

To Sheffield

FR258

P 19

ALLEGHENY
NATIONAL FOREST

FR330

Gas well
clearing

Hector
Falls

Waterfall Hikes of North-Central Pennsylvania

In places, Little Fourmile Run is a continuous waterfall (hike 25).

20 Round Island Run Falls

This waterfall walk rewards those who find its remote trailhead every step of the way deep within scenic Sproul State Forest. You will leave a ridgetop road then descend along an ever-enlarging stream flanked by scads of rhododendron and yellow birch. Sidle alongside a tributary of Round Island Run to emerge at the opening where Round Island Run Falls makes its gambit, dashing over layered stone before pushing onward. An easy hike and multiple photography angles make this a desirable cataract to visit.

Waterfall height: 16 feet
Waterfall beauty: 5
Distance: 1.6-mile out-and-back
Difficulty: Easy
Hiking time: About 1 hour
Trail surface: Natural
Other trail users: None

Canine compatibility: Leashed pets allowed
Land status: State forest
Fees and permits: None
Maps: Sproul State Forest Public Use Map; USGS Sinnemahoning
Trail contact: Sproul State Forest, (570) 923-6011, www.dcnr.state.pa.us/forestry

Finding the trailhead: From Karthaus, take PA 879 west for 1.3 miles, then turn right onto Quehanna Highway and head north for 1.7 miles to Pottersdale Road. Turn right and follow Pottersdale Road for 7.6 miles, then turn left on Kings Mountain Road. Follow Kings Mountain Road for 3.2 miles, then make an acute left on Dutchman Road and follow it for 1.6 miles to Round Island Road. Turn right and follow Round Island Road for 1.8 miles to the trailhead on your left. Look for the post with "Waterfall, Round Island Trail" just past some cabins. Parking is limited and can be done on the roadside here with caution. GPS: 41.263150, -78.002967

The Hike

Round Island Run Falls isn't close to anywhere, but on the other hand, what better place for a waterfall getaway? The hike is pretty from beginning to end, and the reward of Round Island Run Falls completes the picture. Located within massive 305,000-acre Sproul State Forest, the Round Island Run watershed is one of many streams cutting through the Allegheny Plateau to feed the West Branch Susquehanna River. This part of north-central Pennsylvania is known as the Pennsylvania Wilds region, an agglomeration of vast state forests, noteworthy state parks, and clear waterways in thirteen counties where outdoor recreation is always close at hand. Round Island Run Falls is in Clinton County.

Areas like the Pennsylvania Wilds are where waterfall hikers like us prefer to find ourselves. Once on the Round Island Run Trail, you will join a doubletrack path through an upland forest of pine, spruce, and hardwoods. The path circles behind a cabin adjacent to the trailhead, then begins dropping off the Allegheny Plateau. You sidle alongside a creeklet that then joins the unnamed stream along which Round Island Run Falls is located. In actuality, Round Island Run Falls is not on Round Island Run, but rather an unnamed tributary just before the tributary flows into Round Island Run.

However, why should we focus on technicalities such as this when there is a waterfall to see? Sidle alongside a clear, rock-strewn highland stream, dancing downward, tumbling amid maples and birch and rhododendron. Cascades and lesser rapids entertain the water watcher while delving deeper into the stream valley.

Round Island Run Falls noisily announces its presence screened by scads of rhododendron. Make your way to the top of the 16-foot falls and scoot behind its flow. The top-down look is favorable for absorbing the atmosphere of the falls but not for photography. Work your way to the fall's base, then shoot away or simply admire

Round Island Run Falls flows through a frame of rhododendron.
RUSTY GLESSNER

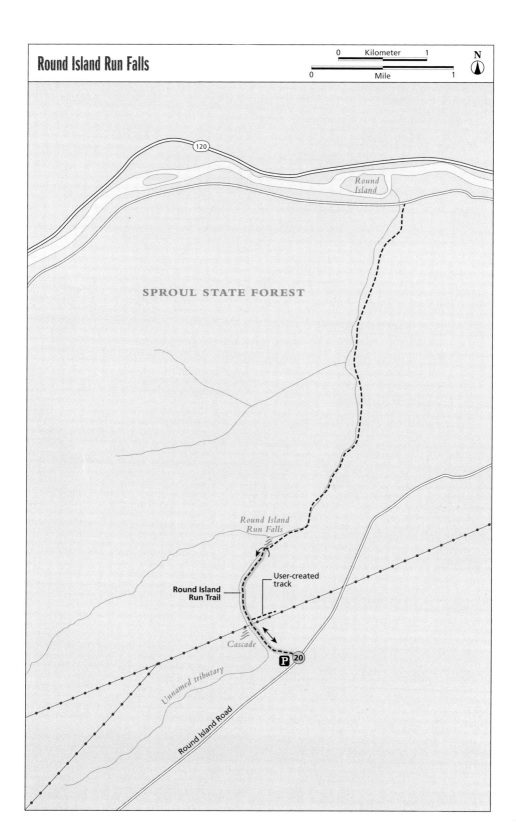

Round Island Run Falls

0 Kilometer 1

0 Mile 1

N

120

Round Island

SPROUL STATE FOREST

Round Island Run Falls

User-created track

Round Island Run Trail

Cascade

P 20

Unnamed tributary

Round Island Road

the two-tiered pour-over that first drops as a curtain about 6 feet and then makes a 10-foot curving descent over naked rock into a smallish plunge pool. The upper ledge has an overhang to the left of the falls. Lesser drops below the main waterfall enhance the overall scene. The adjacent campsite adds an overnighting possibility to this waterfall hiking adventure.

Miles and Directions

0.0 Leave the trailhead on the Round Island Run Trail, briefly starting as a doubletrack then quickly narrowing to come along a small streamlet. A cabin lies across the watercourse.

0.2 Come alongside the stream of Round Island Run Falls. The path becomes rocky.

0.3 Look for a small set of cascades as the stream squeezes past a boulder field. Just beyond these cascades come to a power line crossing and a user-created track leading up to the plateau portion of the power line clearing. Continue deeper into the vale on a picturesque trail.

0.5 Pass an angled overhanging rock on your right. Rhododendron rises, and moss thickens on still rocks.

0.8 Round Island Run Falls becomes audible. Reach the first short spur path to the cataract. This one leads to the top of the falls, where you can peer down into the widening glen where the spiller makes its rocky dive. There is a rocky area to your right where you can work your way down or simply backtrack to the main trail and take the other spur path to the falls, which leads to a small campsite and the base of Round Island Run Falls. Backtrack to the trailhead.

1.6 Arrive back at the trailhead, having ascended from Round Island Run Falls.

21 Yost Run Falls, Kyler Fork Falls

Grab a two-for-one waterfall reward on this pretty little hike in vast Sproul State Forest. The trek starts high then works its way down into a flowery mountain vale as you devolve from gated road to foot trail, finding yourself walking along a dashing stream to first find symmetrical and scenic Yost Run Falls then view curtain-like Kyler Fork Falls flowing into Yost Run. The walk is easy but does drop 500 feet en route to the two waterfalls.

Waterfall height: 12 feet and 8 feet, respectively
Waterfall beauty: 5
Distance: 2.6-mile out-and-back
Difficulty: Easy to moderate
Hiking time: About 1½ hours
Trail surface: Natural
Other trail users: None

Canine compatibility: Leashed pets allowed
Land status: State forest
Fees and permits: None
Maps: Sproul State Forest Public Use Map; USGS Snow Shoe NW
Trail contact: Sproul State Forest, (570) 923-6011, www.dcnr.state.pa.us/forestry

Finding the trailhead: From exit 147 on I-80 at Snow Shoe, take PA 144 south for 16 miles to reach the signed Chuck Keiper trailhead on your left (there will also be a sign stating "Yost Run Loop, Eddy Lick Loop"), located in the Sproul State Forest, a little before crossing the Clinton County line. GPS: 41.175333, -77.878883

The Hike

This area of Sproul State Forest is great for hiking, and the walk to Yost Run Falls and Kyler Fork Falls uses a portion of the 8.2-mile Yost Run Loop. Therefore, you can easily extend this adventure, changing it from a 2.6-mile out-and-back hike to a longer circuit. The descent to the two cataracts leads you past a pair of camps, in reality cabins that are inholdings within Sproul State Forest, providing a getaway for their users. These camps are the reason for the initial path being doubletrack.

After passing the second camp, the Yost Run Loop morphs into a bona fide hiking trail. Descend along the gorgeous Yost Run hollow, where moss and evergreens shade skipping Yost Run. The valley here is rich with an eye-catching concentration of painted trillium in the spring. One of my favorite wildflowers, painted trillium is unmistakable, its center ringed in red atop wavy white petals smaller than your typical trillium. Painted trillium—like other trilliums—has three petals and three leaves, hence the "tri" in its name.

In the United States, painted trillium (*Trillium undulatum*) grows from Georgia in the South up the Appalachians into Pennsylvania, north to Maine, and west to Michigan. One of its biggest threats is being overeaten by deer. Therefore, when deer become overpopulated in Pennsylvania's woods, plants such as painted trillium can be overgrazed as a result.

No matter what time of year, you should enjoy the next highlight—Yost Run Falls. The trail takes you directly beside this three-tiered jewel of a cataract, bordered in mossy gray rocks and rhododendron. Look at the symmetrical increase of Yost Falls: The first tier is narrowest and drops about 2 feet. The second tier widens and drops about 4 feet. The third and final tier widens further still and spills about 6 feet before quickly flowing downstream. The entire waterfall is easy to view and photograph.

Kyler Fork Falls is less easy to access, since it is across Yost Run. However, you cannot miss the falls—just go downstream along a cliff line, keeping your eye peeled on Kyler Fork entering Yost Run. After crossing Yost Run, you will find a small campsite then Kyler Fork Falls. The falls, about 8 feet in totality, makes a two-tiered drop, though its upper tier is minimal—less than 2 feet. The second tier drops curtain style from its mouth, pouring over an undercut ledge, spraying onto rocks, then flowing amid stone to meld its waters with Yost Run.

Enjoy the walk back up to the trailhead the way you came, or consider making the whole Yost Run Loop. It heads about 2.5 miles farther down Yost Run before turning up Second Fork and returning to the highlands and the trailhead for an 8.2-mile circuit.

Miles and Directions

0.0 From the trailhead signboard, join a doubletrack road heading west. Mature oaks tower above smaller oaks and maples. Mountain laurel is prevalent.

0.2 The doubletrack splits and reaches a pair of gates. Head left, passing around a brown-and-yellow state forest gate, still descending. Note the paint blazes designating the Yost Run Loop. Start descending into Bloom Draft (*draft* is another word for stream or valley).

0.6 Reach Camp Bloom, a rustic two-story building in a clearing. Continue down the paint-blazed doubletrack, which becomes rougher deeper into Bloom Draft.

0.8 The trail and creek crisscross one another. The hillside to your right becomes very rocky.

1.1 Reach the lower camp in a small clearing near the confluence of Bloom Draft and Yost Run. Join a singletrack foot trail heading north down Yost Run after bridging Bloom Draft one last time. Look for painted trillium in great numbers here in the spring.

1.3 Reach Yost Run Falls, directly beside the trail on the left. Note the three nearly symmetrical tiers. Continue downstream just a bit to view Kyler Fork Falls flowing above Kyler Fork's confluence with Yost Run. A small campsite stands at the confluence. If the water is up, you may have trouble reaching Kyler Fork Falls dry-shod, though it is a breeze to simply walk through Yost Run. Backtrack to the trailhead.

2.6 Arrive back at the trailhead after your 500-foot ascent from the pair of waterfalls.

Kyler Fork Falls near its confluence with Yost Run is worth the hike.

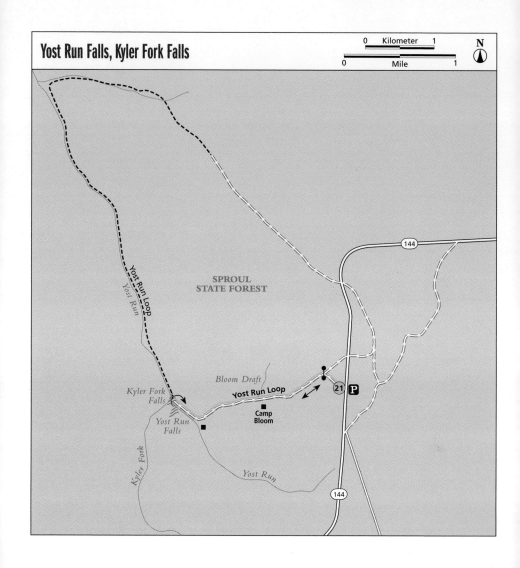

Yost Run Falls can be absolutely stunning in winter.
RUSTY GLESSNER

22 Stone Quarry Run Falls, Water Tank Run Falls

This pleasant hike uses a portion of the Pine Creek Trail, a 62-mile rail trail, to penetrate the Pine Creek Gorge and visit a pair of tributaries showing their descending flows of white. The nearly level rail trail makes for easy hiking, and the beauty of the gorge enriches the entire waterfall hiking experience.

Waterfall height: 14 feet and 34 feet, respectively
Waterfall beauty: 4
Distance: 5.0-mile out-and-back
Difficulty: Easy to moderate
Hiking time: About 2½ hours
Trail surface: Pea gravel
Other trail users: Bicyclers

Canine compatibility: Leashed pets allowed
Land status: State natural area
Fees and permits: None
Maps: Tioga State Forest Public Use Map; USGS Cedar Run
Trail contact: Tioga State Forest, (570) 724-2868, www.dcnr.state.pa.us/forestry

Finding the trailhead: From Morris, take PA 414 west for 5.3 miles, reaching a large parking area, the McCullough Boater Access, on the left just before the PA 414 bridge crossing over Pine Creek. GPS: 41.556367, -77.381533

The Hike

The Pine Creek Trail, a 62-mile rail trail running from near Wellsboro to Jersey Shore on the Susquehanna River, is Pennsylvania's most celebrated rail trail. Sure, there are other worthy rail trails in the Keystone State, namely the Great Allegheny Passage Trail and the Lehigh Gorge Trail, but when outdoor enthusiasts mention the Pine Creek Trail, they talk in reverent whispers of the spectacular yet changing scenery while traversing the Pine Creek Gorge, known as the "Grand Canyon of Pennsylvania."

Interestingly, the Pine Creek Trail is just one element of the outdoor offerings available within the Pine Creek Gorge, another of which is waterfalling. We waterfall hikers are just one subset of the recreational users—you will also find paddlers floating down the mostly Class I rapids of Pine Creek, anglers vying for bass and trout on the river, bicyclers pedaling the rail trail, and backpackers trekking the outlying paths of the greater Tioga State Forest and Tiadaghton State Forest through which the trail travels.

A rail line was first laid through the Pine Creek Gorge in 1883 and the railroad era lasted until 1988, when Conrail abandoned the line through the gorge. About this time, rail trails were gaining steam, and the line through the scenic canyon became a likely candidate for conversion from transportation and shipping line to recreation destination. It took eight years for the first trail segment to open, but eventually the whole trail was ready for business by 2007. You can still see vestiges of the former rail line, such as stone mile markers. Today the Pine Creek Trail serves as a model for other rail trails throughout Pennsylvania and beyond, bringing tourist dollars to the local economy and opportunities to exercise in a scenic setting.

You will get a taste of the Pine Creek Trail on this waterfall hike. By the way, just like Pine Creek, the best time to float the river or visit these waterfalls is from winter through spring, though summer thunderstorms can bring the waters of the Pine Creek Gorge up. A good online water gauge to check is the USGS gauge at Pine Creek at Cedar Run, PA. It will give you an idea as to whether Pine Creek is up or not, which will help to determine if the tributaries of Pine Creek are flowing as well.

Starting at the hamlet of Blackwell, the walk takes you up the gorge, passing a few houses before entering state forest land. The nearly level pea gravel surface makes the hiking very easy, especially when you consider how some other waterfall hikes go up and down on challenging surfaces. After leaving the last of the houses at Blackwell, it is nothing but the trail, the creek, the gorge, and the sky—and maybe a few of your fellow Pine Creek Trail users.

Note the blasted trailside bluffs, now grown over with mosses and dripping with water in wet times. Some trail sections are shaded with sycamore and ash, while others are open overhead. Clear views of Pine Creek are frequent, and the wooded walls of the canyon rise high overhead.

Find your first waterfall upon reaching Stone Quarry Run. This two-tiered 14-foot spiller is visible from the Pine Creek Trail. It makes a smaller drop followed by a curtain descent then runs under the trail bridge.

Continue up the trail, curving with the curves of the gorge, and soon you are at Water Tank Hollow, where Water Tank Run flows from the top of the gorge. And just below the confluence of the two-pronged stream, the flow of those tributaries combines to make one impressive waterfall. Here Water Tank Run squeezes through a gap in the stone promontory above then charges over a rock face, spreading on its 34-foot descent into rubble at its base.

Foolhardy waterfallers continue to climb around the right side of this fall to access an upstream cataract, but it seems a dangerous proposition. Perhaps you may just want to enjoy your surefooted stroll back down to the trailhead at Blackwell along the sure winner that is the Pine Creek Trail.

Miles and Directions

0.0 Leave the McCullough Boater Access Area, with restrooms, pump well, and ramp. Walk east 150 feet on PA 414, away from the PA 414 bridge, and reach the Pine Creek Trail. Head left (northbound) on the Pine Creek Trail, passing around a pole gate and by a few houses bordering the rail trail. The gravel track makes for easy hiking.

0.3 Pass around a second pole gate. Keep north.

0.7 Leave all the houses behind and pass rail trail mile marker #24. Markers are placed each mile throughout the length of the Pine Creek Trail to help users keep apprised of their whereabouts.

0.8 Jerry Run comes in from the far side of the creek. If the water is up, you may hear its falls.

1.2 Reach Stone Quarry Run Falls, visible from the Pine Creek Trail. A short user-created trail leads to the two-tiered 14-foot cataract. After viewing this waterfall, continue up the Pine Creek Trail.

1.3 Bohen Run flows into Pine Creek on the other side of the gorge.

1.7 Reach rail trail marker #23.

2.4 Come to the trail bridge over Water Tank Run flowing from Water Tank Hollow. Here a spur trail leads right, up the angled bank of the creek.

2.5 Reach 34-foot Water Tank Run Falls after working your way past pools and drops to reach the primary, unmistakable fall. Backtrack to the trailhead.

5.0 Arrive back at the McCullough Boater Access Area, completing the waterfall hike.

Bright-red columbine grace the edge of the Pine Creek Trail.

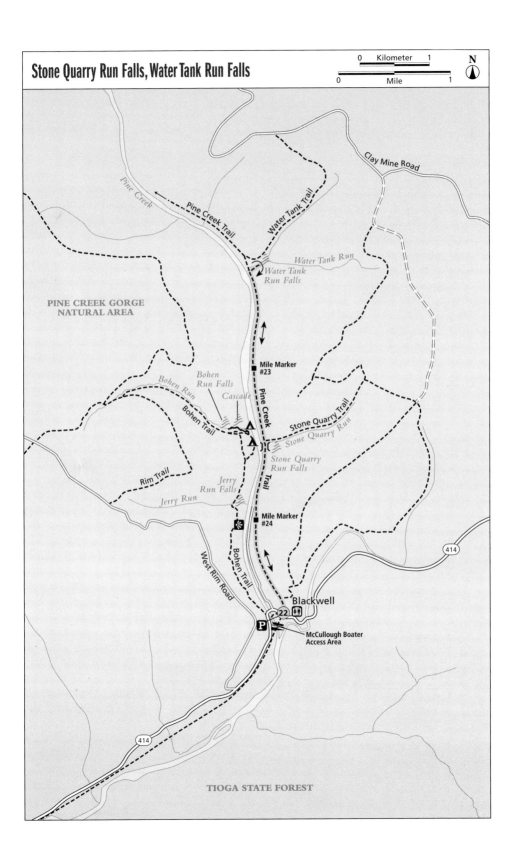

0   Kilometer   1

0   Mile   1

N

PINE CREEK GORGE
NATURAL AREA

Pine Creek

Pine Creek Trail

Water Tank Trail

Clay Mine Road

Water Tank Run

Water Tank
Run Falls

Mile Marker
#23

Bohen
Run Falls

Cascade

Bohen Run

Bohen Trail

Pine Creek Trail

Stone Quarry Trail

Stone Quarry Run

Stone Quarry
Run Falls

Rim Trail

Jerry
Run Falls

Jerry Run

Mile Marker
#24

414

West Rim Road

Bohen Trail

Blackwell

22

McCullough Boater
Access Area

P

414

TIOGA STATE FOREST

Water Tank Hollow Falls creates an expanding veil of white after a heavy spring rain.

23 Jerry Run Falls, Bohen Run Falls

Starting on the lower end of the Pine Creek Gorge at the community of Blackwell, this waterfall hike heads up the side slope of the gorge, first passing tumbling Jerry Run Falls before heading to flats at the confluence of Bohen Run and Pine Creek. Head up Bohen Run past campsites and cascades before reaching high and mighty Bohen Run Falls, a classic spiller sliding over a rock face. Next, visit the top of Bohen Run Falls before returning to the trailhead. The entire hike is quite attractive.

Waterfall height: 25 feet and 30 feet, respectively
Waterfall beauty: 4
Distance: 3.6-mile out-and-back with mini-loop
Difficulty: Moderate
Hiking time: About 2½ hours
Trail surface: Natural

Other trail users: None
Canine compatibility: Leashed pets allowed
Land status: State natural area
Fees and permits: None
Maps: Tioga State Forest Public Use Map; USGS Cedar Run
Trail contact: Tioga State Forest, (570) 724-2868, www.dcnr.state.pa.us/forestry

Finding the trailhead: From Morris, take PA 414 west for 5.3 miles, reaching a large parking area, the McCullough Boater Access, on the left just before the PA 414 bridge crossing over Pine Creek. GPS: 41.556367, -77.381533

The Hike

Bohen Run and Jerry Run are two tributaries of Pine Creek, located within the Pine Creek Gorge Natural Area of the expansive Pine Creek Gorge, much of which is within the Tioga State Forest. The natural area encompasses 12,163 acres of the greater 165,052-acre Tioga State Forest. Three state parks also lie within the gorge. Furthermore, a part of the Pine Creek Gorge—including the part where this hike takes place—was designated a National Natural Landmark in 1968. Pine Creek itself is a Pennsylvania State Scenic River. Obviously, all this means this area is something special. A hike to Jerry Run Falls and Bohen Falls will bear that out.

Formerly, the Seneca Indians used Pine Creek Gorge as a connecting route between settlements in what became New York and settlements down along the Susquehanna River in what became Pennsylvania. However, after our Revolutionary War, a fellow named John English received the gorge area as a war service land grant. He settled in what was the back of beyond, establishing good relations with the Seneca.

The area remained very sparsely settled until the 1820s, when timber operations moved in, eventually taking down the forests of the region, at first floating the giant old-growth logs down Pine Creek to mills on the Susquehanna River. During the latter part of the century-long timber era, a rail line was established to transport the wood from the gorge to the outside world. The line later was used to move coal, freight, and people through the region. In 1988 the last train left Pine Creek.

Since the 1920s the forest of the area has continued to recover. The establishment of the Tioga and Tiadaghton State Forests hastened the improvement, with the state forest service replanting trees and establishing erosion barriers, as well as building sustainable roads and trails and other recreation facilities.

Today the Pine Creek Gorge lives up to its multiple designations. You will find that out on the hike to these two falls. The first order of business is to cross Pine Creek on the PA 414 bridge and pick up the Bohen Trail on the west side of the gorge. Get a taste of the steepness of the gorge as the Bohen Trail works up the side of the canyon, climbing well above Pine Creek. Rocky outcrops and hemlocks as well as maples, ferns, oaks, and mountain laurel stand astride the path. You cannot miss a certain flat rock outcrop beside the trail. It seems no hikers can resist the temptation to walk onto the flat rock protrusion, though the views only warrant a visit when summer's leaves are absent.

Jerry Run Falls presents beauty on a chilly, wet winter day.
RUSTY GLESSNER

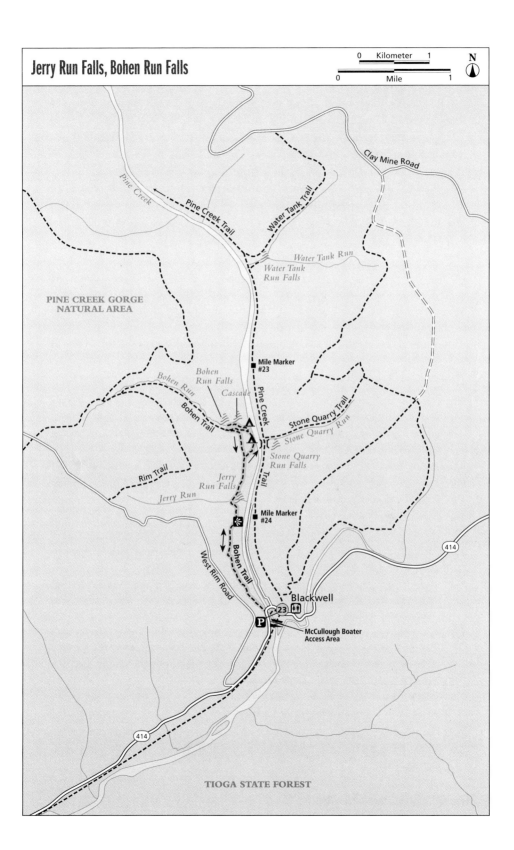

Jerry Run Falls, Bohen Run Falls

Pine Creek

Clay Mine Road

Pine Creek Trail

Water Tank Trail

Water Tank Run

Water Tank
Run Falls

PINE CREEK GORGE
NATURAL AREA

Mile Marker
#23

*Bohen
Run Falls*

Bohen Run

Cascade

Bohen Trail

Stone Quarry Trail

Pine Creek

Stone Quarry Run

Stone Quarry
Run Falls

Rim Trail

*Jerry
Run Falls*

Jerry Run

Mile Marker
#24

414

West Rim Road

Bohen Trail

Blackwell

23

P

McCullough Boater
Access Area

414

TIOGA STATE FOREST

Mountain laurel grows in profusion before reaching Jerry Run and Jerry Run Falls. Hikers can enjoy good looks of the cataract as it dives over a rock lip into a tight-knit gorge that is difficult to reach. Most hikers simply observe the falls from the top and from the outcrops on the south side of the creek. Only dedicated photographers and waterfall enthusiasts scramble to the base of this 25-foot falls.

The hike then leads to a rock hop of Jerry Run and an easier segment of trail. Look for paper birch and firs in the woods. The trail leads down toward Pine Creek as it keeps north. You then come to the loop portion of the hike. Here a blue-blazed spur trail leads down to Pine Creek and lowermost Bohen Run. To view Bohen Run Falls from the bottom, hikers must pick up a user-created trail heading directly upstream alongside Bohen Run. Along the way you will pass a slide cascade and alluring swimming hole. Finally, the user-created trail dead-ends at the base of Bohen Run Falls. Here, enjoy a stellar view of the angled spiller dashing from 30 feet over a widening rock face into its own plunge pool before aiming for Pine Creek.

Do not try to climb the steep gorge wall from this spot; instead, backtrack to Pine Creek then join the blue-blazed trail that then rejoins the Bohen Trail. Here, amid rocks and pines, you can see big Bohen Run Falls from the top down. After this final view, head back on the Bohen Trail, returning to the trailhead at the PA 414 bridge.

Miles and Directions

0.0 Leave the McCullough Boater Access Area, with restrooms, pump well, and ramp. Use the PA 414 bridge to cross Pine Creek. Just beyond the bridge, step over a guardrail and pick up the Bohen Trail, a singletrack path that briefly cruises a flat before ascending the side slope of the gorge using stairs, clinging to the mountainside in thick woods.

0.6 The trail turns into a hollow and picks up an old roadbed. The slope lessens.

0.8 Pass an obvious rock outcrop to the right of the trail. It juts toward Pine Creek, but the view is partly obscured by trees in summer.

1.0 Come to Jerry Run Falls and an overlook. Just ahead, rock hop Jerry Run then view the falls from the other side. The trail keeps northbound in the Pine Creek Gorge.

1.3 Split right from the Bohen Trail, joining a fainter blue-blazed trail dipping right to Pine Creek. Enter a flat filled with pines and a campsite. Continue upriver.

1.6 Find another campsite at the confluence of Bohen Run and Pine Creek. Turn up and follow the user-created trail along Bohen Run. Pass a 10-foot slide cascade with an alluring pool into which it tumbles.

1.7 Reach the base of Bohen Run Falls as the cataract dives from a rock brow and crashes its way down, collects in a pool, and then narrows while working toward Pine Creek. Backtrack to the confluence of Bohen Run and Pine Creek, then climb a mild hill to rejoin the blue-blazed trail climbing well above Bohen Run.

2.0 Meet the Bohen Trail above Bohen Run Falls. Admire the falls from this perch then join the Bohen Trail, heading back toward the trailhead.

2.3 Meet the blue-blazed trail, completing the mini-loop. From here, backtrack to the trailhead.

3.6 Arrive back at the McCullough Boater Access Area after crossing the PA 414 bridge, completing the hike.

24 Falls of the Turkey Path at Colton Point State Park

This waterfall hike in the famed Pine Creek Gorge extends beyond mere appreciation of falling water. It takes you from the gorge rim down an incredible trail, passing overlooks and reaching a 70-foot, two-stage cataract. The hike then follows Fourmile Run through gorgeous woods to reach the bottom of the canyon in a wooded flat where Pine Creek runs more than 500 feet below.

Waterfall height: 70 feet
Waterfall beauty: 5
Distance: 2.6-mile out-and-back
Difficulty: Moderate
Hiking time: About 1½ hours
Trail surface: Natural
Other trail users: None

Canine compatibility: Leashed pets allowed
Land status: State park
Fees and permits: None
Maps: Colton Point State Park; USGS Tiadaghton
Trail contact: Colton Point State Park, (570) 724-3061, www.dcnr.state.pa.us/stateparks

Finding the trailhead: From Wellsboro, take PA 6 west for 11 miles, bridging Marsh Creek in Ansonia. Shortly after this bridge, turn left onto Colton Road, signed for Colton Point State Park, and follow the paved road as it jogs left at 4.4 miles, staying with the paved road, then reach a large parking area on your right at 4.7 miles. GPS: 41.700833, -77.466111

The Hike

The Turkey Path is one of Pennsylvania's most famous trails, deservedly so. The path extends rim to rim across the equally famous Pine Creek Gorge, nicknamed the "Grand Canyon of Pennsylvania." However, there's a little catch: The Turkey Path has no bridge across Pine Creek, leaving it essentially two separate trails, with the western half at Colton Point State Park, described here, and the eastern half at popular Leonard Harrison State Park, also rich with waterfalls and also detailed in this guide.

This western part of the Turkey Path is less visited and has fewer falls, but the hike is still worth your time. The trail is a marvel unto itself, winding downward along an incredibly steep slope that you think no trail can—or should—go. Yet it does. The Turkey Path leaves the parking area near Colton Point, the park's namesake, and first crosses the Rim Trail, another scenic path that runs along the edge of the Pine Creek Gorge.

The Turkey Path comes to the rim of the steep valley cut by Fourmile Run and its tributaries, then executes a series of switchbacks among clinging pines to drop into Rexford Branch, where you can see the upper half of the 70-foot waterfall make a pronounced slide over layered rock before dropping out of sight. Funny thing, few

Falls of the Turkey Path at Colton Point State Park

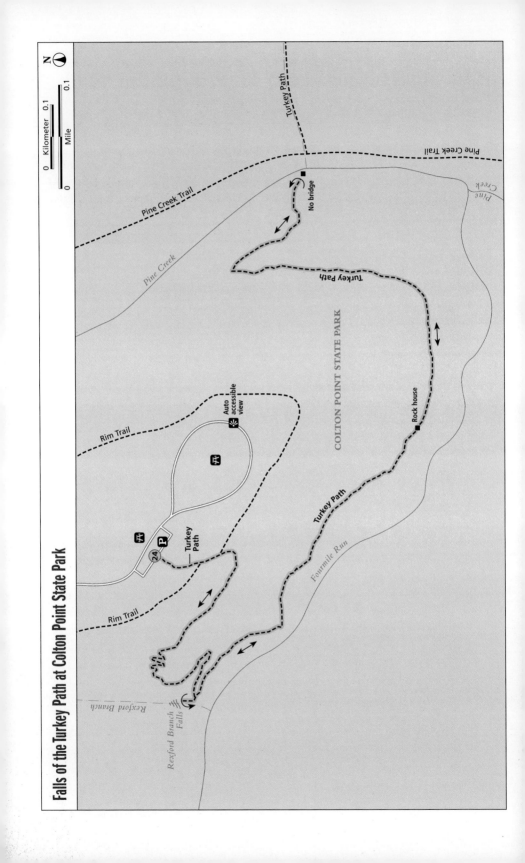

people, if any, reference this cataract as Rexford Branch Falls or even name the falls. However, the 70-foot waterfall is on Rexford Branch, as named on official United States Geological Survey quadrangle maps. Furthermore, this fall is one of those long, angled cataracts with so many segments and incarnations that it is difficult to gauge where the official waterfall begins and ends. In that vein, I think the entirety of the flume exceeds 100 feet.

More carefully constructed switchbacks lead you to the base of the 70-foot fall, where you can see the lower half make an angled slide then drop off a little ledge and execute a final sloped descent before pouring on to contribute its waters to Fourmile Run. It is difficult if not impossible to photograph this fall in its entirety. It seems you must photograph the top or the bottom.

One of many cascades along Fourmile Run is luxurious.
RUSTY GLESSNER

The Turkey Path goes on down the canyon of Fourmile Run. Here, majestic rock bluffs rise above while Fourmile Run crashes in pools and cascades below, separating from the trail the deeper it goes. User-created spur paths head to particularly alluring streamside sights. Finally, the Turkey Path curves into the Pine Creek Gorge and the sounds of that stream overwhelm the watery songs of Fourmile Run. You end up in a gorgeous little flat along Pine Creek where a campsite lies near the stream. Across the creek, the Pine Creek Trail travels by and you can see waterfall-rich Little Fourmile Run flowing into Pine Creek.

This waterfall along Fourmile Run may not have a name, but it's an eyeful.
RUSTY GLESSNER

Rexford Branch Falls emphasizes the layered rock that forms the cascade.

The continuation of the Turkey Path climbs along Little Fourmile Run up to the visitor center at Leonard Harrison State Park. These disparate segments of the Turkey Path are best done as separate hikes starting at different trailheads. They both can easily be done in a day, including driving time between the trailheads.

Miles and Directions

0.0 From the parking area, walk down the paved road a bit toward the auto-accessible viewing area, then leave right on the Turkey Path, with a large signboard warning hikers about steep cliffs and long descents. Angle downhill.

0.1 Intersect the Rim Trail, which comes in from the right. Continue angling down the slope, then a few hundred feet later the Rim Trail leaves left while the Turkey Path descends right, dropping steeply toward the edge of the Fourmile Run rim amid pines.

0.2 Make a series of switchbacks, aiming for Rexford Branch, noisily flowing below. The upper half of 70-foot Rexford Branch Falls comes into view. The lowermost switchback takes you along the edge of the angled cascade as it slides over rock. Descend to enter the greater gorge of Fourmile Run. Do not shortcut the switchbacks. It causes erosion and degrades the trail as well as the ecosystem.

0.4 Return to Rexford Branch. A short spur on a ledge takes you to the base of Rexford Branch Falls. Be careful, as this ledge is slippery. After observing the 70-foot falls from the base, continue down the Fourmile Run canyon. Rock bluffs rise above, and the narrow foot trail wanders along a steep slope. Other waterfalls tumble below but are extremely difficult to access due to the steep slope. Watch for user-created spurs heading to the water.

0.9 The trail takes you near an overhanging rock house.

1.0 The trail curves northeast.

1.2 Make a final switchback and descend into the flat alongside Pine Creek.

1.3 Reach Pine Creek and a campsite. You can walk to the edge of Pine Creek and look across at the Pine Creek Rail Trail and the trail bridge spanning Little Fourmile Run. There is no bridge across Pine Creek and fording can be dangerous, especially when the water is up. Do not do it. Backtrack to the trailhead.

2.6 Arrive back at the trailhead after your 500-plus-foot climb out of the Pine Creek Gorge.

25 Falls of the Turkey Path at Leonard Harrison State Park

This very popular trail at very popular Leonard Harrison State Park offers perhaps more falling water per step than any other path in the Keystone State. Your hike starts at the top of the Pine River Gorge, where stellar views await. Next, descend into the canyon, visiting an impressive series of cataracts streaming down Little Fourmile Run. Enjoy waterfalls all the way to the bottom of the gorge, meeting Pine Creek and the Pine Creek Trail. Be advised there is a 700-foot descent, which means a 700-foot climb back to the trailhead. However, the trail is well graded and has steps and walkways to aid your passage.

Waterfall height: 15 feet, 15 feet, 40 feet, 100 feet among many falls
Waterfall beauty: 5+
Distance: 2.2-mile out-and-back
Difficulty: Moderate, does have elevation change
Hiking time: About 1½ hours
Trail surface: Pea gravel, wooden walkways, stairs

Other trail users: None
Canine compatibility: Leashed pets allowed
Land status: State park
Fees and permits: None
Maps: Leonard Harrison State Park; USGS Tiadaghton
Trail contact: Leonard Harrison State Park, (570) 724-3061, www.dcnr.state.pa.us/stateparks

Finding the trailhead: From Wellsboro, take PA 660 west for 10.5 miles to dead-end at the visitor center of Leonard Harrison State Park. Be advised that between Wellsboro and the state park, PA 660 will turn at different intersections, but the signs are clear, so stay with PA 660 the whole route and you will be fine. GPS: 41.696347, -77.454738

The Hike

Leonard Harrison State Park and the Pine Creek Gorge are deserving Pennsylvania natural attractions that spawn other attractions in their midst, from campgrounds to overlook towers, that visitors will stop by on the way to the state park. In other words, Leonard Harrison State Park and the Pine Creek Gorge are popular destinations. After all, everybody should get a look at the "Grand Canyon of Pennsylvania," as the Pine Creek Gorge is known. Furthermore, the waterfalls of Little Fourmile Run, located within Leonard Harrison State Park, are a draw unto themselves. Be forewarned that these falls are much bolder from winter through spring and will steadily decrease their flow into autumn.

Upon hiking to these cataracts, you will see why they draw so many visitors. When the water is flowing, you will be dazzled first by the overlook near the park visitor center then by one waterfall after another all along Little Fourmile Run. The trail to the bottom of the canyon is a marvel itself and hosts scads of waterfall hikers every year. Solitude seekers should come here during the cold season or off times of the week, including early in the morning or evening. On summer holidays, you may find yourself verily elbowing your way down the trail.

This is not to be discouraging—just pick your visitation times wisely at this "must visit" Pennsylvania outdoor destination. Leonard Harrison State Park is as famous for its views as it is for waterfalls. In fact, since the views of the Pine Creek Gorge can be had by walking just a few steps from the park visitor center, it is safe to say more people have seen the vistas rather than the waterfalls. Nevertheless, not only can you gain immediate views from the visitor center, but you can also take the Overlook Trail that leads to Otter View—a magazine-cover-worthy downstream look at the Pine Creek Gorge.

Though coming in at a mere 585 acres, the state park also features several picnic areas and a campground. Hikers can also access the Pine Creek Trail, the 62-mile rail trail running through the Pine Creek Gorge. But the Turkey Path is the star of the show here at Leonard Harrison State Park. It will not take long to see why.

After checking out the park visitor center and soaking in some views of the Pine Creek Gorge, join the wide pea gravel Turkey Path. It wastes no time in angling down to Little Fourmile Run and the base of the gorge. After the first switchback, the track takes you to the edge of the gorge to enjoy yet another canyon view. From there it turns deeper into the valley, where hemlocks increase in number and shade the declining track. A series of switchbacks eases the descent.

Your first fall will be on a feeder branch of Little Fourmile Run, where it makes a relatively small two-tier drop. After seeing the upcoming cataracts, this waterfall will seem inconsequential. First you come to a 15-foot curtain-type fall, followed by a signature cascade that drops 5 feet, followed by a slightly angled 40-foot spiller on a rock face. Wow!

And more is to come. Other decks and observation areas take you to a very long waterfall that could be 100 feet or more, dropping in stages above and below the observation point. When the water is up, Little Fourmile Run can seem a continuous waterfall. Stairs and steps and landings and handrails make the walk much easier, considering the very steep slope.

You will pass a final set of cascades and slides before the stream runs under the bridge of the Pine Creek Trail, the rail trail running through the gorge. Across the creek the rest of the Turkey Path makes its way to the top of the rim at Colton Point State Park. However, there is no bridge across Pine Creek, and your best bet is to drive to the other side of the gorge then hike down from Colton Point. That waterfall hike is also detailed in this guide.

The lowermost fall on Little Fourmile Run tumbles over boulders.

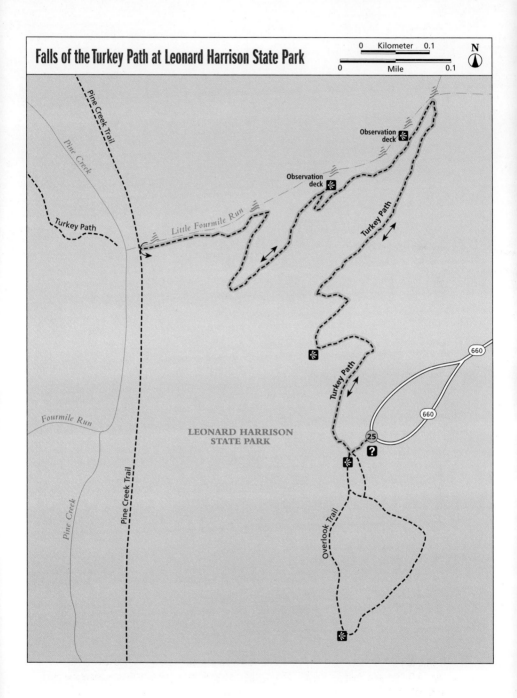

Falls of the Turkey Path at Leonard Harrison State Park

0   Kilometer   0.1

0   Mile   0.1

N

Pine Creek Trail

Pine Creek

Turkey Path

Little Fourmile Run

Observation deck

Observation deck

Turkey Path

Turkey Path

660

660

25

Fourmile Run

LEONARD HARRISON
STATE PARK

Pine Creek Trail

Pine Creek

Overlook Trail

Fog shrouds the Pine Creek Gorge.

Miles and Directions

0.0 Leave the parking area, then walk through the visitor center breezeway (the visitor center offers restrooms, information, and a gift shop). Head out to the views of the gorge on a stone deck, then look right as you are facing into the gorge for the Turkey Path. Join a wide track descending along the edge of the bluff amid evergreens. Make your first switchback.

0.2 Reach a view of the Pine Creek Gorge and a second switchback. Turn back toward Little Fourmile Run on a continual descent.

0.4 Come to your first waterfall at the confluence of a tributary and Little Fourmile Run. The falls on the tributary spills narrowly over a layered ledge then filters through brush to make a second, wider drop before pouring into Little Fourmile Run. Continue down past a bluff.

0.5 Come to the first waterfall on Little Fourmile Run. This one makes a 15-foot ledge drop then spills into a gravelly pool.

0.6 Come to a huge waterfall. A boardwalk takes you to a viewing platform. This fall opens with a 5-foot drop followed by a slightly angled dive dropping a good 40 feet, widening as it goes!

0.7 The Turkey Path passes a cliff line and more cascades.

0.9 Reach another incredible fall with an observation deck. It drops 15 feet, cascades 20 feet, goes past the observation deck, then continues onward below, crashing and dashing, a cavalcade of cataracts perhaps exceeding 100 feet in totality! The trail now follows Little Fourmile Run downstream.

1.1 Pass a final series of lesser stair-step cascades before meeting the Pine Creek Trail, the 62-mile rail trail pushing through the gorge. The west side of the Turkey Path at Colton Point State Park is across Pine Creek, but there is no connecting bridge. Check out Pine Creek and perhaps stroll the Pine Creek Trail, or, better yet, rest before your climb back up to the rim of the gorge. Enjoy the series of astonishing waterfalls a second time as you climb.

2.2 Arrive back at the trailhead, completing the waterfall hike.

This is the first waterfall you see while descending into the Pine Creek Gorge.

26 Sand Run Falls

This easy, straightforward hike leads you to a gorgeous setting at its end—the glen where Sand Run, Babb Creek, and an unnamed stream converge. Here, below sturdy dark cliffs, the waterways meet in a flat after tumbling in two cataracts that add flair to the already scenic spot—big Sand Run Falls and a small spiller nestled in a mini-canyon of its own. Additionally, the trail to Sand Run Falls links to other pathways should you desire a circuit hike.

Waterfall height: In order, 26 feet and 22 feet
Waterfall beauty: 5
Distance: 6.2-mile out-and-back
Difficulty: Moderate
Hiking time: About 3 hours
Trail surface: Natural
Other trail users: None

Canine compatibility: Leashed pets allowed
Land status: State forest
Fees and permits: None
Maps: Sand Run Falls Trail–Tioga State Forest; USGS Cherry Flats
Trail contact: Tioga State Forest, (570) 724-2868, www.dcnr.state.pa.us/forestry

Finding the trailhead: From Williamsport, take US 15 north 29 miles to the Sebring exit. Leave US 15 and head left under the interstate on Blockhouse Road. Follow Blockhouse Road 2.3 miles, then turn left on Lower Arnot Road and follow it for 3.1 miles. Reach a T intersection in Arnot and turn left on Arnot Road. Follow it for 2.4 miles, then look left for the sign "Sand Run Falls Hiking & Ski Trail." Turn left here and reach the small trailhead on your right. There is additional parking on your left, just beyond the first parking area. GPS: 41.681865, -77.154311

The Hike

Have you heard of the Mid State Trail? This ambitious 300-plus-mile path, still in the making, starts near Lawrenceville, Pennsylvania, by the New York boundary and heads southerly all the way to the Maryland state line. The trail's official tagline is "the wildest trail in Pennsylvania," which is a tough slogan to live by. It is also the longest trail entirely in Pennsylvania. The Mid State Trail Association plans to complete the path and officially link it to other trails, creating the Great Eastern Trail, a north-south-running alternative to the Appalachian Trail.

Like many other long-distance paths, in places the Mid State Trail uses already existing trails and overlays its designation upon them. For example, on our waterfall hike, the Mid State Trail runs in conjunction with the Sand Run Falls Trail. The Sand Run Falls Trail was originally constructed by Boy Scouts in the early 1990s.

The path to Sand Run Falls runs through Tioga State Forest, making an easy track along a gentle side slope running parallel to Sand Run, mostly just above the drop-off to the stream bottom. An overhead mix of hardwoods and conifers shades the trail,

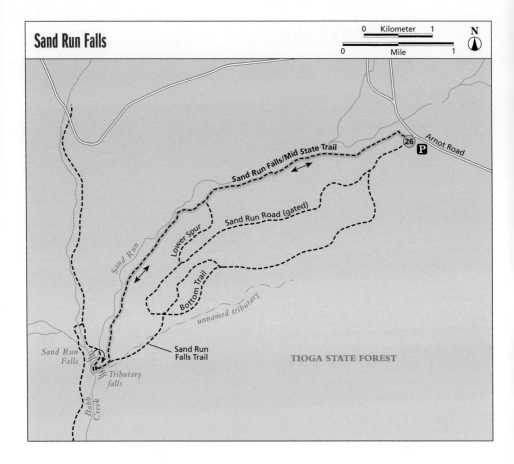

0　　Kilometer　　1

0　　　　Mile　　　　1

N

Sand Run Falls/Mid State Trail

Arnot Road

26　P

Lower Spur

Sand Run Road (gated)

Sand Run

Bottom Trail

unnamed tributary

Sand Run Falls

Sand Run Falls Trail

TIOGA STATE FOREST

Tributary falls

Babb Creek

which is not too rocky. In other words, it is one of those pleasant hikes on which you would like to take a newbie. And the rewards at the end are obvious, true highlights.

Upon reaching the bluffs above Sand Run Falls, you hear the tumbling water echoing off the circular plunge pool. The way down is not easy, but a little scrambling and you are in the glen below the falls. Here the last bit of Sand Run merges with Babb Creek in cool woodland flanked by stately bluffs on all sides. Just around the corner from this stream confluence, you walk down Babb Creek to find a small alcove where a tributary stream makes a classic sloped, widening descent before giving its waters to Babb Creek as well. The whole area of Sand Run Falls deserves exploration. Campsites are situated down here should you desire an overnight backpacking experience.

After enjoying Sand Run Falls, you can simply backtrack or connect to a series of hiking and ski trails traversing the upland plateau above Sand Run. Be advised that the trails can become overgrown in summer, but they are well signed.

Miles and Directions

0.0 From the first small parking area, walk back toward Arnot Road then pick up the Sand Run Falls Trail, a singletrack path heading northwest. Gently descend along the paint-blazed path.

0.1 Curve left, heading more southwest. Begin running parallel to Sand Run, off to your right.

1.1 Glimpse Sand Run, gurgling through bottoms below.

1.5 Come to a signed trail intersection. Here the Lower Spur leaves left toward the nest of ski trails on the plateau above. Stay straight with the Sand Run Trail, still gently descending on the brow of the slope above the bottomland.

2.2 The downgrade sharpens a bit. Sand Run is spilling faster too, in noisy rapids.

3.0 Come to a signed intersection. Head right here, as the trails going left head up to the ski trail network. You will come along a tributary then hear a falls to your left. This is the upper part of the tributary falls. Ahead, a spur trail goes left to look at this upper falls as well as right to Sand Run Falls. Explore the upper unnamed tributary falls, then head right toward Sand Run Falls.

3.1 Come to Sand Run Falls. Admire it from the rim, a majestically surging white curtain pounding into a dark pool. At this point you can access the base of the falls by continuing on the Mid State Trail, fording Sand Run above the falls, and then turning downstream to the bottom below the falls, or simply scramble down the slope a little downstream of the falls. A rope has been placed here in the past. Either way, explore the glen, the falls, the grottoes, and the base of the tributary falls. This is one scenic slice of the Keystone State. Backtrack to the trailhead.

6.2 Arrive back at the trailhead, completing the waterfall hike.

*A head-on view
of Sand Run Falls
reveals its stone tiers.*
RUSTY GLESSNER

27 Fall Brook Falls

Take a short walk through an old picnic area along Fall Brook to visit a pair of falls rushing through the gorge cut by the stream. Though the falls and the fascinating geology of the immediate canyon have remained constant through the years, the area around Fall Brook has undergone many a change.

Waterfall height: In order, 20 feet and 8 feet
Waterfall beauty: 3
Distance: 0.6-mile out-and-back
Difficulty: Easy
Hiking time: About ½ hour
Trail surface: Natural
Other trail users: None

Canine compatibility: Leashed pets allowed
Land status: State forest
Fees and permits: None
Maps: Tioga State Forest Day Use Map; USGS Gleason
Trail contact: Tioga State Forest, (570) 724-2868, www.dcnr.state.pa.us/forestry

Finding the trailhead: From the US 15 exit at Blossburg, take Bloss Mountain Road north for 0.9 mile, then turn right on Main Street and follow it 1.6 miles (it turns to Gulick Street along the way), leaving Blossburg to turn left on Morris Run Road. Follow Morris Run Road for 4 miles (along the way it changes to River Road), reaching a parking area on your right just before bridging Fall Brook, across from Carey Road. At the parking area you will see a yellow gate and oil equipment. GPS: 41.678963, -76.989365

The Hike

Fall Brook Falls is scenically wonderful but somewhat strange. The spot used to be a picnic area with trails leading to Fall Brook Falls and the immediate gorge of Fall Brook, but the picnic locale was abandoned, left to nature's devices. Now we have a stone bridge and well-used trail leading to the falls with handrails guarding precarious areas and little else in the way of relics from the picnic area. To cause additional hesitation among waterfall hikers, the trailhead parking area is fronted by a gate, and behind it stands energy industry equipment.

However, the story of Fall Brook is intertwined with Pennsylvania's energy industry. Though it is not evident, the area around the trailhead was once the thriving coal town of Fall Brook, having a population of over 3,000 souls just before the Civil War. Later the coal played out and the residents moved to greener pastures, but the name Fall Brook remained, now populated by a few scattered folk who like their neighbors far afield.

The immediate area across from Fall Brook holds mine-water discharge reclamation ponds. To this day, oil and gas are extracted from the greater area but do not affect the beauty of Fall Brook Falls, other than the out-of-the ordinary trailhead. The hike quickly takes you into woods to sidle alongside Fall Brook, running smooth above the

Fall Brook Falls

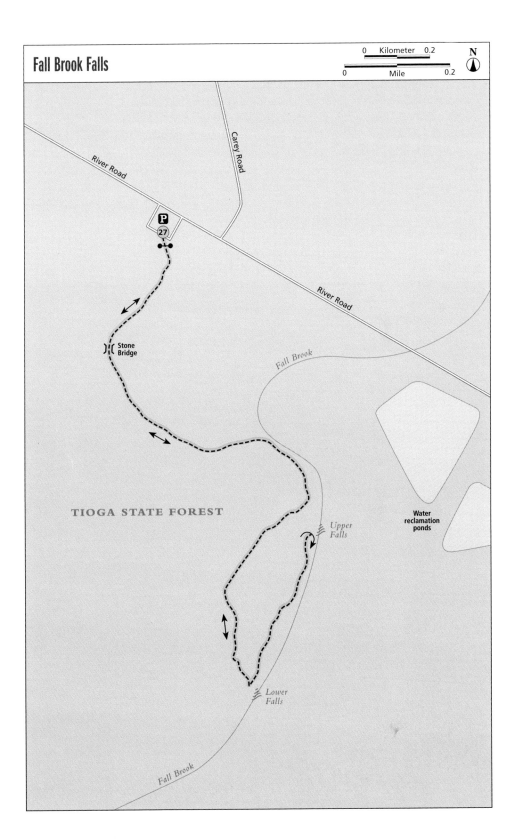

0   Kilometer   0.2

0   Mile   0.2

N

River Road

Carey Road

P

27

River Road

Stone Bridge

Fall Brook

TIOGA STATE FOREST

Upper Falls

Water reclamation ponds

Lower Falls

Fall Brook

falls. Note the quaint stone bridge. Stay along Fall Brook, then come to Fall Brook Falls, with its slide leading to a curtain-style drop pouring into an overhung gorge. The slide drops about 6 feet, while the main curtain-type drop is about 14 feet. You can get top-down looks at the falls from the precarious bluff edge.

The walk traces user-created trails downstream back from Fall Brook, where you eventually work back to the creek. At a flat-topped boulder at Fall Brook, Lower Falls drops just downstream, about an 8-foot spiller. Here you can access the inside of the gorge, but use care. It seems easier to walk upstream to reach the base of Upper Falls than it is to scramble down to reach the base of closer Lower Falls. No matter whether you scramble or not, the geology of the Fall Brook Falls area is a remarkable sight.

Upper Falls dives off a ledge, ensconced in a stone gorge.
RUSTY GLESSNER

Miles and Directions

0.0 From the parking area, walk around a yellow gate, passing energy management equipment to your left. Fall Brook is off to your left. Immediately enter woods on a footpath. Angle left, crossing a little stone-lined bridge, a leftover from the days when this was a picnic area. Enter dark evergreen forest.

0.1 Reach the top of Fall Brook Falls, also known as Upper Falls. The trail is bordered by a metal handrail. Below, the falls makes a long slide then drops off a ledge into a pool bordered by an impressive bluff, especially on the side of the trail. Continue downstream at the top of the bluff, tracing user-created paths.

0.2 Return to Fall Brook just a little above Lower Falls of Fall Brook Falls. It's challenging to access Lower Falls' base—use caution. However, to reach the base of Upper Falls, scramble up the left bank of the stream, carefully picking your way along the water as a bluff rises to your left.

0.3 Reach the base of Fall Brook Falls and its plunge pool. When the water is lower, it is easier to scramble to photography spots. The bluff to your left rises imposingly. Backtrack to the trailhead.

0.6 Arrive back at the trailhead, completing the walk.

Watch the water travel downstream along Fall Brook toward Lower Falls.

28 Jacoby Falls

This hike in the Loyalsock State Forest first takes you through a wetland by boardwalk then up the 600-foot-deep hollow cut by Jacoby Run. The trek culminates at the base of a cliff, where boulders and rocks of all sizes lie strewn below the falling curtain of 29-foot Jacoby Falls, a worthy goal. The aforementioned boulders double as ideal repose and photography spots for capturing the falls.

Waterfall height: 29 feet
Waterfall beauty: 5
Distance: 3.4-mile out-and-back
Difficulty: Easy
Hiking time: About 2 hours
Trail surface: Natural, a little boardwalk
Other trail users: None
Canine compatibility: Leashed pets allowed

Land status: State forest
Fees and permits: None
Maps: Jacoby Falls Trail Map and Guide; Loyalsock State Forest Public Use Map; USGS Bodines
Trail contact: Loyalsock State Forest, (570) 946-4049, www.dcnr.state.pa.us/forestry

Finding the trailhead: From exit 21 on I-180 near Montoursville, east of Williamsport, take PA 87 north for 4.4 miles to PA 973. Turn left and join PA 973 west, crossing Loyalsock Creek. After bridging Loyalsock Creek, turn right onto Wallis Run Road and follow it for 4.3 miles to the Jacoby Falls trailhead on your right. GPS: 41.376833, -76.920267

The Hike

On some waterfall hikes, it is the journey to the waterfall that is the highlight. However, here at Jacoby Falls, despite the hike being an enjoyable scenic trek, the waterfall is the star of the show. Here you enter a closing hollow, steepening and narrowing then ending as a rock wall rises in the background. Jacoby Run makes its plunge from the stone rampart, splattering into a menagerie of boulders and rocks, gathering steam then slaloming among yet other rocks and boulders downstream beyond the falls.

The landscape is worth deliberation, a place to relax and truly soak in the scene, not merely snap a picture to say you were there then move on. When hiking here, give yourself a little time at Jacoby Falls. *Note:* Camping is not allowed along the Jacoby Falls Trail.

The hike features an unusual start. Here, in order to stay on state forest land, the Jacoby Falls Trail traces a long narrow boardwalk spanning a vegetated wetland. The straight wooden track is a bit bouncy when you cross the wetland, and it continues into the forest until solid ground is reached. Ironically, the trail surface then becomes quite rocky as it first works down the Wallis Run valley before turning up Jacoby Run Hollow.

Jacoby Falls makes its 29-foot plunge followed by lesser cataracts.

As you work up the hollow, it is hard not to contrast the wild side of the creek—where the trail lies—with the more-groomed private land side. That side also harbors the pipeline maintenance road, with which the Jacoby Falls Trail briefly runs before the two separate prior to reaching the falls. At that point the path enters an increasingly rugged gorge, and it comes as no surprise the falls would be in this jagged section of rocks and boulders, steep-sided hills, and tall trees.

Then Jacoby Falls comes into view, a scenic white curtain with something to offer in every season—the gushing torrent of spring, the cooling spray of summer, the color-bordered trickle of autumn, and the ice sculpture of winter. Soak it in.

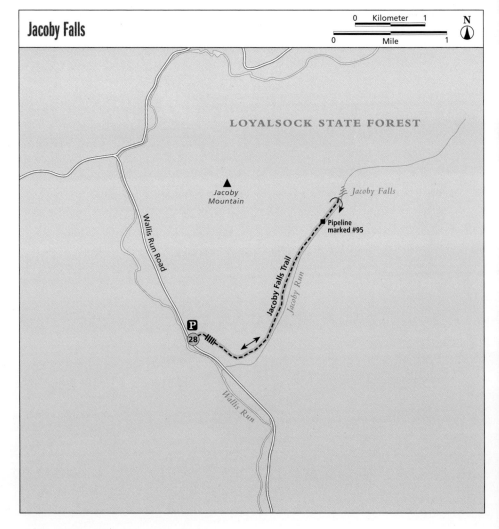

Jacoby Falls

LOYALSOCK STATE FOREST

Jacoby Mountain

Jacoby Falls

Pipeline marked #95

Wallis Run Road

Jacoby Falls Trail

Jacoby Run

Wallis Run

Miles and Directions

0.0   Leave the large Jacoby Falls trailhead and signboard, joining a narrow boardwalk spanning a wetland. Once across the wetland, the Jacoby Falls Trail turns right (southeast), working down the wide valley of Wallis Run.

0.4   Curve left into the hollow of Jacoby Run. Private posted property is to your right, across the creek at this point. The blazed trail stays in the Loyalsock State Forest.

1.2   The gorge narrows and you stay along the left bank.

1.5   Stay left as a grassy well access road leads right near a pipeline with the number 95.

1.7   The trail dead-ends at the base of 29-foot Jacoby Falls. Here you can explore and ramble among the rocks and boulders, aiming for the best view, even getting alongside the base of the rock shelf over which Jacoby Falls flows. Backtrack and do not use the pipeline access road on your return trip.

3.4   Arrive back at the trailhead after making the final leg of the hike on the wetland boardwalk.

29 Angel Falls, Gipson Falls

This waterfall hike combines a legendary path—the Loyalsock Trail—and a legendary cataract—Angel Falls—along with bonus cascades. Situated on aptly named Falls Run, Angel Falls is easily one of Pennsylvania's ten most exciting waterfalls. The hike climbs from creek bottoms onto a high, dry ridge before crossing upper Falls Run and then turning down to view impressive Angel Falls, diving 70 feet to its bottom. A steep downgrade takes you to Gipson Falls and a third unnamed spiller on Falls Run. From there, hikers can backtrack. Use of the unmaintained trail from Ogdonia Road to Angel Falls is strongly discouraged due to erosion of the resource.

Waterfall height: In order, 70 feet, 15 feet, 10 feet
Waterfall beauty: 5
Distance: 3.4-mile out-and-back
Difficulty: Moderate
Hiking time: About 2¼ hours
Trail surface: Natural
Other trail users: None
Canine compatibility: Leashed pets allowed
Land status: State forest
Fees and permits: None
Maps: Loyalsock State Forest Hiking Trail Map and Guide; Loyalsock State Forest Public Use Map; USGS Hillsgrove
Trail contact: Loyalsock State Forest, (570) 946-4049, www.dcnr.state.pa.us/forestry

Finding the trailhead: From Montoursville, take PA 87 north for 21 miles to Ogdonia and Ogdonia Road. Turn right on Ogdonia Road and follow it for 3 miles to a road split. Here, head left on Brunnerdale Road and follow it for 0.2 mile to the Loyalsock Trail trailhead on your left. GPS: 41.385150, -76.668517

The Hike

Like much of Pennsylvania's rural mountainous regions, what became Loyalsock State Forest was completely logged over, this area by the Central Pennsylvania Lumber Company. These scarred lands were then purchased by the Commonwealth of Pennsylvania to conserve and rehabilitate the terrain, not only to replant the forests but also to revegetate the land to prevent erosion and flash flooding and to improve habitat for the flora and fauna that once thrived in these majestic highlands.

About the time Pennsylvania was buying the forests—in the 1930s—the Great Depression was under way and the federal government had started a works program called the Civilian Conservation Corps (CCC). The CCC employed young men to develop and rehabilitate parks and forests such as the Loyalsock. Within the bounds of this particular state forest, six different CCC companies worked the land, planting trees, building nonerosive roads and trails, and constructing the original buildings of the Hillsgrove Ranger Station.

Today the forest has come full circle and the Loyalsock now harbors 114,000 acres of wildland—including waterfalls—to explore. The Loyalsock State Forest as a unit of the Pennsylvania state forest system was created in 2006 by combining parts of the former Wyoming State Forest, Tiadaghton State Forest, and Tioga State Forest. The agglomeration of these lands was then named after the primary stream of the region, Loyalsock Creek.

You will hike the master path of the forest—the Loyalsock Trail—en route to Angel Falls. In case you were wondering (I was), the unusual name Loyalsock is the corruption of an Algonquin name for the stream that became Loyalsock Creek. The Loyalsock Trail is named for the creek. The Loyalsock Trail runs for 59 miles through the state forest and is popular with backpackers. On that note, camping is not allowed along the Loyalsock Trail around Angel Falls to protect the resource.

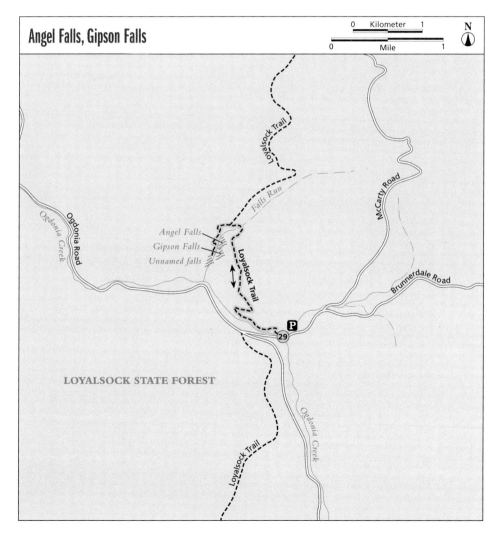

Angel Falls, Gipson Falls

The hike to Angel Falls starts with a pair of crossings of Ogdonia Creek. That will give you an idea of what the water levels are here. Cruise down the attractive stream valley of Ogdonia Creek. You then leave the valley, climbing a steep, heavily wooded ridge rising well above the creek. The Loyalsock Trail joins and leaves former logging grades as it makes its way uphill. After ascending 400 feet, the track levels off and turns into the upper valley of Falls Run, gently and innocently babbling and belying its steep, waterfall-heavy nature below.

However, the Angel Falls Trail takes you to the action, first leading to the top of the falls combined with a partial view into the forest beyond. The outcrops here will leave those with a fear of heights shaking in their boots. Nevertheless, others will be thrilled. You can work your way around the bluff to the base of Angel Falls, watching it fearlessly plunge from its rock precipice to make a short drop, then widen and spread and spill and splash over layers of stratified stone, delivering different looks at different water levels before slowing—but not for long.

Follow Falls Run downstream, once again working around cliffs. Here you can see Gipson Falls start even more narrowly then tumble in steps, never quite making a definable end—Falls Run just keeps falling. Work your way down to the next fall (unnamed). This classic ledge cataract makes a 10-foot drop over overhung rock strata, slows in a pool, and then makes more spills just for show.

From here it is best to backtrack, staying on maintained trail, as the Loyalsock State Forest discourages hikers from making the straight off-trail trip from Ogdonia Road to the falls on Falls Run. This was once the route of the Loyalsock Trail, but erosion caused it to be rerouted.

Miles and Directions

0.0 Leave the Loyalsock Trail trailhead on Brunnerdale Road and follow it west, immediately hopping over Ogdonia Creek. Continue downstream and cross Ogdonia Creek a second time. The stream is much larger here, as Brunnerdale Run has added its flow. When the water is up, this may be a ford.

0.4 Leave the Ogdonia Creek valley for the uplands. Switchback uphill, going on and off old logging tracks. Beech, cherry, and maple shade the route.

1.2 Turn left on the Angel Falls Trail. Step over Falls Run, climb to the other side of the hill, and then begin descending downstream parallel to Falls Run.

1.4 Begin dropping sharply toward Falls Run.

1.5 Reach the top of 70-plus-foot Angel Falls. Look down from an outcrop and out beyond the Falls Run valley. From here, work downhill along the rim of the gorge on a user-created trail—be careful, the drop is a doozy. Pick your way around the cliff line, then make your way to the base of the falls.

1.7 Reach Gipson Falls after once again working around a cliff line. Here the slender cataract jumps off a precipice then bounds down in stages. Look left for a small cave in the cliffs. Travel downhill yet again to see a third and final ledge drop of 10 feet with a wet rock house behind it. Backtrack toward the Loyalsock Trail; avoid continuing downhill toward Ogdonia Road.

3.4 Arrive back at the trailhead on Brunnerdale Road, staying on maintained trail.

Angel Falls is a magnificent cataract.

Gipson Falls makes its own worthy drop.
RUSTY GLESSNER

30 Rode Falls

The hike to Rode Falls is more than just a waterfall hike—it is an adventure. Join the impressive Loyalsock Trail as the highlight reel of a path first works along a high bluff hundreds of feet above Ketchum Run. Pass two notable westerly overlooks where the Loyalsock Creek valley cuts a swath through the mountains. Continue the descent to reach Ketchum Run and find Rode Falls pitching over a crag into a stony-framed plunge pool. Admire the waterfall, then climb a ladder to the 12-foot overhang from which Ketchum Run spills. Follow the Loyalsock Trail a bit more to complete a mini-loop using an alternate connecting path for hikers who want to avoid the ladder beside Rode Falls. Be advised that the hike involves a 600-foot descent followed by the climb out.

Waterfall height: 12 feet
Waterfall beauty: 4
Distance: 3.5-mile out-and-back with mini-loop
Difficulty: Moderate
Hiking time: About 2 hours
Trail surface: Natural
Other trail users: None

Canine compatibility: Leashed pets allowed
Land status: State forest
Fees and permits: None
Maps: Loyalsock State Forest Hiking Trail Map and Guide; Loyalsock State Forest Public Use Map; USGS Hillsgrove
Trail contact: Loyalsock State Forest, (570) 946-4049, www.dcnr.state.pa.us/forestry

Finding the trailhead: From the intersection of PA 187 and PA 154 in Forksville, take PA 154 east for 2.3 miles to Worlds End Road. Turn right and follow Worlds End Road for 2 miles, then turn right onto the Bridle & Ski Trail, which is actually a road but may be gated in winter (the gate should be open during the warm season). This road/trail was formerly known as Coal Mine Road and may be listed as such on some maps and directions. Follow the gravel track for 2 miles, then look left for a small clearing and little-used parking area on a right turn, just before the Loyalsock Trail crosses the Bridle & Ski Trail. The parking area—to the left of the road—is not obvious but does have some stone underneath to harden the spots to park your vehicle. GPS: 41.456850, -76.628383

The Hike

The Loyalsock Trail is one of Pennsylvania's finest hiking paths, and the trip to Rode Falls is just one more example of this fine trail displaying its beauty. On this hike you will have to earn it, though. Starting at the heights well above Loyalsock Creek, you join the singletrack Loyalsock Trail, cruising along the brow of the gorge dropping to Ketchum Run. Stunted oaks and other trees grow along the edge of the bluff dropping hundreds of feet below, where you will be later. It is not long before the Loyalsock Trail takes you to your first reward—Upper Alpine Overlook, a westerly vista extending down the Loyalsock Creek valley framed by distant hills beyond. The path then continues along the rim's edge before making a sharp dive that makes you begin to contemplate the return trip back to the trailhead.

Nevertheless, there is a waterfall to see and, before that, another overlook. After losing elevation—but not too much—you will come to the rock outcroppings of the Lower Alpine Overlook and another surprisingly rewarding panorama of the Loyalsock State Forest and surrounding lands. This rocky cliff is bordered by ferns and mosses and is just one of those places that makes you want to stop, relax, and contemplate the natural beauty.

Yet Rode Falls beckons. Therefore, we work our way down toward Ketchum Run and then reach a trail intersection. Here the Loyalsock Trail gives hikers an alternate route if they want to avoid the ladder beside Rode Falls. However, being the adventurous waterfall hikers that we are, we go for the ladder and for Rode Falls, using the ladder-avoiding alternate trail later to make a mini-loop.

Down we go more until Ketchum Run is running off to our right. Despite the sounds of the crashing and dashing stream, we soon hear a louder, deeper rumble, that of Rode Falls. Here an elevated berm provides a convenient viewing platform whereupon we see white froth charging over a line of rock, widening a bit before splashing along an angled lower shelf, then slowing in a mossy rock-walled nest before pushing on through shallow rocks. This aquatic feature complements the two overlooks, together creating a fun trek.

The rock walls on both sides of the waterfall are steep and complete enough to offer no passage. Therefore, a ladder has been placed on the left side of the rock shelf, allowing you to scale the cliff walls where no route exists. That is excitement! And to think they offer an alternate to avoid this Pennsylvania waterfall hiking thrill.

Beyond Rode Falls you dodge through the lower Ketchum Run gorge before the Loyalsock Trail turns away from the creek and climbs. This is where the ladder-avoiding alternate path comes in. We simply take it, making a little loop, and then backtrack our way up to the high country and the trailhead, another Pennsylvania waterfall hike under our belt.

Miles and Directions

0.0 Leave the obscure parking area on the curve of what was Coal Mine Road and is now the Bridle & Ski Trail and walk 300 feet northwest on the road/trail before reaching the single-track Loyalsock Trail as it crosses the Bridle & Ski Trail. Head left on the Loyalsock Trail and continue northwest along the brow of the mountain among hemlock, beech, and oak.

0.3 Reach the Upper Alpine Overlook and a campsite. From this perch you can gaze down toward Ketchum Run below and Loyalsock Creek beyond. Continue on the Loyalsock Trail, enjoying more rim running.

Rode Falls is at its best during the spring flow.
RUSTY GLESSNER

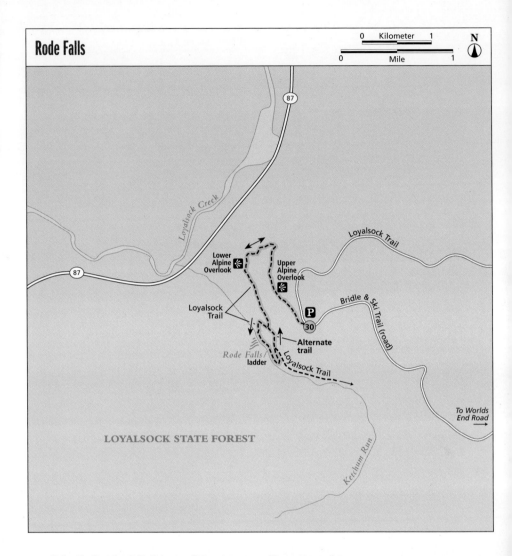

0   Kilometer   1

0   Mile   1

N

0.6   The Loyalsock Trail drops off the plateau, making a steep dive.

0.8   The descent eases and soon you cross a boggy flat on a level bench. Head for the edge of the mountainside.

1.0   Come to the Lower Alpine Overlook. The immediate scenery with mosses, ferns, and shade trees complemented by a fine view leaves many hikers preferring this lower vista.

1.1   Resume descending. The path goes on and off old logging roads, but the blazes of the Loyalsock Trail make the way clear.

1.4   Reach a trail intersection. Here the official Loyalsock Trail goes right, and this is the way to Rode Falls and the ladder at the falls. The lesser-used alternate trail avoids the ladder and shortcuts the Loyalsock, but it also misses Rode Falls. Go right with the official Loyalsock Trail. Descend.

1.5 The Loyalsock Trail cuts left and aims for Ketchum Run. Soon come to the creek and begin working up the valley.

1.6 Come to Rode Falls. Here the cataract jumps off a rock rim into a stone-lined cathedral, splashing in a pool, and then enters rocky shallows. A natural berm provides a good contemplation spot. The ladder looms to the left. When you are ready, climb the wooden ladder over the waterfall rim and continue up Ketchum Run.

1.9 The Loyalsock Trail turns away from Ketchum Run.

2.0 Reach an intersection. Now the more-trodden Loyalsock Trail heads right, while the ladder-avoiding alternate splits left. Stay with the fainter alternate trail.

2.1 Complete the alternate trail and the mini-loop. From here, backtrack on the Loyalsock Trail, making the 500-plus-foot ascent back toward the trailhead.

3.5 Arrive back at the trailhead, completing the waterfall hike.

Lower Alpine Overlook affords a magnificent view.

31 Cottonwood Falls

Combine a waterfall trip with an overall fun little hike at picturesque Worlds End State Park. Cottonwood Falls is a modest cascade, but you will appreciate not only the falls here but also the aquatic scenes on the well-developed trail system. In addition, Worlds End State Park offers other land and water attractions.

Waterfall height: 10 feet
Waterfall beauty: 3
Distance: 1.4-mile lollipop loop
Difficulty: Easy, does have 300-foot climb
Hiking time: About 1 hour
Trail surface: Natural
Other trail users: None

Canine compatibility: Leashed pets allowed
Land status: State park
Fees and permits: None
Maps: Worlds End State Park; USGS Eagles Mere
Trail contact: Worlds End State Park, (570) 924-3287, www.dcnr.state.pa.us/stateparks

Finding the trailhead: From the intersection of PA 187 and PA 154 in Forksville, take PA 154 east for 3 miles to the Chapel and Double Run Nature Trail trailhead on your right, a 0.5-mile beyond the left turn into the park visitor center. There is limited parking for 4 or 5 cars here. GPS: 41.465950, -76.578600

The Hike

Driving here on winding roads may make you think you are at the world's end, but if this is the end of the journey, then it will be worth it. Early in Pennsylvania's history, settlers used a faint path that is now the Pioneer Road Trail and Worlds End Road to reach this seemingly forlorn spot along Loyalsock Creek. Purportedly the settlers looked down upon the gorge of Loyalsock Creek and proclaimed it the end of the world.

The name Worlds End stuck and began appearing on maps. Interestingly, some local residents objected to the name, saying this spot was really called Whirl's Glen, for a swirling pool in Loyalsock Creek. The objectors undertook a letter-writing campaign, and the state changed the name of the park to Whirls Glen. In response, a greater, more effective letter-writing campaign led the State Geographic Board to change the name back to Worlds End State Park.

My own preference is Worlds End. I admit that before my first visit, the name had me intrigued. The preserve is completely enveloped by the Loyalsock State Forest, effectively adding to the wildness and remoteness of the 780-acre park within the Endless Mountains. It truly is kind of far from anywhere, so I encourage you to make more than a waterfall day hike when visiting the park, which was developed in the

1930s by the Civilian Conservation Corps and features their signature rustic wood and stone architecture.

For starters, the park offers nineteen cabins as well as a seventy-site shaded campground. Half of the campsites have electricity. Shower houses are available for those who stay in cabins as well as campers. The park is laced with over 20 miles of hiking trails, including the famous, long Loyalsock Trail. The waters of Loyalsock Creek draw

Cottonwood Falls slides down "steps" before making its vertical dive into a pool.
RUSTY GLESSNER

in anglers vying for trout, stocked regularly. Paddlers come here in spring and tackle the creek's whitewater. However, most visitors enjoy the waters of Loyalsock Creek at the dammed swimming area, open during the summer.

The hike to Cottonwood Falls heightens your Worlds End State Park experience. The trek joins the Double Run Nature Trail, working upstream alongside singing Double Run under beech, yellow birch, maple, and evergreens. The well-marked and -maintained footpath soon passes an oft-fished pool below a little cascade. Ahead, bridge a wetland before coming to the loop portion of the hike. Hiker trail bridges help to keep your feet dry.

Stay with the Double Run Nature Trail as it climbs high and away from water, making you wonder if you are on the right path. After all, this is a waterfall hike. The hike then officially leaves Worlds End State Park for the Loyalsock State Forest, but you will not know the difference other than a sign. The forest and trail management are the same here. You then descend to the lushly wooded West Branch Double Run valley.

Heading downstream, you soon come to Cottonwood Falls, located within sight of the trail. A user-created track leads to the substantial pool below the pour-over. Here the pool and a low but long cliff line frames the 10-foot cataract as it discharges from a cleft in the rock. The geography favors moving around to get different viewpoints of the cataract.

Continuing down West Branch, you will see other small falls, waterslides, and intriguing water features that enrich the hike. All too soon, you are backtracking toward the trailhead, wondering what else to do here at the end of the world.

Note: You will see another waterfall shown on the Worlds End State Park map—High Falls. However, the falls is well below the trail and can be seen neither from the trail nor from Loyalsock Creek below. The park strongly discourages hikers from attempting to visit High Falls. Don't do it!

Miles and Directions

0.0 Leave the Double Run/Chapel trailhead, joining the hiker-only Double Run Nature Trail.

0.1 Pass an oft-fished pool on Double Run.

0.2 Come to a trail junction. The Loyalsock Trail comes in on your left. At this point go right and cross Double Run on a wooden hiker bridge. Reach another trail intersection. Go left here on the Double Run Nature Trail, making a clockwise circuit. Climb away from Double Run, working up the ridge dividing Double Run from West Branch Double Run.

0.6 After climbing 300 feet, start your descent for West Branch Double Run.

0.7 Switchback to the right, still descending. West Branch Double Run is visible and audible below.

0.8 After utilizing wood steps, bridge West Branch Double Run and reach a trail intersection. Turn right, still on the Double Run Nature Trail, tracing West Branch Double Run downstream, passing a warm-up cascade just below the bridge.

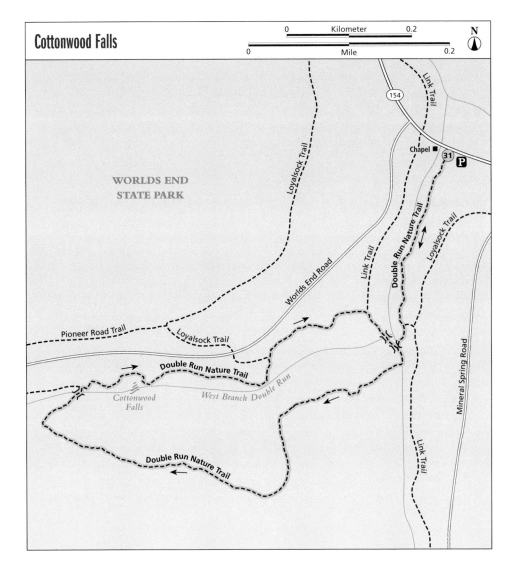

0.9 Reach 10-foot Cottonwood Falls as it spills into a cliff-lined pool. Access is easy. Continue down the mini-gorge, looking for a little slide cascade.

1.0 Pass another lesser falls of 6 feet, then meet the Loyalsock Trail. Stay right, downhill.

1.1 Reach another trail intersection. Here the Link Trail lives up to its name and leaves left to link to the main park day-use facilities. Our hike turns right to cross West Branch Double Run on a hiker bridge.

1.2 Come to another intersection and the bridge over Double Run. You were here before. Head left, crossing Double Run on the hiker bridge, now backtracking.

1.4 Arrive back at the trailhead, completing the waterfall hike.

32 Alpine Falls

Start this hike at a remote trailhead deep in the regal Loyalsock State Forest. First you trace the Crane Spur, a woodsy doubletrack, then join the Loyalsock Trail, descending to incised East Branch Big Run, where you find Alpine Falls making its long and varied tumble, first crashing over a rim into a naked rock channel, then flattening out on a stone slab and hopping down a stone-lined gorge and out of sight, onward to feed Loyalsock Creek.

Waterfall height: 25 feet
Waterfall beauty: 4
Distance: 1.4-mile out-and-back
Difficulty: Easy, though reaching base of falls is tough
Hiking time: About 1 hour
Trail surface: Natural
Other trail users: None

Canine compatibility: Leashed pets allowed
Land status: State forest
Fees and permits: None
Maps: Loyalsock State Forest Hiking Trail Map and Guide; Loyalsock State Forest Public Use Map; USGS Eagles Mere
Trail contact: Loyalsock State Forest, (570) 946-4049, www.dcnr.state.pa.us/forestry

Finding the trailhead: From the intersection of PA 187 and PA 154 in Forksville, take PA 154 east for 1.3 miles and turn left on obscure but signed Loyalsock Road. The turn is located just before a private cabin. If you miss the turn, continue to the entrance to Worlds End State Park on your left, then turn around and backtrack for 0.5 mile to make the turn onto Loyalsock Road. Once on Loyalsock Road, set your odometer and drive for 7.1 miles to the Crane Spur on your right (at 6.8 miles, on a sharp turn, you will pass a cabin known as the Cubs Nest). The Crane Spur trailhead is not an elaborate trailhead by any means. In fact, it is nothing but a narrow pull-off, with limited parking for only 1 or 2 cars. Here you will see a doubletrack blazed trail heading southwest into the woods. Additionally, the other end of the Crane Spur is only 0.1 mile farther on your right. Do not accidentally leave from this second Crane Spur trailhead or the whole hike will be confusing to the extreme. GPS: 41.484850, -76.545167

The Hike

When en route to more-popular waterfalls at Pennsylvania's state and national forests and parks, signs guide the way to these preserves and help build your anticipation. You then see signs for the trailhead and then the trail itself. Reaching your desired waterfall is simply a matter of executing the hike. The trip to Alpine Falls features none of the above. Rather, a bit of unease settles in from the beginning. Few signs are to be seen on the way to the trailhead. The last part of the drive is 7 miles on an obscure gravel road traveling through a forgotten portion of a lonesome state forest. Then, upon reaching the supposed trailhead, there is neither a large established parking area

The uppermost stage of Alpine Falls is just a prelude to the final act.

nor signs pointing the way to the falls. Instead, a single blaze on a tree gives you hope that this is the right track.

You begin following a half-grown-over logging road now dubbed the Crane Spur (the Crane Spur is shown on Loyalsock State Forest maps). A hiker track is overlain on the roadbed amid a classic northern hardwood forest of beech and birch. Then comes the decisive moment—a split in the old logging road/trail. Here the blazed Crane Spur goes left, but we go right. Neither route at this point is encouraging, but at least the right (and correct) path has a beaten-down footbed. After a short period of uncertainty, we come to the signed and blazed Loyalsock Trail. Yay!

Trepidation evaporates like waterfall mist in the rising sun. We follow the Loyalsock Trail down to the sound of tumbling water, our mood changing to excitement at seeing a new waterfall for the first time, hoping for plentiful water and perhaps photography opportunities, or maybe just a chance to relax by moving water in a scenic Pennsylvania setting.

Alpine Falls delivers on all counts, cutting through the stony chasm draining off the plateau dividing Loyalsock Creek from Little Loyalsock Creek. It is easy to peer down into the gorge below, admiring the varied falls of the remote pour-over. Reaching the base of the falls is another matter altogether. There is no good route. My only advice is to scout up and down along the old logging road running parallel to the stream down here. This level roadbed also serves as a campsite and hangout astride Alpine Falls. If you reach the base of the falls, explore the intriguing rock houses on the bluffs at the far side of the lower cataract.

On your return trip, after successfully finding this little piece of Pennsylvania paradise, you will be smiling the whole way—despite the uphill—and looking forward to sharing the beauty of Alpine Falls with others so they can experience the trepidation, anticipation, then triumph that comes with visiting this cataract.

Miles and Directions

0.0 From the parking area at the first Crane Spur trailhead, walk southwest on a blazed doubletrack with a slight downhill. Small seeps cross the track in places. East Branch Big Run is gurgling off to your right in ferny woods, and trees are growing in the old roadbed. In summer, scenic fern glades are found nearby.

0.5 Come to a split in the roadbed. The official Crane Spur goes left, but we go right on an obvious roadbed overlain with a singletrack footbed.

0.6 The roadbed opens to a small campsite and the Loyalsock Trail. Turn right and descend a footpath. The sounds of East Branch Big Run drift into your ears.

0.7 Reach East Branch Big Run and another campsite on another logging road. Alpine Falls is just downstream of the crossing of the Loyalsock Trail here. The narrow, thin, three-stage drop that is Alpine Falls is nestled deep in the gorge. Be careful approaching this cataract. Backtrack to the trailhead.

1.4 Arrive back at the trailhead, completing the waterfall walk.

Alpine Falls

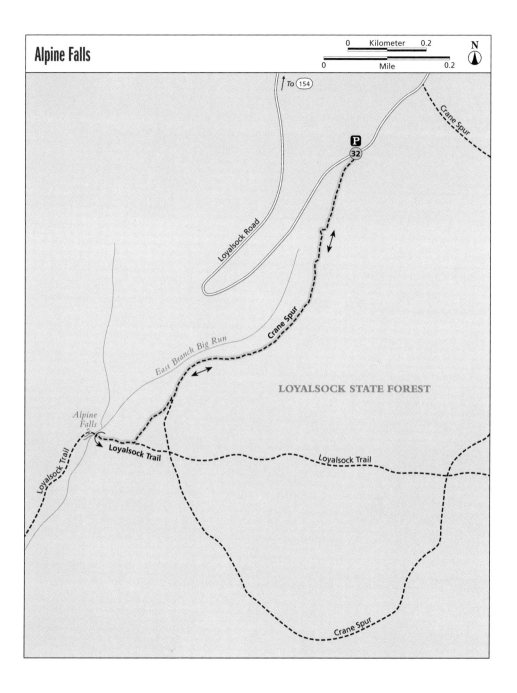

Kilometer 0 0.2

Mile 0 0.2

N

To 154

Crane Spur

P
32

Loyalsock Road

Crane Spur

East Branch Big Run

LOYALSOCK STATE FOREST

Alpine Falls

Loyalsock Trail

Loyalsock Trail

Loyalsock Trail

Crane Spur

The second stage of Alpine Falls presents a spectacular sight!
RUSTY GLESSNER

33 Dutchman Falls

Located on a spur path at the eastern end of the famed Loyalsock Trail, Dutchman Falls makes its double descent just before reaching Loyalsock Creek. Whether you catch the spiller with a lot of water or a little, you will find a changing waterfall exhibiting fluctuating flow patterns, each of them displaying something special for the Pennsylvania waterfall hiker. The walk to the falls, though short, is deceptively difficult due to the irregular trail bed and steepness.

Waterfall height: 27 feet
Waterfall beauty: 4
Distance: 0.6-mile out-and-back
Difficulty: Moderate due to irregular trail bed
Hiking time: About ½ hour
Trail surface: Natural
Other trail users: None
Canine compatibility: Leashed pets allowed

Land status: State forest
Fees and permits: None
Maps: Loyalsock State Forest Hiking Trail Map and Guide; Loyalsock State Forest Public Use Map; USGS Laporte
Trail contact: Loyalsock State Forest, (570) 946-4049, www.dcnr.state.pa.us/forestry

Finding the trailhead: From the intersection of Main Street and US 220 in Laporte, take US 220 north and follow it for 2.9 miles to Mead Road. Turn left on Mead Road and follow it 0.2 mile to the right turn into the easterly terminus of the Loyalsock Trail. GPS: 41.448222, -76.453180

The Hike

The Loyalsock Trail is a Pennsylvania hiking icon. The nearly 60-mile end-to-end pathway wends its way through the 115,000-acre Loyalsock State Forest, passing streams, mountains, overlooks, and deep woods, traveling to or near many highlights of the state forest, including Dutchman Falls. It also features a historic component—traveling by historic structures, along a former railroad grade, and tracing a precolonial Indian path.

Whether they are thru-hiking the entire distance of the Loyalsock Trail from its eastern end near Laporte to the western terminus near Montoursville or engaging a shorter endeavor, backpackers find overnight backcountry camping spots in seeking their mileage goals. A small portion of the Loyalsock Trail passes through Worlds End State Park.

Elevations along the Loyalsock Trail range from a little over 600 feet to 2,140 feet. Thanks to the maintenance of the Alpine Club of Williamsport, the Loyalsock Trail remains in good shape. The club has been at it for over seven decades, though the path was originally laid out by Boy Scouts. Several waterfalls can be found along the trail's length, including Angel Falls, Alpine Falls, and this one—Dutchman Falls—all detailed in this guide. The eastern terminus of the Loyalsock Trail—the starting point for this waterfall hike—accommodates many a car, for not only backpackers but also day hikers visiting Dutchman Falls and another nearby feature known as Haystack Rapids on Loyalsock Creek.

From the trailhead, you descend the Loyalsock Trail—surprisingly rough and rocky at this point—toward Loyalsock Creek. After briefly joining an old logging railroad grade, you cross Loyalsock Creek on the old railroad bridge (check out the stonework by the railroad masons on this culvert). You then pick up a blue-blazed spur

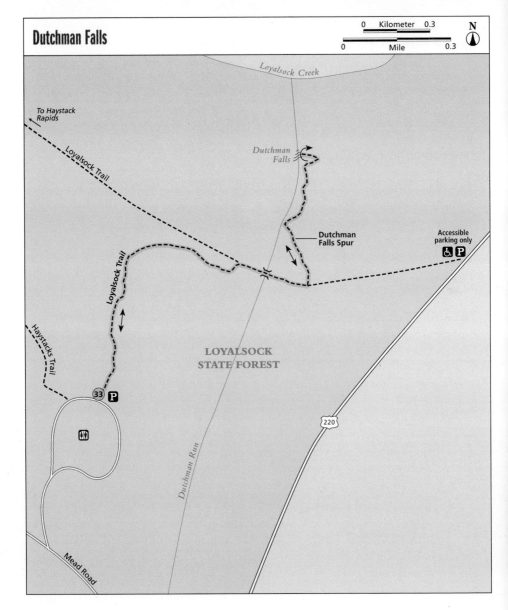

Dutchman Falls

0 Kilometer 0.3

0 Mile 0.3

N

Loyalsock Creek

To Haystack Rapids

Loyalsock Trail

Dutchman Falls

Dutchman Falls Spur

Accessible parking only

Loyalsock Trail

Haystacks Trail

LOYALSOCK STATE FOREST

33 P

220

Dutchman Run

Mead Road

leading down along Dutchman Run to the base of the falls shortly before Dutchman Run feeds Loyalsock Creek. Here you can safely walk to the base of Dutchman Falls to view, admire, and photograph the spiller. The uppermost 6-foot drop of the falls cannot be seen from here, but the stair-stepping final 21-foot cascade can.

Avoid user-created trails leading alongside the falls. They are dangerous and erosive. While down here, note the stone tongue over which Dutchman Run flows just before meeting big Loyalsock Creek.

Lengthening your hike is easy. Simply either follow the Loyalsock Trail west along the creek or trace the railroad grade 2 miles to Haystack Rapids, a geological/aquatic feature where unusual rock formations are found on Loyalsock Creek. Part of your return trip can be on the Haystacks Trail, which takes you back to the parking lot where you started.

Dutchman Falls spills in numerous tiers.

Dutchman Falls in winter.
RUSTY GLESSNER

Miles and Directions

0.0 Leave the eastern terminus of the Loyalsock Trail trailhead at the lowermost end of the parking area, then join the Loyalsock Trail on a rocky, irregular path heading sharply downhill. Watch your footing. Hiking poles help here.

0.2 Reach the old Williamsport and North Branch Railroad grade. Head right here, going over Dutchman Run on the old rail span. Note the grade extends out to US 220, where only accessible parking is permitted. On the far side of Dutchman Run, look for the blue-blazed path leading down along the run, briefly following an old roadbed then switchbacking and safely working its way toward the base of Dutchman Falls. Admire the 6-foot upper drop of Dutchman Falls on the way down.

0.3 The end of the trail makes a sharp switchback just before reaching Loyalsock Creek. Reach the base of the oft-photographed lower tier of Dutchman Falls. Backtrack to the trailhead.

0.6 Arrive back at the trailhead, completing the waterfall walk.

34 Sullivan Falls

Though the walk to the falls barely qualifies as a hike, the quarter-mile jaunt to Sullivan Falls will reward you with a fine aspect of this imposing spiller as it nosedives from a cliff into a swirling, circular pool bordered by steep sides. The land where this falls is found—State Game Lands No. 13—hosts several other falls that can be visited by experienced, prepared, and intrepid waterfallers.

Waterfall height: 34 feet
Waterfall beauty: 4
Distance: 0.2-mile out-and-back
Difficulty: Easy
Hiking time: About ¼ hour
Trail surface: Natural
Other trail users: None

Canine compatibility: Leashed pets allowed
Land status: State game lands
Fees and permits: None
Maps: State Game Lands 013; USGS Red Rock
Trail contact: Pennsylvania Game Commission, (833) 742-4868, www.pgc.pa.gov

Finding the trailhead: From Dallas, take PA 415 north for 1.6 miles, then turn left and follow PA 118 west for 18 miles to Red Rock. At Red Rock, turn right on PA 487 north and follow it for 3.8 miles to Sullivan Falls Road, just past the entrance to Ricketts Glen State Park on your right. Turn left on gravel Sullivan Falls Road and follow it downhill, bridging a stream at 1.7 miles, then reach the trailhead at 2.1 miles. Look for the parking area and inscribed stone on your right. GPS: 41.334933, -76.339390

The Hike

It is no surprise that Sullivan Falls and other impressive cataracts are situated along the East Branch Fishing Creek watershed. After all, it is the next major watershed over from the waterfall-rich streams of Ricketts Glen State Park.

Flowing off North Mountain, a series of tributaries of East Branch Fishing Creek—notably Sullivan Branch, where Sullivan Falls is found, and Heberly Run—are home to numerous cataracts. However, unlike Ricketts Glen State Park, these waterfalls are on state game lands, basically undeveloped as far as hiking trails are concerned. One can only imagine a loop trail visiting the waterfalls of Sullivan Branch and Heberly Run. While maybe not as great as the waterfall loop hike at Ricketts Glen State Park, it still would be one of the top waterfall hikes in the Keystone State. Download the map of State Game Lands No. 13 and explore the possibilities for yourself. The USGS quadrangle Red Rock shows additional cataracts.

There are intrepid waterfallers who execute such an undertaking, visiting falls on Heberly Run such as Twin Falls and Lewis Falls as well as other unnamed cataracts. Alas, at least we have the short and easy walk to Sullivan Falls. And it is on a trail. The trailhead is even marked with an inscribed stone slab. Here you can take the walk to

In springtime Sullivan Falls fairly gushes into its big pool.

Sullivan Falls, then work your way down to the plunge pool of the 34-foot diver. The deep waters below the cataract are popular with summertime swimmers.

It is also easy to access the top of the falls. Here you can peer down on the cavernous walls upon which Sullivan Falls echoes. Also, look upstream just above the brink of the falls. At this point Sullivan Branch makes a narrow S-curve around the erosion-resistant rock before flattening out and diving off its perch.

In addition, if you are enjoying the waterfalls of Ricketts Glen State Park, it is but a short drive to the Sullivan Falls trailhead and a short walk to the falls. Therefore, even if you are not up for off-trail hiking the waterfalls of State Game Lands No. 13, at least make the easy walk to Sullivan Falls.

Miles and Directions

0.0 From the signed trailhead, follow the well-trod trail leaving the lower end of the parking area, heading northwest. The sound of Sullivan Falls rises.

0.1 Come to the rim of the walls into which 34-foot Sullivan Falls tumbles. From here, you can scramble down to the base and plunge pool of the falls or head right and walk to the cusp of the cataract. Backtrack to the trailhead.

0.2 Arrive back at the trailhead, completing the waterfall walk.

Sullivan Falls is a worthy destination even in the grip of winter.
RUSTY GLESSNER

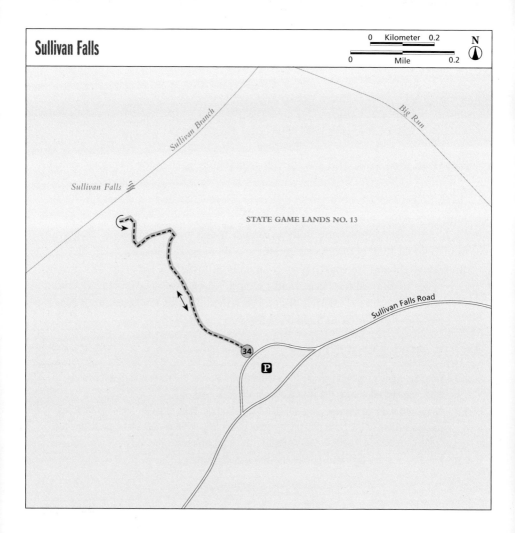

Sullivan Falls

0   Kilometer   0.2

0   Mile   0.2

N

Sullivan Branch

Big Run

Sullivan Falls

STATE GAME LANDS NO. 13

Sullivan Falls Road

34

P

35 Falls of Ricketts Glen

Hiking to the twenty-one named falls of Ricketts Glen State Park over a nearly 7-mile loop is considered to be *the* singular waterfall hiking experience in Pennsylvania, perhaps even America's greatest waterfall hike. At this state park you will head up Kitchen Creek and a tributary, seeing fall after fall, cataract after cataract, on a remarkable trail system that has to be walked upon to be truly appreciated.

Waterfall height: 11 to 94 feet
Waterfall beauty: 5+
Distance: 6.7-mile lollipop loop
Difficulty: Difficult due to stone steps and elevation changes
Hiking time: About 4 hours
Trail surface: Natural, stone
Other trail users: None

Canine compatibility: Leashed pets allowed
Land status: State park
Fees and permits: None
Maps: Ricketts Glen State Park; USGS Red Rock
Trail contact: Ricketts Glen State Park, (570) 477-5675, www.dcnr.state.pa.us/stateparks

Finding the trailhead: From Dallas, take PA 415 north for 1.6 miles, then turn left and follow PA 118 west for 16.5 miles to reach the large Falls Trail parking area on your right, just before bridging Kitchen Creek. GPS: 41.300293, -76.273191

The Hike

For some Pennsylvania waterfall hikers, Ricketts Glen State Park is all they need. Why? There simply is no other place that compares to this preserve—a place where you can not only enjoy twenty-one named waterfalls but also old-growth forest and a remarkable preserve that is one of the finest state parks in the entire country.

In addition to stunning natural scenery, Ricketts Glen State Park offers numerous outdoor recreation opportunities along with a campground, cabins, and cottages for overnight pleasure (these accommodations are snapped up during the summertime). Not only does the park offer waterfall-laden streams, but it also features the alluring Lake Jean. Here water enthusiasts can swim at a beach during summer or fish the 245-acre lake. Boaters can tool around on the water. Canoes, kayaks, rowboats, and paddleboats are available for rent should you want to explore the impoundment that feeds the waterfalls of Ricketts Glen.

The Falls Trail is undoubtedly the most popular hiking here, yet there are other pathways for both hikers and equestrians. A total of 26 miles of trails course through the park, where the forests are lush and the game is plentiful. This is wild country—bears are known to roam the preserve.

But Ricketts Glen has always been a wild place. Back in 1868, Colonel R. Bruce Ricketts bought this tract along Kitchen Creek—and an additional 80,000 acres in order to harvest its timber. Word got back to Colonel Ricketts that the streams through his land not only were good for fishing but, perhaps more importantly, housed a stunning number of waterfalls in addition to old-growth pines, oaks, and hemlocks. He did not harvest along the waterfalls of Kitchen Creek, but instead built a trail system whereby the waterfalls can be visited.

Ricketts's descendants later sold a huge swath of land to the Pennsylvania Game Commission, but not the falls area. However, in 1942 the falls area was sold to Pennsylvania to create a state park. More land was purchased around the falls until the 13,000-acre park was fully realized. Over the decades, facilities of Ricketts Glen State Park have improved and continue to progress, yet the waterfalls cannot be improved upon. Taken in their entirety, it is hard to believe this many scenic cataracts can be found in one area on one hike. Thus, it is easy to see why some waterfallers believe they need no other destination than Ricketts Glen. And the hike is a Pennsylvania classic, a must-do Keystone State trail endeavor.

The trek starts at the large PA 118 parking area. The Falls Trail begins making its way up Kitchen Creek on a wide and well-maintained path, designed to handle significant foot traffic. A little over a mile into the hike, you reach your first waterfall— Murray Reynolds Falls. Colonel Rickett named many of the waterfalls for friends, family members, and American Indian tribes.

You pass two more cataracts before coming to a spot known as Waters Meet, the point where Kitchen Creek and a tributary creating Ganoga Glen come together. The hike then heads up the vale of Ganoga Glen, visiting a series of mind-boggling waterfalls, including 94-foot Ganoga Falls, a towering shower of white. And there are even more dischargers in myriad forms showcased in Ganoga Glen—ten named waterfalls in all.

After climbing a thousand feet, the circuit hike then joins the Highland Trail as it works its way atop the Allegheny Plateau in rich woodlands pocked with rock outcrops. One of these formations is known as Midway Crevasse. Ultimately, you return to Kitchen Creek, where you are now heading downstream, passing still more waterfalls taking multiple forms. You will also undoubtedly appreciate the remarkable stonework that was undertaken to enable hikers a way through the gorge that is a geological wonder. In some places the pathway takes you directly alongside the cataracts themselves. The whole adventure is thrilling—not only the waterfalls, not only the trails, but the entire experience that is the Falls Trail at Ricketts Glen.

The waterfalls along this stretch of Kitchen Creek range from 15 to 60 feet in height. Some are tall like Ozone Falls, while others are wide such as Wyandot Falls. Undoubtedly, you will find a waterfall that really captures your fancy. My two favorites are Ganoga Falls, simply due to its huge majestic drop and sizable plunge area, and R. B. Ricketts Falls with its double drop complemented by a tributary of Kitchen Creek plummeting into the same plunge pool as does the falls.

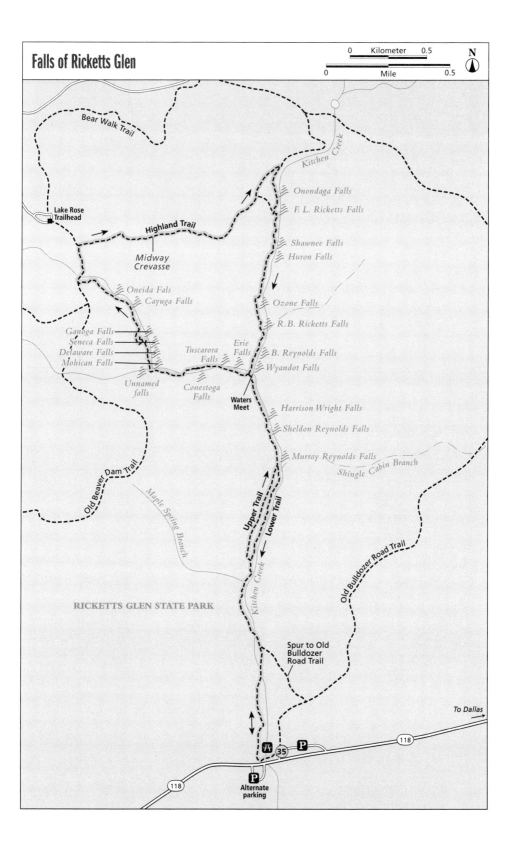

Falls of Ricketts Glen

Bear Walk Trail

Kitchen Creek

Onondaga Falls

F. L. Ricketts Falls

Lake Rose Trailhead

Highland Trail

Midway Crevasse

Shawnee Falls

Huron Falls

Oneida Fals

Cayuga Falls

Ozone Falls

R.B. Ricketts Falls

Ganoga Falls

Seneca Falls

Delaware Falls

Mohican Falls

Tuscarora Falls

Erie Falls

B. Reynolds Falls

Wyandot Falls

Unnamed falls

Conestoga Falls

Waters Meet

Harrison Wright Falls

Sheldon Reynolds Falls

Murray Reynolds Falls

Shingle Cabin Branch

Old Beaver Dam Trail

Maple Spring Branch

Upper Trail

Lower Trail

Old Bulldozer Road Trail

RICKETTS GLEN STATE PARK

Kitchen Creek

Spur to Old Bulldozer Road Trail

To Dallas

118

35

P

P

Alternate parking

118

0   Kilometer   0.5

0   Mile   0.5

N

A word of caution: Since this is a spectacular hike, the trailheads can fill quickly, especially the ones leaving from the high country near Lake Jean. These upper trailheads allow a shorter, smaller loop to be undertaken, where you see eighteen of the twenty-one waterfalls. However, when coming here go for the classic, most rewarding event and start your hike down at the PA 118 trailhead. There is a little bit of backtracking but you get to see all twenty-one waterfalls and experience the prodigious natural beauty found in the gorges of Kitchen Creek and Ganoga Glen.

Give yourself plenty of time, especially if you are a photographer. In fact, waterfall hikers planning to take many pictures can expect the hike to take ten or twelve hours—no joke. Casual hikers snapping quick shots with their phones will take but four or five hours. Also, try to come here during off times such as early in the morning or on weekdays. The trail is closed during winter because the mist from the waterfalls renders the trails icy to the extreme, making them downright dangerous. However, ice climbers and hikers properly equipped with a minimum of ice axe, rope, and crampons can explore the falls after signing in and out with the park office.

The trails around the waterfalls are usually wet. Trekking poles can really help here. Proper footwear is essential—do not wear flip-flops or sandals. Remember, the hike requires a 1,000-foot elevation change if making the full loop. Finally, make sure to have a good time, for the experience at Ricketts Glen is what waterfall hiking is all about!

Miles and Directions

0.0   From the trailhead, join the Falls Trail heading west. Pass through a picnic area.

0.1   Bridge Kitchen Creek and a stream braid of the creek. Begin hiking up the left bank of the stream among big hemlocks and hardwoods. Note the occasional service roads used by park personnel to maintain the trail system. Enter the Glens Natural Area, a Pennsylvania preserve and National Natural Landmark.

0.3   Bridge Kitchen Creek again. Notice the reddish rock contrasting with the green vegetation. The stream also exhibits a darkish iron tint. Look at the large old-growth forest in the wooded flats rich with wildflowers.

0.6   Pass the spur trail leading right to the Old Bulldozer Road Trail. Keep straight on the Falls Trail. Ahead, use a low bridge to span a braid of Kitchen Creek, then cross the stream braid a second time.

0.9   Cross over to the left-hand bank of Kitchen Creek, then find a trail intersection and take the Upper Trail. Climb a bit then level off, cruising the side slope of the valley.

1.3   Meet the Lower Trail at Murray Reynolds Falls. This cataract tumbles 16 feet from a U-shaped cleft in the rock then splits, divided by a boulder before slowing. You have reached your first waterfall at Ricketts Glen! Resume up the gorge.

1.4   Come to 36-foot Sheldon Reynolds Falls. This showstopper makes a classic vertical dive over a horizontal ledge then lands about two-thirds the way down, crashing on an angled overlayered rock.

1.5   Come to the curtain-like 27-foot Harrison Wright Falls. It plummets from a wide rock brow into a semicircular amphitheater and plunge pool. The path climbs along the left side of

R. B. Ricketts Falls on the left is complemented by a tributary making a delicate drop.

the amphitheater, affording multiple photograph opportunities. Curve to the top of the falls before continuing up the canyon. The trail is directly alongside the creek.

1.7 Reach Waters Meet and a trail junction. Head left, up Ganoga Glen. Before continuing on, note that you can see parts of waterfalls on each stream above Waters Meet.

1.8 Pass back-to-back 47-foot waterfalls, first tall and narrow Erie Falls. The trail goes directly alongside Erie Falls using stone steps hewn into the rock, delivering an up-close and personal view of the pour-over. Next comes stair-stepping Tuscarora Falls. It features a straight drop, an angled slide, and then a final drop. It also has stone steps going along its heights.

1.9 Come to 17-foot Conestoga Falls, making its drop followed by a run down a flat stone slab.

2.2 Cross a tributary. Look up the tributary for an unnamed ledge falls partly screened by vegetation. Quickly return to the stream of Ganoga Glen, squeezing past 39-foot Mohican Falls. The cataracts come fast and furious now. Pass multistage 37-foot Delaware Falls then 12-foot Seneca Falls, a smaller cascade-like spiller.

2.3 Approach massive and majestic Ganoga Falls, the tallest waterfall here at 94 feet. Walk down to its base and huge plunge pool area, delivering a misty drizzle. Next, rejoin the main trail, ascending a series of stone steps that are a wonder unto themselves. Admire the multitiered widening wonder that is Ganoga Falls while climbing. You come near the top of the falls, then turn away, paralleling a cliff line. Work above the cliff line, then once again head upstream through Ganoga Glen after a second switchback.

2.6 Come alongside the 11-foot ledge that is Cayuga Falls with its overhanging grotto. Once again the trail theatrically takes you directly alongside the cataract before moving on.

2.7 Pass 13-foot Oneida Falls, another shelf drop pouring from a horizontal rim that is wider than it is high, making a slight horseshoe. Only one more named waterfall remains along Ganoga Glen. Join a stone walkway. Ahead—if the water is flowing—a tributary across the creek creates a continuous cascade.

2.9 Reach the plateau and a trail intersection. Here the Old Beaver Dam Trail goes left. You go right, staying with the Falls Trail.

3.0 A spur goes left to the Lake Rose trailhead parking area. Stay right here, joining the Highland Trail. Traverse the plateau in conifers, hardwoods, and rock outcroppings.

3.0 Step over a small stream on a remarkable low stone bridge, yet another example of the superlative trail construction here at Ricketts Glen State Park. The walking is easy and level. For a while you walk the rim of the gorge, 1,000 feet above the trailhead.

3.4 Punch through a boulder garden known as the Midway Crevasse.

3.8 Reach the shortcut to F. L. Ricketts Falls. Do not take it; if you do, you will miss Onondaga Falls. Keep straight, stepping over a few streamlets flowing off the plateau.

3.9 Come to an intersection. Here the trail you are on keeps straight for Beach Lot #2. We turn sharply right, descending along Kitchen Creek.

4.0 Bridge over to the left bank of Kitchen Creek. The gorge tightens.

4.1 Reach 15-foot Onondaga Falls after descending steps along its left side. Curve around to its plunge pool for a head-on gander.

4.2 Intersect the shortcut trail to F. L. Ricketts Falls and the falls itself. Here the Falls Trail circles around the right-hand side of the cataract.

4.4 The stone slab trail leads to the brink of 30-foot Shawnee Falls. Walk along the curving cataract with a direct view of a tall bluff on the far side of the creek. Huron Falls, 41 feet, comes directly thereafter. Both the two falls and the path along them create a dramatic scene.

4.7 Bridge over to the right-hand bank of Kitchen Creek, then come to 60-foot Ozone Falls, the tallest cataract on Kitchen Creek. It starts narrow and vertical, then widens as it dances down layered stone strata, briefly levels out, squeezes past a boulder, then slides a ways before making a final tumble. The bottom-up view reveals the trail bridge above the falls.

4.8 Come to stellar R. B. Ricketts Falls, coming in at 36 feet in two primary drops. Enjoy the look from the base, where you can admire the double drop of Kitchen Creek along with a veillike drop of an unnamed tributary into the same plunge pool.

4.9 Reach B. Reynolds Falls after bridging Kitchen Creek again. This spiller makes a curtain dive from a rock lip overhanging an inverted cliff. The trail takes you to a side-on view of the cataract to see its dive close-up.

5.0 Pass powerful 15-foot Wyandot Falls, the last of the spillers before returning to Waters Meet. You have been here before. Begin backtracking down Kitchen Creek. Pass Harrison Wright, Sheldon Reynolds, and Murray Reynolds Falls a second time.

5.4 Reach a trail intersection. Head left on the Lower Trail. At points this path passes along gravel bars astride Kitchen Creek. In other places the trail works up side slopes amid the rugged terrain along the stream.

5.8 Complete the Lower Trail. From here, resume backtracking toward the PA 118 trailhead.

6.7 Arrive back at the trailhead, completing the unforgettable waterfall hike.

A scenic pedestrian bridge crosses Wyandot Falls.
RUSTY GLESSNER

These stepping stones take you alongside Kitchen Creek.

*Mohican Falls
charges in white
during early April.*
RUSTY GLESSNER

Waterfall Hikes of Northeast Pennsylvania

A rung of the Indian Ladders (hike 49)
RUSTY GLESSNER

36 Falls of Salt Springs State Park

This out-of-the-way state park not only hosts three fine waterfalls on Fall Brook but also offers fascinating human and natural history, a fine little tent campground, and additional trails that make this preserve a fun getaway.

Waterfall height: In order, 15 feet, 10 feet, 10 feet
Waterfall beauty: 4
Distance: 0.6-mile lollipop
Difficulty: Easy to moderate, does have some rock scrambling along Fall Brook
Hiking time: About ¾ hour
Trail surface: Natural

Other trail users: None
Canine compatibility: Leashed pets allowed
Land status: State park
Fees and permits: None
Maps: Salt Springs State Park; USGS Franklin Forks
Trail contact: Salt Springs State Park, (570) 945-3239, www.dcnr.state.pa.us/stateparks

Finding the trailhead: From Montrose, drive north on US 29 for 5.5 miles to Buckley Road. Turn left and follow Buckley Road for 1.5 miles to Salt Springs Road, just after bridging Fall Brook. Turn right on Salt Springs Road and drive for 0.5 mile to the parking area on your left just before reaching the Wheaton House. GPS: 41.911978, -75.865072

The Hike

What is now Salt Springs State Park is layered in human and natural history. Located in the northern portion of Pennsylvania's Endless Mountains, this area has attracted visitors for not only the waterfalls splashing through the Fall Brook Gorge but also the salt springs for which the park was named. Well before white settlers ever made it to this part of what became Pennsylvania, local aboriginals were extracting salt from this spring located against a bluff near the confluence of Fall Brook and Silver Creek. It was a matter of removing the water from the spring and then boiling it down to the salt remnant. After this area became part of the American frontier, early settlers also used the salt springs to obtain this valuable mineral, instrumental in preserving food, among other uses.

The proximity of the salt springs to Fall Brook Gorge popularized this area, making it a regular tourist destination for over two centuries. This indirectly preserved the old-growth hemlocks that still stand astride the gorge, despite the threat of the exotic hemlock woolly adelgid, a pest from Asia that is killing Pennsylvania's hemlocks.

In 1840 the Wheaton family settled at the mouth of the Fall Brook Gorge next to the salt springs. Their dairy farm was in continuous operation for 130 years. They welcomed visitors to the gorge and kept the area under their wing. During this same time, a mill and woolen manufacturer harnessed the power of Fall Brook, diverting its water with a flume at the lowermost waterfall to operate their machinery before closing up shop. Attempts were also made to commercially obtain salt from the springs, but several operations failed one after another—there simply wasn't enough salt to make it worthwhile.

By the 1970s the old-growth hemlock forest here became recognized as one of the few virgin woodlands left in Pennsylvania. An effort was undertaken to preserve this forest, as well as the salt springs and the Fall Brook Gorge, and in 1973 Salt Springs State Park came to be. Trails, a picnic area, and a campground were established. Later a philanthropic unit known as Friends of Salt Springs Park arose and purchased 437 adjacent acres, effectively doubling the size of the park. Friends of Salt Springs Park

The upper falls at Salt Springs State Park make their stair-step dance under an evergreen awning.
RUSTY GLESSNER

also helps maintain and manage this underutilized northeastern Pennsylvania getaway. I recommend this park not only for the waterfalls but also for its beauty and atmosphere. It is truly a place to relax and enjoy the special scenery.

The importance of this park is also borne out in the establishment of the Fall Brook Natural Area, a state-designated parcel within the park protecting the ancient forest here as well as the stream corridor containing the waterfalls you will see on this hike.

The hike itself is unusual. After crossing the bridge over Fall Brook, you head directly up the left bank on the Fall Brook Trail, except it does not look like a trail. You end up squeezing your way between the water and the nearly vertical gorge wall. When Fall Brook is high, this trail is untenable. However, at lower water levels, it is a matter of scrambling and rock hopping on the exposed rock. Nevertheless, the exposed rock may be wet. During winter this route can be very difficult to do without getting your feet wet. During that time you may want to head along the stream as far up as you can go, then backtrack and circle around on the Hemlock Trail.

Whatever you do, do not shortcut your way up the side of the gorge. Over time, visitors have torn up the vegetation and caused erosion. The park has had to install signs declaring the side of the gorge off-limits. Either stay along the creek, walking the rocks, or backtrack and circle around to the top of the gorge.

You will soon come to the first and in my opinion most impressive waterfall, Lower Falls, a 15-foot-high and 20-foot-wide angled spiller pouring over layered rock into a wide basin. Beyond here the Fall Brook Trail necessitates scrambling up the left side of the falls (undoable at high flow) to reach Middle Falls, a shorter version of Lower Falls except with a shallower basin.

At this point you are feeling comfortable with the unusual route and then reach Upper Falls. This two-tiered spiller is the smallest fall, but the complete forest canopy overhead makes it easier to photograph. Head left here to join the Hemlock Trail near an observation deck.

You will view Penny Rock on the return trip at the top of the gorge. On this stone, visitors have crammed the coins into the crevices of the layered rock, purportedly for good luck. The custom's origin is long forgotten.

The Hemlock Trail is bordered with old-growth trees, mostly hemlocks. Sometimes an old-growth forest is not as evident as people expect. Before you imagine a continuous stand of giant trees, realize that authentic old-growth woodland is not an agglomeration of even-aged trees. On the contrary, even-aged trees are a sign of disturbance—it means before the even-aged trees rose simultaneously, something happened to cause the trees growing there earlier to fall at the same time, usually storms or timbering.

An old-growth forest will have many big trees along with younger trees that grow when they get the chance. A growth opportunity is created when a big tree falls, creating a light gap. Young trees sprout in this light gap, and other somewhat-grown trees thrive in the additional sun. Trees are continually growing and dying as older trees

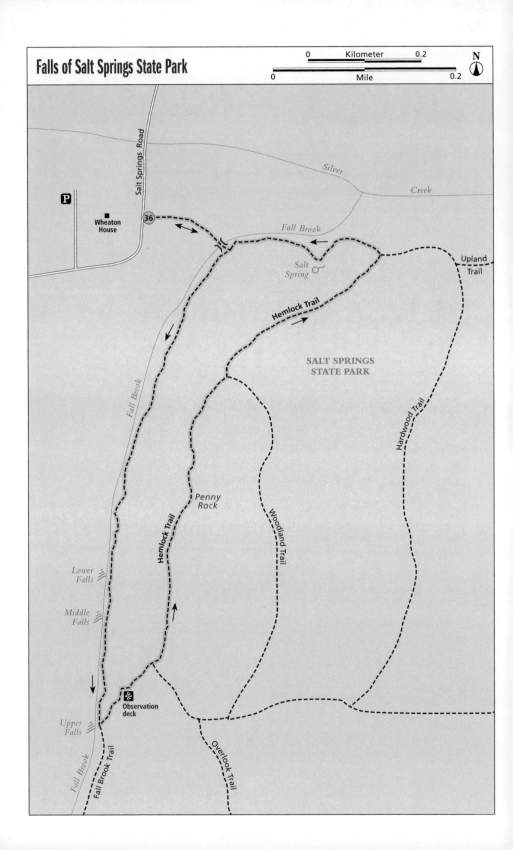

Falls of Salt Springs State Park

Kilometer
0   0.2

Mile
0   0.2

N

Silver

Creek

P

Salt Springs Road

Wheaton House

36

Fall Brook

Salt Spring

Upland Trail

Hemlock Trail

SALT SPRINGS STATE PARK

Fall Brook

Hardwood Trail

Penny Rock

Hemlock Trail

Woodland Trail

Lower Falls

Middle Falls

Observation deck

Upper Falls

Fall Brook

Fall Brook Trail

Overlook Trail

Lower Falls shows off its splendor on a prime May waterfall day.
RUSTY GLESSNER

succumb to lightning strikes, disease, or old age, creating a mosaic of all-aged trees, even in old-growth forests such as this one at Salt Springs State Park.

Your final order of business is to visit the salt springs, banked against the bluff near the confluence of Fall Brook and Silver Creek. You may see the well bubbling a little bit, the escape of sulfurous gas. The water has a combination of briny and sulfuric taste. You are then back at the trailhead. Nearby, you can visit the Wheaton House, open weekends during the warm season, or maybe pitch your tent in the primitive campground just across Silver Creek. At least have a picnic here at this attractive and historic state park in addition to your waterfall hike.

Miles and Directions

0.0 Leave the parking area, then walk around the Wheaton House, cross Salt Springs Road, and reach the trailhead, inscribed with stone markers. Head right up Fall Brook directly along the stream, where it seems no trail should be.

0.1 Come to Lower Falls, the 15-foot layered cascade. If the water is low, scramble up the left bank; otherwise, backtrack to the trailhead then head up the Hemlock Trail. Do not climb the side of the gorge and cause erosion. Next, come to and then work around 10-foot Middle Falls.

0.3 Reach two-tiered Upper Falls, then head left up to the Hemlock Trail near an observation deck. Head back down the gorge, passing Penny Rock.

0.4 Keep straight as the Woodland Trail leaves uphill to the right. Descend toward Silver Creek.

0.5 Reach the bottomland along Silver Creek. Here the Hardwood Trail leaves right but we head left, crossing an open grassy space. Ahead you will come to the salt springs, complete with interpretive signage.

0.6 Arrive back at Salt Springs Road, completing the walk.

Coins are crammed into crevices at Penny Rock.

37 Nay Aug Falls

A beautiful waterfall set in a rugged gorge in the middle of downtown Scranton? Yep, it is true. Nay Aug Falls on truly Roaring Brook makes a 20-foot tumble in a rocky wooded canyon that—with a little imagination—seems the back of beyond rural Pennsylvania. The walk is easy; it is finding the right trailhead amid the maze of roads, trails, and buildings of Nay Aug Park that is the hard part.

Waterfall height: 20 feet
Waterfall beauty: 5
Distance: 0.6-mile out-and-back
Difficulty: Easy
Hiking time: About ½ hour
Trail surface: Gravel, natural
Other trail users: None

Canine compatibility: Leashed pets allowed
Land status: City park
Fees and permits: None
Maps: Nay Aug Park; USGS Scranton
Trail contact: Nay Aug Park, info@nayaugpark
.org, www.nayaugpark.org

Finding the trailhead: From exit 184, River Street, on I-81 northbound, turn left onto River Street and follow it 0.1 mile to Meadow Avenue. Turn right and follow it 0.2 mile, then turn left onto Moosic Street/PA 307 and follow it 0.2 mile. Turn right onto Harrison Avenue and follow it 0.3 mile, then turn right onto Mulberry Street and follow it 0.2 mile to enter Nay Aug Park. The official address for the park is 1901 Mulberry St. Once inside the park, follow the main outside road loop right, toward the Wildlife Center, passing the David Wenzel Tree House to reach Parking Lot I, on the right just past the Wildlife Center. You will see a sign for the John and Gertrude Galdieri Memorial Fountain near the trailhead. GPS: 41.402837, -75.638045

The Hike

The gorge created by Roaring Brook came first, along with Nay Aug Falls, the 20-foot classic ledge-drop cataract forming the centerpiece of this hike. After Scranton came to be, the wooded hills above Roaring Brook and Nay Aug Falls became a retreat of sorts for local Scrantonians, despite being next to downtown. Since the early 1900s what is now Nay Aug Park has housed the Everhart Museum, an amusement park, and a zoo. The park is now managed by the City of Scranton, which has developed a nest of trails integrated into the park roads, forests, and buildings.

When coming to Nay Aug Park for the first time, you will be faced with an immediate array of choices of where to go after somehow navigating (with or without your phone's help) through downtown Scranton. Fret not, for everybody is faced with the same dilemma on their first outing here. After all, the current incarnation of the park houses pavilions, a greenhouse, a museum, a water park, war memorials, gardens, a wildlife center—even a tree house. Therefore, do not be embarrassed to ask for directions, even if you are a man.

By the way, the David Wenzel Tree House is another highlight you want to visit while here. The all-access trail leads to a covered platform—actually built into a tree rising 150 feet above Roaring Brook—that is close enough to the falls to see them from afar and certainly hear them. (Full disclosure: You will also hear the drone of cars on nearby I-81.)

After following park signs, you will reach the proper parking area, which is a little past the David Wenzel Tree House on your right and the Wildlife Center on your left. Even there you are faced with choices. Don't go for the circular trail near the fountain; rather, drop southwest on a path toward the Paul Kanjorski Bridge, making your way down, trying to stay on the correct trail despite a host of potentially confusing user-created trails. Keep going toward the water and you cannot miss the bridge, the only way across the Roaring Brook Gorge. In fact, before this bridge was built in 2007, the far side of the Roaring Brook Gorge was inaccessible.

Additionally, the roofed bridge makes an excellent spot to look up and down Roaring Brook. You will likely be surprised at the geology of the gorge—it seems like there is nothing but rock and water down there flanked by a line of trees on both banks. This view will explain why Nay Aug Falls and its gorge was designated a National Natural Landmark.

Once across the bridge, you travel downstream in lush woods of birch, pine, and rhododendron that could be anywhere in a back-of-beyond Pennsylvania state forest. Soon you reach the first of two overlooks opening to Nay Aug Falls. The first view is from a wooden deck looking down on the waterfall diving from a naked rock ledge into an impressive plunge pool, enclosed in stone on three sides. The next overlook, set partly under an overhanging ledge, gives you a straight-on view of the 20-foot cataract and also allows you to appreciate the geology of Roaring Brook.

While here at the park, take full advantage of all the offerings at this Scranton icon.

Miles and Directions

0.0 Leave Parking Lot I, near the Wildlife Center, and descend on a path leading downhill. Immediately come to another trail, split right, and walk a few feet, then turn left to join the Mufasa Trail.

0.1 Reach a wide gravel path. Turn right, toward the Paul Kanjorski Bridge. Soon reach the roofed span and enjoy views of Roaring Brook. After crossing the bridge, turn right and follow Roaring Brook downstream in rich woods.

0.3 Come to the first overlook of Nay Aug Falls. This is a top-down view. Curve around a rock outcropping then reach the second view, more of a straight-on approach, still elevated. You may also hear commotion in the direction of the David Wenzel Tree House. Backtrack to the trailhead.

0.6 Arrive back at the trailhead, completing the urban waterfall walk.

You'll find a great view downstream of Roaring Brook from the Paul Kanjorski Bridge.

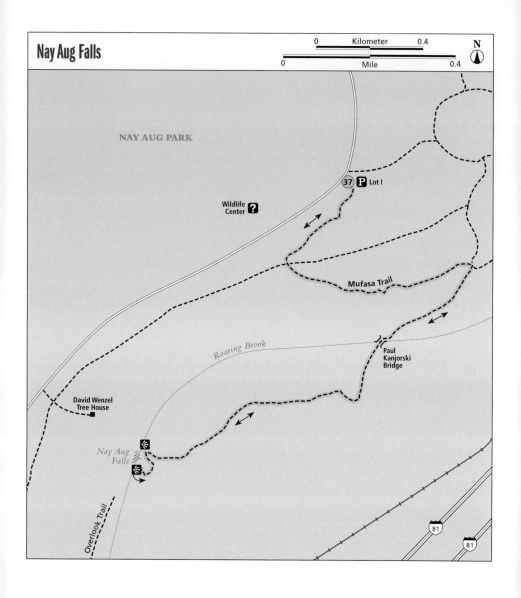

0   Kilometer   0.4

0   Mile   0.4

N

NAY AUG PARK

37 P Lot I

Wildlife Center ?

Mufasa Trail

Roaring Brook

Paul Kanjorski Bridge

David Wenzel Tree House

Nay Aug Falls

Overlook Trail

81

81

Nay Aug Falls dives from its stony precipice into a stone-encircled plunge pool.
RUSTY GLESSNER

38 Seven Tubs

Popular Seven Tubs encompasses aquatic features along Laurel Run and tributaries on a tract of the Pinchot State Forest just outside Wilkes–Barre. This preserve houses the Seven Tubs, a series of pools divided by waterfalls cutting through an incised canyon you have to see to believe. The rest of the hike traverses upland woods on the Audubon Loop before turning down another tributary of Laurel Run at a cascade, then follows Laurel Run past lesser cataracts before returning to the trailhead.

Waterfall height: 5 to 15 feet
Waterfall beauty: 5
Distance: 2.1-mile loop
Difficulty: Easy to moderate
Hiking time: About 1 hour
Trail surface: Natural, a little pavement near trailhead
Other trail users: None

Canine compatibility: Leashed pets allowed
Land status: State forest
Fees and permits: None
Maps: Pinchot State Forest–Seven Tubs and Deep Hollow Tracts; USGS Wilkes-Barre East
Trail contact: Pinchot State Forest, (570) 945-7133, www.dcnr.state.pa.us/forestry

Finding the trailhead: From exit 170 on I-81 near Wilkes-Barre, take PA 115 south for 1.7 miles to the signed entrance to Seven Tubs Nature Area (Bear Creek Boulevard). Turn right and follow the road for 0.4 mile to dead-end at a large parking area on your right. GPS: 41.235417, -75.810533

The Hike

The Seven Tubs is a Pennsylvania geological wonder. When you see it for the first time, the reason for the name is evident. Here Wheelbarrow Run has sculpted a deeper-than-wide chasm through pure bedrock, complete with sweeping curves, as if you were carving with a knife through room-temperature butter. Waterfalls divide each of the seven tubs from one another, slender spirals of white sculpting the mini-canyon, calling to mind the slot canyons of Utah.

A bridge crosses Wheelbarrow Run on the lower end of the Seven Tubs, allowing you a direct upstream view and a downstream look. Fact is, without the bridge the slot canyon is so narrow, it is hard to see the Seven Tubs. Official trails travel along both sides of the slot canyon, yet visitors cannot resist working their way into the individual swirling pools.

And there are still other waterfalls. Very near the trailhead you will come to a wide, shallow, sloping waterslide of a cascade at the confluence of Wheelbarrow Run and Laurel Run. This is a popular play area and the land around it is a little beaten down, but the 15-foot slide adds another water feature to the former county park that was taken over by the Pinchot State Forest. Forest personnel improved the trails,

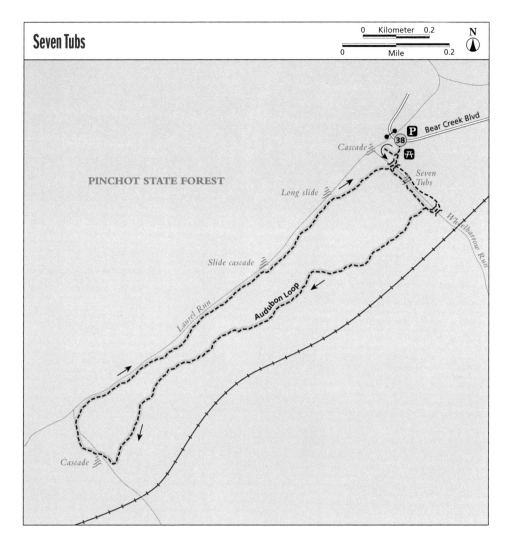

0   Kilometer   0.2

0   Mile   0.2

N

PINCHOT STATE FOREST

Bear Creek Blvd

P

38

Cascade

Seven Tubs

Long slide

Slide cascade

Laurel Run

Audubon Loop

Wheelbarrow Run

Cascade

made a large parking area, and put in some picnic tables. The very first part of the trail is all-access, allowing wheelchair-bound waterfall enthusiasts to grab a look at the Seven Tubs.

You will see all the aforementioned attractions at the beginning of the loop hike. From there, the marked Audubon Loop travels over rock outcrops and oak woods before returning to the water. At this point an unnamed tributary of Laurel Run makes yet another slide cascade, this one on a smaller scale. The hike then joins Laurel Run, where outstanding scenery continues. Although devoid of singular majestic waterfalls, the Laurel Run valley exudes wooded Pennsylvania mountain magic punctuated with occasional cascades that are worth a look.

Note: Being so close to Wilkes-Barre and Scranton, the Seven Tubs can become very busy during warm-weather weekends and summer holidays. The immediate area

The Seven Tubs connected by slender ribbons of waterfalls can be counted from the bridge.

A sliding cascade marks the confluence of Wheelbarrow Run and Laurel Run.

around the trailhead suffers from an abundance of user-created trails; therefore, try to stay on the path and protect the resource. Pick your visitation times wisely and you will be well rewarded. I have come here early in the morning on a late spring weekday and nearly had the place to myself.

Miles and Directions

0.0   From the signboard at the trailhead, take the asphalt path past picnic tables. Note the cool rock landscaping. Look for a trail with built-in steps leading down and to the right. Follow this track down to the confluence of Wheelbarrow Run and Laurel Run. Here you will find the longest waterfall in the nature area, a wide, sloped slide. Backtrack up to the asphalt path and continue hiking.

0.1   Reach the bridge spanning Wheelbarrow Run. From this span, you can look both upstream and down as Wheelbarrow Run cuts its gorge in a frenzy of white alternating with slower areas—the tubs of the Seven Tubs. The all-access trail ends here, while trails go up along both sides of Wheelbarrow Run. Yet another trail goes right, down to Laurel Run. This will be your return route. For now, head up the right bank of Wheelbarrow Run, examining the falls and tubs.

0.2   The trail splits. Go left for a moment, following Wheelbarrow Run to a footbridge spanning the creek. Look upstream for the historic railroad tunnel through which Wheelbarrow Run flows. Backtrack, then resume the clockwise Audubon Loop, ascending over rock. Roll through xeric upland woods, heavy with oaks and pines with a blueberry understory.

0.7 Cut under a transmission line.

0.8 Step over a streamlet.

1.1 Drop alongside an unnamed tributary of Laurel Run. Look left as this waterway soon makes a pyramid-shaped cascade, slowing in a long pool. Continue downstream.

1.2 Turn northeast and begin walking alongside Laurel Run, singing over rocks and shoals, amid mountain laurel and other evergreens.

1.4 The whole of Laurel Run tips over a low ledge cutting across the stream at an angle. Ahead, look for other shoals.

1.6 Pass a slide cascade making a 10-foot descent over 30 feet of flowing water. The rerouted trail works farther away from the stream.

1.7 A boardwalk helps you span a spring seep flowing over smooth rock.

1.9 Look for a long slide and the biggest pool of the area. The Audubon Loop pulls away from Laurel Run.

2.0 Return to the bridge over Wheelbarrow Run, completing the loop portion of the hike. Backtrack to the trailhead.

2.1 Arrive back at the trailhead, completing the waterfall hike.

39 Choke Creek Falls

Head to a wide and scenic waterfall deep in the Pinchot State Forest. The walk traces forest roads for the first part of its distance, then splits off to a primitive path, cruising along Choke Creek. Reach a rock protrusion over which Choke Creek makes its double drop. Adjacent stone promontories enhance the aquatic scenery and make excellent picnicking/relaxation spots.

Waterfall height: 16 feet in 2 stages
Waterfall beauty: 4
Distance: 1.6-mile out-and-back
Difficulty: Easy
Hiking time: About 1 hour
Trail surface: Gravel, natural
Other trail users: Bicyclers on forest road

Canine compatibility: Leashed pets allowed
Land status: State forest
Fees and permits: None
Maps: Pinchot State Forest–Thornhurst Tract; USGS Thornhurst
Trail contact: Pinchot State Forest, (570) 945-7133, www.dcnr.state.pa.us/forestry

Finding the trailhead: From exit 13 on I-380 southeast of Scranton, take PA 507 south briefly toward Gouldsboro, then turn left on PA 435 north and follow it for 1.6 miles to Clifton Beach Road. Turn left and follow Clifton Beach Road for 5.8 miles, then turn right on Pine Grove Road. Follow Pine Grove Road for 1.5 miles, then meet Bear Lake Road where you turn right, go for 0.1 mile, and turn left onto Tannery Road. Follow Tannery Road for 1.2 miles, then turn acutely left onto Phelps Road. Follow Phelps Road for 2.2 miles to reach a point where it makes a 90-degree right turn. Park here but do not block the gate of the unnamed southwest-bound forest road on which you will soon be hiking. GPS: 41.174683, -75.609083

The Hike

This hike gets straight to the point, er, waterfall. Choke Creek Falls is one of those cataracts that comes up in conversation among waterfall enthusiasts, but the waterfallers may not have been there in person. I heard of Choke Creek Falls from an old-timer I ran into at another waterfall. We were discussing our favorite cataracts in the Keystone State, and he positively raved about Choke Creek Falls.

It is neither very high nor voluminous nor overly dramatic. However, the combination of unmoving rock and rushing waters with a living frame of azaleas, hardwoods, and evergreens creates an overall mosaic of beauty that is worth a visit.

Choke Creek flows fast then reaches a wide, level precipice over which it drops about 10 feet. This upper part of the fall is twice as wide as it is tall, lending a spillway effect, wide and imposing, though at lower water levels a protrusion is exposed in this upper drop. On the lower drop Choke Creek makes a slanting slice of white foam through gray stone, slowing in a deep and dark plunge pool that serves as a summertime swimming hole.

The upper drop of Choke Creek Falls is broad and wild.

These rock gates work as excellent waterfall-viewing locales as well as ideal relaxation and picnicking areas. The swimming hole is accessed downstream. Allow yourself plenty of time to hang out at Choke Creek Falls, because this is one hike where it is the destination and not the journey.

You start your route to Choke Creek Falls by following an unsigned, gated gravel track accessed off Phelps Road in the Pinchot State Forest. The route's obscure nature helps keep Choke Creek Falls lesser visited. Even the parking is less than obvious. The hike follows a gravel forest road to a clearing and a split. After passing around a second gate, the path becomes more primitive before reaching Butler Run. Here a log bridge crosses the smallish stream and joins the rerouted Pinchot Trail. Beyond Butler Run, follow the Pinchot Trail running parallel to Choke Creek to your left, sometimes slowed by beaver dams in this locale.

Ahead, the sound of water falling urges you on. The track emerges at a rock outcropping, and behold—Choke Creek Falls. You are standing on the brink of the lower drop, while the upper drop is dead ahead. Go ahead and explore the partly vegetated rock outcropping, gaining different views of the spiller. A campsite lies in a grassy clearing nearby. This is a good wildflower area, and you will see wild pink azaleas in season.

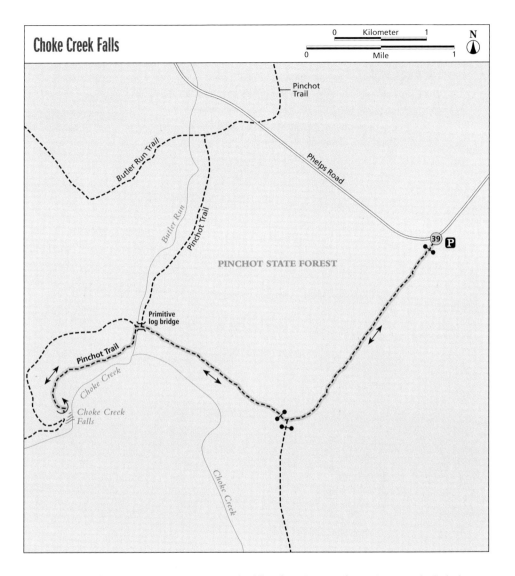

Pinchot
Trail

Butler Run Trail

Phelps Road

Butler Run

Pinchot Trail

PINCHOT STATE FOREST

39 P

Primitive
log bridge

Pinchot Trail

Choke Creek

Choke Creek
Falls

Choke Creek

During the summertime you may find locals enjoying the swimming hole below the falls. If you are in the Scranton and Wilkes-Barre area, check out Choke Creek Falls—you may be happily surprised.

Miles and Directions

0.0   From the curve on Phelps Road, take the black-and-yellow-gated forest road southwest. The walking is easy and level on the gravel doubletrack bordered with oaks and witch hazel. Just ahead, a gated clearing lies off to the left. Keep straight.

0.3   Descend to a clearing, with two gated tracks leaving away from it. Split right and walk around the right gate, now heading northwesterly on a more primitive track. Choke Creek and Butler Run become audible in the distance. To your left, Choke Creek is often dammed from beavers.

0.6 Come to a primitive log bridge over Butler Run. Cross the bridge then immediately turn left, following Butler Run downstream toward Choke Creek, joining the Pinchot Trail. Come along Choke Creek, cruising above the waterway in thick woods.

0.8 Emerge onto the outcrop beside Choke Creek Falls. The lower drop is at your feet, while the upper drop is dead ahead. Explore the outcropping and adjacent areas, as well as getting a full-on frontal view of the falls from the big, dark plunge pool. Backtrack to the trailhead.

1.6 Arrive back at the trailhead, completing the waterfall hike.

40 Tobyhanna Falls

Enjoy a walk to a wide, low riverine waterfall that is the centerpiece of a 130-acre preserve along Tobyhanna Creek. Additional trails, a picnic area, and waterside geology enhance the Austin T. Blakeslee Natural Area experience.

Waterfall height: 8 feet
Waterfall beauty: 3
Distance: 0.8-mile out-and-back
Difficulty: Easy
Hiking time: About ¾ hour
Trail surface: Natural
Other trail users: None
Canine compatibility: Leashed pets allowed

Land status: County natural area
Fees and permits: None
Maps: Austin T. Blakeslee Natural Area; USGS Blakeslee
Trail contact: Tobyhanna Township Parks & Recreation, (570) 646-1212, https://tobyhannatownshippa.gov

Finding the trailhead: From exit 284 on I-80 near Blakeslee, take PA 115 north for 0.5 mile and turn left into the Austin T. Blakeslee Natural Area, just after bridging Tobyhanna Creek. Immediately reach the trail parking area near the park pavilion. GPS: 41.083100, -75.584450

The Hike

Tobyhanna Falls is an atypical waterfall located at an atypical park. The waterfall is a wide, powerful surge of white flowing over an equally wide and low—and formidable—rock bed. You might even call Tobyhanna Falls a powerful rapid. The falls makes a very angled descent about 8 feet into a humongous plunge pool that seems to be in a constant swirling rotation. The cataract can be seen from multiple angles along the north bank of Tobyhanna Creek, especially with the presence of the wide rock slab creating the falls. This area is particularly popular with anglers, although waterfall enthusiasts and locals come to hike trails here at Austin T. Blakeslee Natural Area on a regular basis.

One of the things that makes the park unusual is its origins. The former farm was first converted to Harrison Park. The nature getaway was popular with locals until a flood on Tobyhanna Creek devastated the preserve in 1955. The park was never reopened. Although you could still see relics of the park such as the foundations of the stone buildings, roller-skating rink, and an artesian well, the land that was Harrison Park lay fallow for six decades.

The area was then reopened in 2009 with a new name: Austin T. Blakeslee Natural Area. Part of the reason this 130-acre preserve was reopened as a natural area was its funding source—the Pennsylvania Department of Conservation and Natural Resources. They wanted this scenic spot along Tobyhanna Creek to remain in a

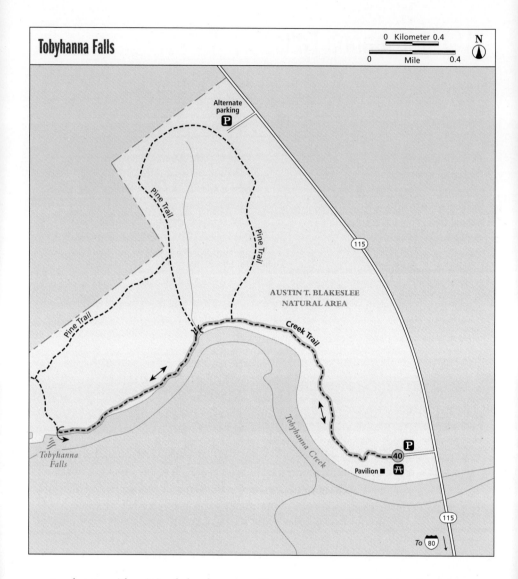

natural state with minimal development. However, a condition of the development was to create a trail network so we can visit Tobyhanna Falls. Furthermore, a nice little pavilion and picnic area is set beside the trailhead parking area.

On the walk, you will run parallel to Tobyhanna Creek the entire distance. Although Tobyhanna Falls is not high, the powerful rumbler is unmistakable. You first wander through planted red pines, then cruise on a bluff above the river. Perennial feeder springs cross the trail, creating wetlands over which steps lead that will help keep your feet dry.

Enjoy good looks at the stream before reaching the falls. Walk out onto the massive stone slab and check out Tobyhanna Falls from behind and from the side. You can then work your way downstream along the bank on anglers' trails to get an upstream look at the churning froth of white. The massive plunge pool below it prevents a direct straight-on upstream perspective. However, it does not take multiple angles to realize this is a surge of water deserving to be the centerpiece of a county natural area.

Miles and Directions

0.0 Leave the parking area and join the Creek Trail through red pines. Tobyhanna Creek flows to your left.

0.1 Cross a spring seep on a bridge, then climb a little bluff above the river. Cross a second seep using elevated wood stepping "stones."

0.2 The Pine Trail leaves right for the upper parking area. Stay straight on the Creek Trail.

0.3 Bridge a little creek, then meet another arm of the Pine Trail. Keep straight, still on the Creek Trail. Ahead, step over more seeps and stay along the river.

0.4 Open onto a flat granite outcrop stretching from the wooded hill to Tobyhanna Creek. Here is Tobyhanna Falls, spilling over the stone where the creek was narrowed. Below the falls, Tobyhanna Creek widens in a substantial pool. Backtrack to the trailhead, though opportunities for extended hiking exist here at the 130-acre natural area.

0.8 Arrive back at the trailhead, completing the waterfall hike.

A close-up shot of Tobyhanna Falls reveals the power of the water.
RUSTY GLESSNER

Tobyhanna Falls drops over a wide rock slab.

41 Hawk Falls

This is a short but scenic waterfall walk to an impressive cascade in one of Pennsylvania's more popular state parks—Hickory Run. Hikers will descend a deepening valley to find Hawk Run making its leap over exposed rock into a major plunge pool before the stream contributes its waters to Mud Run. The plentiful exposed rock in and around the falls creates fine waterfall seating as well as areas to explore above, beside, and below Hawk Falls.

Waterfall height: 25 feet
Waterfall beauty: 4
Distance: 0.8-mile out-and-back
Difficulty: Easy
Hiking time: About ¾ hour
Trail surface: Natural
Other trail users: None

Canine compatibility: Leashed pets allowed
Land status: State park
Fees and permits: None
Maps: Hickory Run State Park; USGS Hickory Run
Trail contact: Hickory Run State Park, (272) 808-6192, www.dcnr.state.pa.us/stateparks

Finding the trailhead: From exit 284 on I-80 near Blakeslee, take PA 115 south for 1.8 miles to PA 903. Turn right and follow PA 903 for 4 miles to PA 534 west, then turn right and follow PA 534 for 2.5 miles to reach the trailhead on your left just before driving under the Pennsylvania Turnpike (I-476). GPS: 41.010651, -75.634189

The Hike

Being situated between the Wilkes-Barre and Allentown metropolitan areas, plus being easily accessible from New Jersey and New York, has made Hickory Run State Park a popular destination for all kinds of outdoor recreation, including waterfalling. Best suited as a nature getaway, the rugged landscape has always made it a challenge to carve out a living in what became the nearly 16,000-acre state park. The thick forests, deep swamps, and rocky soil even kept American Indians from calling this area home. Pennsylvania settlers who had been given Revolutionary War land grants turned their back on the area they dubbed "shades of death."

However, being along the Lehigh River, where a shipping canal was built, and also being in the direct path between Wilkes-Barre and Allentown brought travelers to the Hickory Run region, as well as residents serving those traveling by canal or stagecoach. That era did not last long, but the unforgiving soil did grow enough trees to be logged over, next bringing loggers to the region but leaving the land subject to flood and fire for decades. Then along came a fellow named Harry Trexler of nearby Allentown. He saw the Hickory Run area as a potential park for Pennsylvania

Hikers admire Hawk Falls from the top.

residents, especially families, to reconnect with nature and hunt at a well-managed wildlife hunting reserve.

Mr. Trexler died before his dreams were realized, but he had purchased land that became the wellspring for the current park. The National Park Service purchased the rest of what we see today, and used the Civilian Conservation Corps (CCC) to develop a recreation demonstration area. The CCC's work forms the backbone of the park's roads and trails and many buildings. In 1945 Hickory Run became a state park. Today it is a beloved destination in eastern Pennsylvania and far beyond the Keystone State boundaries.

The large preserve is bordered by state game lands as well as Lehigh Gorge State Park, further enlarging the wild area. However, the park is chock-full of facilities, from the large campground and cabins to lakes for swimming and fishing, as well as fishing streams. The preserve includes a whopping 44 miles of trails that are enjoyed year-round. I have camped and hiked here and pronounce the park a wonderful family getaway, just as Harry Trexler envisioned a century ago.

We waterfall enthusiasts will put visiting Hawk Falls at the top of our Hickory Run State Park to-do list. Although the trailhead and hike are not far from the Pennsylvania Turnpike, the auto throughway has no negative bearing on the adventure.

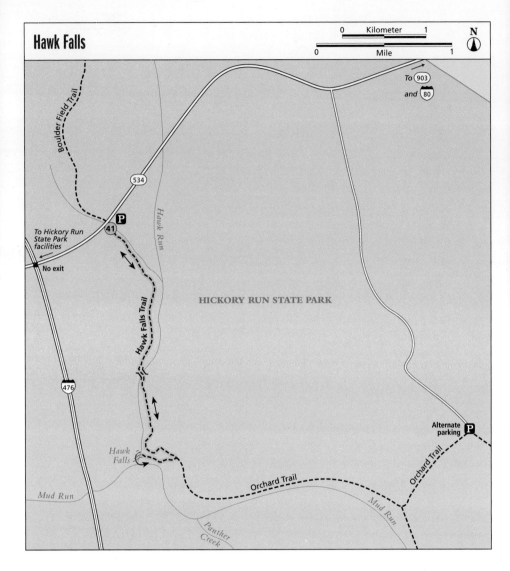

From the parking area, you walk toward the turnpike then pick up the Hawk Falls Trail on the far side of a bridged tributary of Hawk Run. The natural-surface widish trail heads south, winding toward Hawk Run. Rhododendron crowds the noisy creek, which you bridge after a short bit. The hike then works down the left bank of the stream as the waterway continues to cut a deepening gorge of its own. You will then come to a very rocky area laced with user-created spur trails aiming for Hawk Falls. Take one of them and walk out to the brink of the cataract. Here you can see the falls pirouette from its perch into the carved stone basin replete with a sizable plunge pool that shallows on its lower end. The payoff.

Hawk Falls mimics a wedding cake, even at a lower flow.
RUSTY GLESSNER

It is just a few more feet before Hawk Run gives its waters up to Mud Run. You can walk down to the bottom of the falls by circling around the rock shelf then aiming for the confluence of Hawk Run and Mud Run. Enjoy the face-on view of Hawk Falls, which I believe to be the best look, certainly for waterfall photography.

Miles and Directions

0.0 From the parking area, walk west on PA 534, crossing the bridge over the tributary of Hawk Run. Here you will find the signed start of the Hawk Falls Trail. Join the natural-surface path, working around some vehicle barrier boulders. Yellow birch and rhododendron crowd the trail.

0.1 The descent steepens.

0.2 Reach a trail bridge and cross Hawk Run. Continue the downgrade.

0.3 Find the spur going right to the top of the falls. Walk out onto the rock and view the falls, as well as the Pennsylvania Turnpike bridge over Mud Run in the distance. To reach the lower viewing area, return to the main trail.

0.4 Come to the base of the falls after taking the right spur down through a rhododendron copse to Mud Run and its confluence with Hawk Run. Use some deft steps to work your way to a face-on view of Hawk Falls. If you want to extend your hike, join the Orchard Trail as it continues along Mud Run then loops back to an alternate parking area. Otherwise, backtrack to the trailhead.

0.8 Arrive back at the trailhead, completing the waterfall hike.

42 Buttermilk Falls, Lukes Falls

This fun little trek uses one of Pennsylvania's historic rail trails to make an easy hike to reach two waterfalls from the same trailhead. Located deep in the canyon of the Lehigh River at Lehigh Gorge State Park, you trace the nearly level Lehigh Gorge Trail to view precipitous Buttermilk Falls, extending 60 exciting feet. Your next order of business is to visit Lukes Falls, a lower-flow cataract that will still get your blood flowing.

Waterfall height: 60 feet and 50 feet, respectively
Waterfall beauty: 5
Distance: 1.2-mile out-and-back
Difficulty: Easy
Hiking time: About ¾ hour
Trail surface: Pea gravel
Other trail users: Bicyclers, snowmobilers in winter

Canine compatibility: Leashed pets allowed
Land status: State park
Fees and permits: None
Maps: Lehigh Gorge State Park; USGS Weatherly
Trail contact: Lehigh Gorge State Park, (272) 808-6192, www.dcnr.state.pa.us/stateparks

Finding the trailhead: From exit 273 on I-81 near White Haven, take PA 940/Church Street south for 0.6 mile to Lehigh Gorge Drive. Turn left and follow Lehigh Gorge Drive for 6.2 miles to Rockport Road. Turn left and follow Rockport Road for 1.1 miles to dead-end at the Rockport Access of Lehigh Gorge State Park. If the lower parking area is full, backtrack on Rockport Road to an upper parking area. GPS: 40.966650, -75.755017

The Hike

This hike takes place on one of Pennsylvania's best rail trails—the Lehigh Gorge Trail. The history of this path goes beyond being a converted railroad line. Initially, in the late 1700s, coal was discovered in the upper Lehigh River valley. A budding United States needed energy, and entrepreneurs sought to access the coal using canals, which were starting to be developed throughout the East. A system of dams, locks, and canals were built on the Lehigh River to maintain an adequate supply of water to float the coal down to the Lehigh and onward to its mother stream, the Delaware River. Once on the Delaware the "black gold" could be floated to Philadelphia and points beyond.

However, the story of the canal in the Lehigh Valley follows the pattern of canals everywhere—the rise of the much more efficient railroad did away with the less efficient and more troublesome canal. Here, in places on the Lehigh River, the railroad simply built over the canal tow passageway.

After the railroad line was abandoned, the Lehigh Gorge Trail came to be, overlain on the former tracks. The 26-mile pathway stretches down the Lehigh River from

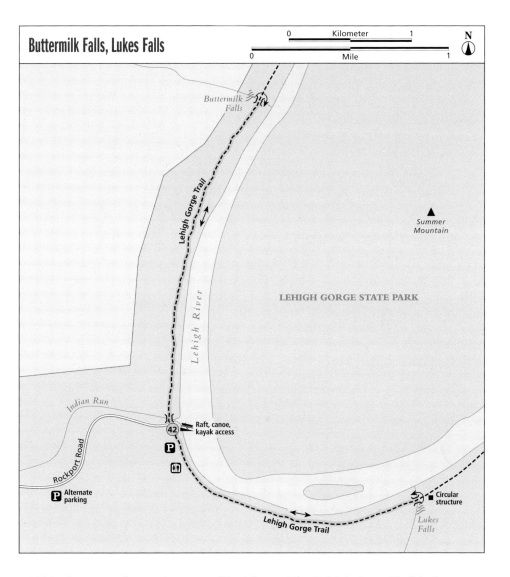

0   Kilometer   1

N

0   Mile   1

Buttermilk Falls

Lehigh Gorge Trail

▲ *Summer Mountain*

LEHIGH GORGE STATE PARK

Lehigh River

Indian Run

Raft, canoe, kayak access

42

P

Rockport Road

P Alternate parking

Lehigh Gorge Trail

Circular structure

Lukes Falls

White Haven to the tourist town of Jim Thorpe. The Lehigh Gorge Trail is also part of the greater Delaware & Lehigh Trail, an incomplete yet expanding pathway that will ultimately stretch 165 miles from Wilkes-Barre almost to Philadelphia, along both the Lehigh and the Delaware Rivers. When complete, this pathway will be a fantastic addition to Pennsylvania's recreation network.

Luckily for us, the Lehigh Gorge Trail is complete and you can use it to visit two waterfalls from one trailhead, the Rockport Access. The first waterfall takes the Lehigh Gorge Trail northbound, upstream, crossing the bridge over Indian Run. The Lehigh River powers around a sharp bend below, and Summer Mountain rises across the river.

Start upriver on a nearly level, pea gravel track. The walking is as easy as one can ask for when waterfall hiking. You will pass a raft slide on your right. This is used by whitewater enthusiasts to take on the Lehigh's Class II–III rapids in the springtime, when the water is up. Interestingly, whitewater paddlers face the same problems shippers of coal did concerning the Lehigh River—not enough water during the summer and fall. The coal shippers built the dams and canals to ensure the constant water levels necessary to float the coal downstream. Whitewater paddlers can only catch the Lehigh River when it is up.

Bluffs rise high to your left, some of them cut when the rail line pushed through this rugged canyon. It is not long before you find a bridge and Buttermilk Falls. Above you, an unnamed stream makes a slender splashing debut, sliding and channeling its way over an irregular rock face a good 60 feet before crashing and flowing under the trail bridge. This bottom-up view is the only angle you can get of this waterfall without risking life and limb.

Buttermilk Falls flows under the Lehigh Gorge Trail.

Buttermilk Falls makes its slender dive toward the Lehigh River.

Are you ready for Lukes Falls? Backtrack to the trailhead, then walk the Lehigh Gorge Trail south, curving with the curve of the river. On the way, you can gain superlative views of the flowing Lehigh. The walk to Lukes Falls follows a similar refrain, except your gradient is slightly downhill. You reach a trail bridge where narrower Lukes Falls spills in ragged stages, stairstepping to squeeze through a rock cleft then sliding its way below the bridge before dashing a few more feet to meet the Lehigh River. The cataract could exceed 50 feet, but it is hard to see its apex. Lukes Falls can become obscured by vegetation in summer, revealing a thin veil of white bordered by greenery. Look for the round structure beyond Lukes Falls, part of the history of the Lehigh Gorge.

It is likely you will want to explore more of the Lehigh Gorge Trail, so walk on if you please. Remember that both of these falls are best enjoyed when the water is up—late winter through spring—though winter can reveal incredible ice sculptures on Buttermilk Falls.

Miles and Directions

0.0 Leave the Rockport Access northbound on the Lehigh Gorge Trail. Immediately bridge Indian Run on a wide, pea gravel path.

0.3 Come to the trail bridge and Buttermilk Falls, spilling 60 feet to flow under the span. Note the stone abutments on the bridge, likely from earlier railroad days. Backtrack to the trailhead.

0.6 Arrive back at the trailhead, then continue south on the Lehigh Gorge Trail, curving with the curve of the Lehigh River.

0.9 Reach a trail bridge and Lukes Falls. This long, tapered flume spills at least 50 feet, slender as a rope in spots. However, it has a small watershed and can run very low by late summer. Backtrack to the trailhead.

1.2 Arrive back at the Rockport Access, completing the waterfall rail trail walk.

Lukes Falls makes a narrow drop that cannot be seen in its entirety.

43 Wild Creek Falls

This is one of those out-of-the-way waterfalls that is better than you might expect. Located at Beltzville State Park—better known as a lake destination rather than a moving water destination—a short hike on interconnected nature trails takes you to a cool glen and a sightly scene where Wild Creek tumbles over an irregular bulbous stone face, lending an unusual appearance. If the hike is a bit too short, simply enjoy the extended nature trails linked to the falls access trail.

Waterfall height: 14 feet
Waterfall beauty: 4
Distance: 0.6-mile out-and-back
Difficulty: Easy
Hiking time: About ½ hour
Trail surface: Natural
Other trail users: None

Canine compatibility: Leashed pets allowed
Land status: State park
Fees and permits: None
Maps: Beltzville State Park; USGS Pohopoco Mountain
Trail contact: Beltzville State Park, (610) 377-0045, www.dcnr.state.pa.us/stateparks

Finding the trailhead: From exit 74 near Parryville on I-476 (the Pennsylvania Turnpike), join US 209 north for 0.1 mile, then turn left on Harrity Road and follow it for 0.1 mile. Turn right on Pohopoco Drive and stay with it for 6.9 miles, then make a right turn into the Wild Creek trailhead parking area, just before bridging Wild Creek. Drive to the south end of the large parking area and reach the Wild Creek trailhead, avoiding all other entrances to Beltzville State Park. GPS: 40.890360, -75.562795

The Hike

Located in the southern foothills of the Poconos, Beltzville State Park came to be in 1972 when the US Army Corps of Engineers, as a flood control project, dammed Pohopoco Creek, which drains the Poconos to the north. Pohopoco Creek eventually feeds the Lehigh River. The Corps deeded the shoreline to the Commonwealth of Pennsylvania, and this was how Wild Creek Falls became a protected cataract within a state park.

Later, when trails were laid out, it was only natural to lead a path by the falls within a trail network often used for cross-country skiing in the winter. Springtime—and other times of the year—finds a few straggling waterfall enthusiasts visiting Wild Creek Falls.

Beltzville State Park is water-centric, with multiple boat launches, fishing, and motorboating on the 949-acre lake. The 500-foot-wide sand beach and swimming area are major summertime draws. Swimming is not allowed in Wild Creek. The preserve has a total of 15 miles of hiking trails and a few miles of mountain-biking trails. Camping is not offered, but the park does have numerous picnicking areas.

A stone observation platform allows a close look at Wild Creek Falls.

The walk to Wild Creek Falls is easy and straightforward, and you soon find yourself at the bridge crossing over Wild Creek. This is a scenic area—an idyllic combination of cool clear water, expansive tree cover, and gray rock protrusions. As you walk up the Wild Creek valley, a raised rock promontory delivers your first vista of Wild Creek Falls while making its bumpy yet beautiful white descent. The site will make you want to come closer, and you can work around the promontory and come to the side of the falls atop more rock.

Here Wild Creek Falls pours over an angled, knobby rock strata, giving it an out-of-the-ordinary appearance. At this point the Falls Trail curves away from Wild Creek and makes a little mini-loop before returning to the stream. Still other trails can be used to extend your hike at this worthy Pennsylvania state park.

Miles and Directions

0.0 From the trailhead, pass around a pole gate, heading south on a doubletrack path amid a mix of brush and trees. After 200 feet, come to a trail intersection. Here an arm of the Christman Trail leaves right while a user-created trail goes left to Wild Creek. Keep straight, still on the doubletrack path, in a mix of evergreens and hardwoods.

0.2 Reach an intersection. Split left here with the Falls Trail. Drop to crystalline Wild Creek, then span the stream on a hiker bridge and walk into a wooded flat. Here the loop part of the Falls Trail leads right and also connects to the Cove Ridge Trail, which wanders along the shore of Wild Creek Cove, an arm of Beltzville Lake. Keep hiking upstream along Wild Creek. This is a pretty area.

0.3 Reach an elevated stone promontory affording your first view of Wild Creek Falls as it makes an irregular descent. Work around the stone outcrop, then return to the water for an up-close sidelong look at the 14-foot spiller. Either backtrack or follow the Falls Trail as it makes a mini-loop up and down an adjacent hill.

0.6 Arrive back at the trailhead, completing the walk.

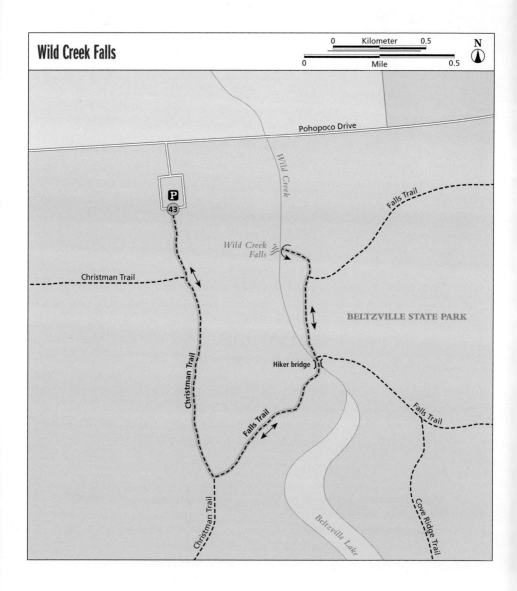

Wild Creek Falls

A picturesque hiker bridge crosses Wild Creek.

44 Hackers Falls

This is one of the least visited—yet still popular—waterfalls along waterfall-rich Raymondskill Creek. Jump off and on old pre-park roads on a well-signed track leading to powerful fan-shaped Hackers Falls. From here, you can backtrack through pleasant woods or enhance your adventure with a longer hike using other paths in the Cliff Park trail system of Delaware Water Gap National Recreation Area, perhaps visiting Tristate Overlook.

Waterfall height: 15 feet
Waterfall beauty: 4
Distance: 2.0-mile out-and-back
Difficulty: Easy, does have some hills
Hiking time: About 1 hour
Trail surface: Some gravel, mostly natural surface
Other trail users: None

Canine compatibility: On leash only
Land status: National recreation area
Fees and permits: None
Maps: Cliff Park Trail System; USGS Milford
Trail contact: Delaware Water Gap National Recreation Area, (570) 426-2452, www.nps.gov/dewa

Finding the trailhead: From the intersection of PA 739 and US 209 in Dingmans Ferry, take US 209 north for 4.9 miles. Turn left onto Raymondskill Road and follow it for 0.5 mile to reach the Raymondskill Falls parking lot on your left. *Note:* There are two parking lots on the left within immediate proximity to one another; the first one is better for this hike. This is also known as the Hackers trailhead. GPS: 41.290264, -74.840079

The Hike

The Delaware Water Gap area, along the Delaware River separating Pennsylvania and New Jersey, has long been a popular recreation destination, even before the existence of Delaware Water Gap National Recreation Area. Over a century ago, visitors were flocking to the locale, retreating to cabins and rustic hotels, getting away from the big cities of the Eastern Seaboard and coming here to visit waterfalls, fish, and boat. However, the dearth of public lands hampered hiking.

The situation changed with the establishment of Delaware Water Gap National Recreation Area, which came about as a twist of fate, especially when considering that hiking trails like those we use to reach Hackers Falls and other cataracts within the recreation area were the result.

Back in 1955, Hurricane Diane stormed its way up the Eastern Seaboard, dropping copious amounts of rain, including 16 inches at one recording station in Connecticut. Throughout New Jersey, Pennsylvania, and New England, streams overflowed their banks, reaching record levels. This massive load of water made its way down the Delaware River, leaving a swath of devastation in its wake, especially in the inundated

Poconos of Pennsylvania. Over a hundred people lost their lives in the Keystone State alone.

This flood led authorities to seek ways to prevent such a tragedy from happening again. The plan arose to build a dam along the Delaware River somewhere in the Delaware Water Gap region. By 1965 the US Army Corps of Engineers was authorized to build what became known as the Tocks Island Dam. The land around this 37-mile-long lake was to be part of the Tocks Island National Recreation Area. Land was purchased and people were moved, some via condemnation.

A group arose opposing the dam—the Delaware Valley Conservation Association—which rallied local residents as well as those from afar to halt the project. Citing additional infrastructure that needed to be built to handle what would be a popular lake as well as environmental concerns, the project was halted in 1975. Additionally, the proposed dam site was not geologically sound enough to hold what would have been the largest earthen dam east of the Mississippi.

However, the land for the lake and dam was already purchased. Therefore, the federal government went ahead with a national recreation area that would be based on the undammed Delaware River and the lands and streams draining into it in both Pennsylvania and New Jersey. The result is what we see today, over 70,000 acres

Hikers and dogs alike enjoy access to the water at Hackers Falls.

of history, hills, and waterfalls—and plenty of hiking trails—at Delaware Water Gap National Recreation Area.

The Cliff Park area, home of Hackers Falls, presents 8 miles of interconnected trails with multiple trailheads just south of Milford, Pennsylvania. This trail network runs on and off old roads of pre-park residents, vacationers, and other landowners. For waterfall hikers like us, Cliff Park provides an opportunity to see Hackers Falls while traversing pleasing and relaxing woods.

Our route to Hackers Falls starts at the same trailhead as popular Raymondskill Falls, so do not panic when you see busy parking lots upon arrival. Easily over 90 percent of those parking here will be heading to Raymondskill Falls—Pennsylvania's highest cataract. While here you can easily bag both Hackers Falls and Raymondskill Falls.

The hike leaves from the north side of Raymondskill Road on the Hackers Trail and climbs to quickly join an old woods road. You will be going on and off these intersecting roads, but worry not, for the Park Service has placed trail signs at any and all potentially confusing junctions, whether they are official trails or not. Meander under a changing forest canopy, from oaks and pines to hemlock thickets. Eventually you surmount a hill whereupon the Loggers Path leaves right. From there, wind your way down to Raymondskill Creek and a moist, cool valley.

Sidle alongside a bluff above the stream, then come to Hackers Falls, visible through the trees well before you reach it. From there, the path comes to a rock outcrop where you descend to a fine view of the falls and the plunge pool into which it flows. This pool was once an extremely popular swimming hole. Here reckless cliff divers jumped from adjoining heights into the plunge pool, not always with success, thus causing injuries and rescues. The Park Service has since prohibited all swimming and diving above, in, and below all waterfalls in the Delaware Water Gap National Recreation Area.

Nevertheless, Hackers Falls is a rewarding destination. Here you can see the 15-foot inverted fan-shaped cataract spread its white froth over a widening angled rock shelf bordered by the high cliff to your left as you face the falls. The wide falls basin stands open to the sun, and the flat rock shelf in front of the falls makes for excellent waterfall seating. On your way back, consider looping by the Tristate Overlook on the Cliff Trail for an extensive vista. Enjoy!

Miles and Directions

0.0 Leave the Hackers trailhead and cross Raymondskill Road, north. Walk around a pole gate, then join the doubletrack Hackers Trail. Just ahead, the Cliff Trail goes right and can be used to form a loop. Stay with the Hackers Trail, climbing. Watch the trail signs as the path goes off and on old roads.

0.5 Come to a trail intersection. Here the Loggers Path goes right to meet the Cliff Trail. This is where you can loop back to the trailhead. For now, stay left, leveling off. Soon turn southwest on a straight old road in pines.

0.7 Curve abruptly right, dropping toward Raymondskill Creek. The stream becomes audible.

0.9 Come alongside a bluff above Raymondskill Creek.

1.0 Reach Hackers Falls. A short spur drops left to a large rock outcrop that makes for a natural viewing platform of the inverted fan-shaped spiller set against a high cliff. Backtrack to the trailhead.

2.0 Arrive back at the trailhead, completing the hike.

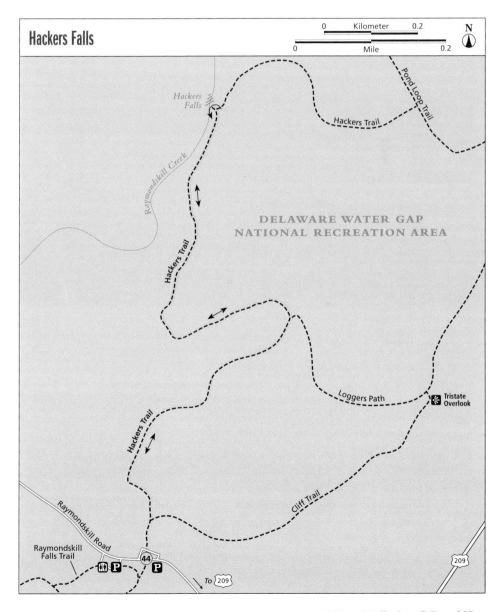

45 Raymondskill Falls

Make a short loop to see Pennsylvania's highest waterfall, tumbling through the Poconos at Delaware Water Gap National Recreation Area. The walk leads from the parking area to the top of 150-foot Raymondskill Falls, then the well-constructed trail curves to the lower part of the massive cataract with a lesser tributary fall spilling nearby.

Waterfall height: 150 feet
Waterfall beauty: 4
Distance: 0.3-mile loop
Difficulty: Easy, does have nearly 200-foot elevation change
Hiking time: About ½ hour
Trail surface: Steps, gravel, some natural surface

Other trail users: None
Canine compatibility: Pets prohibited
Land status: National recreation area
Fees and permits: None
Maps: Raymondskill Falls Trail; USGS Milford
Trail contact: Delaware Water Gap National Recreation Area, (570) 426-2452, www.nps .gov/dewa

Finding the trailhead: From the intersection of PA 739 and US 209 in Dingmans Ferry, take US 209 north for 4.9 miles. Turn left onto Raymondskill Road and follow it for 0.5 mile to reach the Raymondskill Falls parking lot on your left. *Note:* There are two parking lots on the left within immediate proximity to one another. I recommend the second parking lot, with the restroom building, for this hike. GPS: 41.229457, -74.887530

The Hike

Finding the proper starting point to reach Raymondskill Falls can be a challenge. For starters, the trail system emanates from two different yet adjacent parking lots. That alone gets people started on the wrong foot. And having another trail across the road from the parking area casts a bit more doubt on where to go. Therefore, at the Raymondskill Falls parking area (also known as the Hackers trailhead, just to add a little more confusion), you will see uncertain waterfall hikers waiting for someone else to make the right move to reach Pennsylvania's highest fall, generally estimated to be 150 feet, with other estimates rising as high as 180 feet!

However, it is generally agreed that Raymondskill Falls, with three major drops, is the highest cataract in the Keystone State. One reason for this height differential is that the falls cannot be seen in its entirety due to lack of marked and maintained trail. At one time there was a marked and maintained path to the very base of the falls, but erosion and the elements shut it down.

Nowadays we have a marked and maintained trail leading you to the top of the falls, with a second observation deck located near a plunge pool between the second and third stages of the long cataract. From this lower observation deck, you can observe the final stage of Raymondskill Falls but not the whole thing. Some waterfall enthusiasts illicitly scramble to the base of Raymondskill Falls, but that goes against the policy of Delaware Water Gap National Recreation Area, where the falls is located.

Even if you cannot see the whole thing at one time, a trip to Raymondskill Falls is worth your time. Draining swamps and small lakes on the Pocono Plateau, Raymondskill Creek meanders mainly east before reaching the plateau's rim and makes a precipitous drop to meet the Delaware River. Not surprisingly, here is where Raymondskill Falls is found. When flowing boldly the cataract is a loud froth of white, roaring like the highest waterfall in Pennsylvania should. Even at lower autumn water levels, the pour-over still displays a stately demeanor.

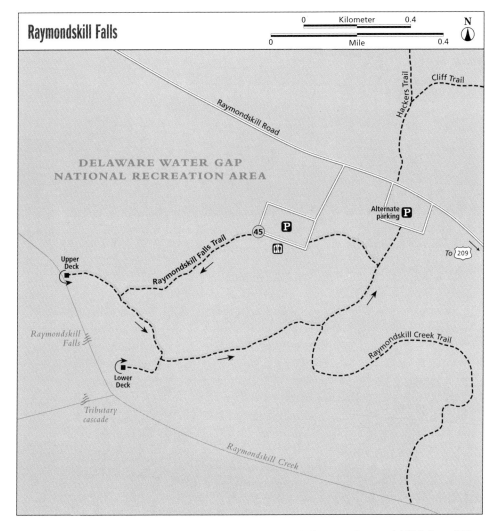

Even though the primary drop of Raymondskill Falls is only one section of the entire cataract, it's still pretty impressive. RUSTY GLESSNER

Your best bet to reach the falls without looking lost is to start in the most westerly parking lot, the second one after coming from US 209. This is a large parking area with a restroom building. Start the walk to Raymondskill Falls by leaving the south-west corner of the parking area and entering woods on a wide, heavily used gravel track. You can already hear the falls. It is not long before you find an observation deck standing at the brink of the falls. You can look upstream at a lesser pool and rapids, but the froth that is Raymondskill Falls spills out of sight from this vantage.

Heading to the lower observation deck, you will pass a dripping cave then walk the spur that leads down to the large plunge pool after the first two stages of the waterfall. This is a safe place to appreciate the spiller as it slaloms betwixt stone flanks. You can also look down at the final stage of the falls and at the sheet cascade of a tributary flowing to meet Raymondskill Creek. As previously mentioned, there was once a trail to the base of the falls but no more.

Hikers then leave the waterfall area and begin climbing. The Raymondskill Creek Trail—also a short path—makes a spur that curves down to the creek several hundred feet downstream of Raymondskill Falls. This side trail can add some mileage—and smaller seasonal waterfalls—to your hike. Otherwise, the ascent continues, passing a spur to the lower parking area. The final part of the loop returns you to the upper, second parking area.

Even if you become temporarily turned around here—as most people do—consider it a badge of honor earned by seeking Raymondskill Falls.

Miles and Directions

0.0 Leave the upper, western parking area on a pea gravel track, descending southwesterly. Shortly reach an intersection. Head right on a spur to reach an observation deck at the top of Raymondskill Falls. Backtrack, then resume the circuit hike.

0.2 Split right on the spur leading to the primary viewing/photography deck below the first two drops, beside a basin above the third and final drop. Look down and to your left at this third drop as well as the sheet cascade of a tributary of Raymondskill Creek. Backtrack and continue the loop, passing the intersection with the Raymondskill Creek Trail. Make a solid uphill climb.

0.3 Arrive back at the trailhead, completing the waterfall hike, after passing a spur to the lower parking area.

A tributary falls emphasizes the size of the lowermost drop of Raymondskill Falls.

46 Factory Falls, Fulmer Falls, Deer Leap Falls

Enjoy an engineering marvel of a trail to view these three also marvelous waterfalls on upper Dingmans Creek at George W. Childs Park. Overlooks, bridges, and steps working through the rugged valley allow waterfall hikers a chance to see this Pennsylvania waterfall magnet from multiple angles and vantages without even having to get their feet wet.

Waterfall height: In order, 18 feet, 56 feet, 30 feet
Waterfall beauty: 5
Distance: 1.2-mile lollipop loop
Difficulty: Easy
Hiking time: About ¾ hour
Trail surface: Pea gravel, boardwalk, some natural surface
Other trail users: None

Canine compatibility: Pets prohibited
Land status: National recreation area
Fees and permits: None
Maps: Dingmans Creek Trail; USGS Lake Maskenozha
Trail contact: Delaware Water Gap National Recreation Area, (570) 426-2452, www.nps.gov/dewa

Finding the trailhead: From the intersection of PA 739 and US 209 in Dingmans Ferry, take PA 739 north for 1.2 miles, then turn left on Silver Lake Road. Follow Silver Lake Road for 1.8 miles, then turn left onto Park Road and quickly turn left into the George W. Childs Park parking area. GPS: 41.237037, -74.919337

The Hike

Back in the early 1800s, settlers of the Poconos saw the waterfalls of Dingmans Creek primarily as a source of energy rather than a source of beauty as we view them today. To grind their wheat and corn into meal, locals built small dams and mills all along Dingmans Creek as it fell toward the Delaware River. Even today, you can still see evidence of these mills, though the fully erect dams have long since washed away.

Still others saw larger commercial ventures possible along the banks of Dingmans Creek. In one particular spot—along this waterfall hike—Joseph Brooks erected a wool-spinning factory in 1826. He even brought in the sheep. Dingmans Creek provided the energy for the wool-spinning machines, run by upwards of threescore employees. However, the sheep did not fare so well, succumbing to predators and disease. Therefore, Mr. Brooks had to transport raw wool to the factory then ship the processed product to Philadelphia, killing his profit margin. Nevertheless, the factory limped along until Mr. Brooks passed away in 1832, then shut down for good. You can still see stone remains of the once three-story-tall structure.

More grinding mills and even a tannery were established along the banks of Dingmans Creek, but the stream's beauty and its falling waters shone through to a man named George W. Childs. He purchased the area around Factory Falls, Fulmer Falls, and Deer Leap Falls in 1892, with the intent to build a park for the general public to enjoy these cataracts. However, Mr. Childs passed away two years later.

Factory Falls is a stunning multifaceted cascade.
RUSTY GLESSNER

His wife eventually deeded the property to the Commonwealth of Pennsylvania in 1912. Ultimately, when the Delaware Water Gap National Recreation Area came to be, George W. Childs Park was brought into the fold and is now managed by the National Park Service.

Upon seeing this trio of cataracts, you will understand Mr. Childs's desire to preserve this part of Dingmans Creek. The park has gone through many transformations, upgrades, and repairs, including where the Civilian Conservation Corps (CCC) laid their hands on the place, leaving their legacy of construction.

Change is afoot again. The trail system took twin hits back in 2018, when back-to-back winter storms tore down trees, destabilized soils, and more. It took a full six years to reopen Childs Park; however, the trail system emerged safer and more resilient than ever, and includes more universally accessible segments. The waterfalls tumble as they always have. Photographers need to know that although they will be able to see the waterfalls from many different angles, the limitations on where they can go may hamper their efforts.

The first part of the hike uses an all-access track winding down to an overlook of Factory Falls. From there, you will employ a combination of trail and stairwells descending to Fulmer Falls, dropping 56 feet, the tallest of the trio. Due to the trail configuration, it is hard to get close to this falls, except at the top. Beyond a bridge crossing of Dingmans Creek, you continue downstream then reach dramatic Deer Leap Falls, where a slender channel pinched in by rock walls shoots forth into an enormous plunge pool. Stand atop the bridge over Deer Leap Falls, then curve around to the falls basin.

From there, the hike uses more stairs to work up the right bank of Dingmans Creek, eventually coming to the overlook at Fulmer Falls. Note how this cataract plunges into a semicircular basin before pushing out into its plunge pool. Next, after admiring the CCC pavilion, check out the stone foundations of the Brooks Woolen Mill. Enjoy yet another perspective of Factory Falls, then take a little side trip to the CCC pump shelter before returning to the trailhead, completing a triple crown of a hike, one of Pennsylvania's finest waterfall treks.

Miles and Directions

0.0 From the trailhead, join the George W. Childs Trail, at this point a winding pea gravel all-access trail. Pass several picnic spots along the path.

0.2 Switchback downhill.

0.3 Reach a trail intersection with a creek bridge dead ahead. Split right, beginning a counterclockwise loop around Dingmans Creek. Walk just a short distance, then take the all-access spur to an overlook of 18-foot Factory Falls as it makes an angled plunge, dropping in stages. Resume the loop, leaving the all-access path behind. Use built-in steps.

0.4 Come to an overlook of 56-foot Fulmer Falls. It is hard to reach this cataract from the bottom due to having to stay on the trail. A large pool lies between you and the pour-over. Just ahead, reach a bridge spanning Dingmans Creek in the depths of the gorge. Stay right here, descending toward Deer Leap Falls.

0.5 Walk to the bridge and stand at the cusp of 30-foot Deer Leap Falls, just above where it slices between stone pillars then lunges out and then down into its enormous basin. Do not cross the bridge. Instead, circle around, continuing downstream, then cross the bridge below the plunge pool of Deer Leap Falls.

0.6 Continue upstream after circling around Deer Leap Falls. Travel up the right-hand side of Dingmans Creek well back from the water.

0.7 Come to the other end of the hiker bridge below Fulmer Falls. Keep ascending.

0.8 Reach an overlook at the top of Fulmer Falls. Note the semicircular hole into which the cataract spills then pushes out to its long plunge pool. Continue the loop, passing the CCC pavilion and the foundations of the Brooks Woolen Mill. Pass another overlook of Factory Falls.

0.9 Reach a trail junction and bridge over Dingmans Creek. Head right, upstream, to visit the CCC pump shelter, then return to the bridge. Cross the bridge and backtrack on the all-access trail toward the trailhead.

1.2 Arrive back at the trailhead, completing the waterfall triple-crown hike.

A hiker bridge runs above Deer Leap Falls, providing a great viewpoint.
RUSTY GLESSNER

Factory Falls, Fulmer Falls, Deer Leap Falls

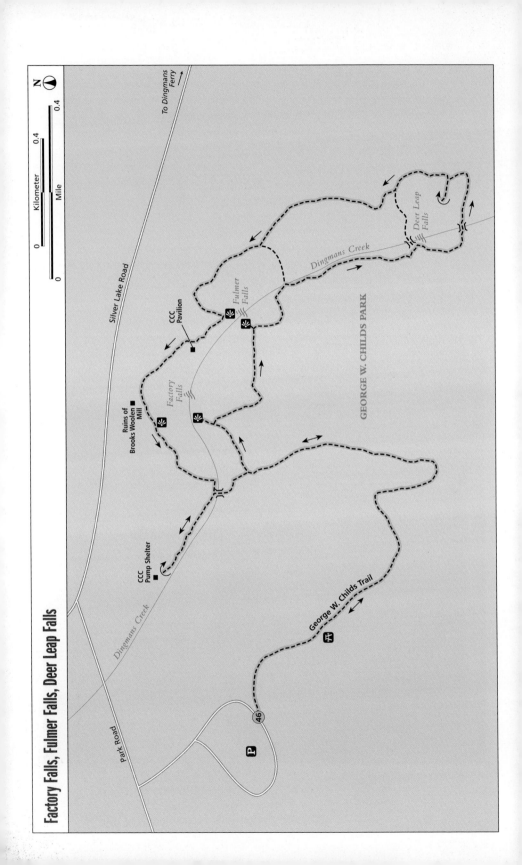

To Dingmans Ferry

Silver Lake Road

Dingmans Creek

GEORGE W. CHILDS PARK

Deer Leap Falls

Fulmer Falls

Factory Falls

CCC Pavilion

Ruins of Brooks Woolen Mill

CCC Pump Shelter

Park Road

Dingmans Creek

George W. Childs Trail

46

N

Kilometer

Mile

0   0.4

0   0.4

This photo captures the upper part of 56-foot Fulmer Falls.
RUSTY GLESSNER

47 Dingmans Falls, Silverthread Falls

Enjoy two tall yet completely different cataracts on this jaunt up lower Dingmans Creek at a historic Pocono tourist destination in operation since the 1880s, now managed by the National Park Service as part of the Delaware Water Gap National Recreation Area.

Waterfall height: 130 feet and 80 feet, respectively
Waterfall beauty: 5+
Distance: 1.0-mile out-and-back
Difficulty: Easy, does have many steps at the end
Hiking time: About ¾ hour
Trail surface: Boardwalk, pea gravel, wooden steps

Other trail users: None
Canine compatibility: Pets prohibited
Land status: National recreation area
Fees and permits: None
Maps: Dingmans Creek Trail; USGS Lake Maskenozha
Trail contact: Delaware Water Gap National Recreation Area, (570) 426-2452, www.nps.gov/dewa

Finding the trailhead: From the intersection of PA 739 and US 209 in Dingmans Ferry, take US 209 south for 0.2 mile to Johnny Bee Road. Turn right and follow Johnny Bee Road for 1.2 miles to dead-end at the Dingmans Falls Visitor Center parking lot. *Note:* This access road is not maintained in winter. GPS: 41.229457, -74.887530

The Hike

Dingmans Falls and its sidekick Silverthread Falls have been drawing visitors to the valley of Dingmans Creek since before the 1880s, when a hotel was erected to cater to waterfall visitors. That same hotel has now been refurbished as the national park visitor center at Dingmans Falls, adding a Victorian flair to the beautiful natural surroundings of this alluring valley.

Of course, being located on Dingmans Creek is no surprise. It seems like everything around here is named Dingman—Dingmans Falls, Dingmans Creek, and the town of Dingmans Ferry, among others. Ol' Dingman got around. It all started in 1735 when 23-year-old Andrew Dingman migrated from his birthplace in New York and came down to the Delaware Valley. (He likely went by the name Andreas Dingerman at the time; the name evolved over the years.) Here he found high and wild mountains rising from the river valley, but around the spot where the creek was to bear his name, he zeroed in on a large and lush river bottom, ideal for agriculture and settlement. There Dingman erected a log cabin, cleared part of the bottomland for crops, and established a ferry that would burnish his name in Pocono lore.

After settling in for the long haul, Dingman built a stone house that was promptly destroyed in the French and Indian War, but he and his now-growing family rebuilt again. A community grew around Dingman and his ferry. By the time the United States came to be after the Revolutionary War, the community of Dingmans Ferry (known then as Dingmans Choice) was in full swing.

In 1834 the first bridge across the Delaware was built at the ferry site, linking Pennsylvania and New Jersey. However, this rickety wooden affair—like a series of other wooden bridges after it—was destroyed by flood. By 1860 a Dingman was once again at the helm of the ferry linking the Keystone State to the Garden State, and for another forty years, until a toll bridge opened in the year 1900, Dingman's ferry stayed in business.

The bridge probably helped the hotel (naturally named Dingmans Hotel) that had been established at Dingmans Falls in the 1880s. But even at that, after the Delaware Water Gap National Recreation Area came to be, the Park Service bought the hotel and you can now enjoy it in its incarnation as a visitor center, opened during the warm season. Restrooms, water, and interpretive information are available there.

The walk to the two waterfalls is fun, easy, and rewarding. The way is all-access to the base of Dingmans Falls; however, the steps to the overlook above the falls are a challenge. Leave the signboard and trailhead between the parking area and the visitor center, joining a wide path—the Dingmans Creek Trail—to soon span Dingmans Creek on a bridge. You immediately reach Silverthread Falls; the faucet-like low-flow spiller is as narrow as an unwound thread of silver. At 80 feet, the flume can put on quite a show when displaying adequate water. At lower levels Silverthread Falls will spill in delicate tendrils dripping their way through the crevice, ending in a unique squared-off channel.

Moving upstream, the boardwalk trail winds through rich woods. After crossing the trouty stream a second time, you move up the left bank of the creek in a steepening vale, a place seeming as if it might have a 130-foot waterfall. You then join an observation deck extending to the base of Dingmans Falls.

The colossal cataract generates a roar and mist that adds to its imposing height. The observation deck allows you to move around, but its wetness can make footing tricky. Swimming is not allowed. From the deck you can look beyond the bluff to your left up at the two-stage drop, first as a mostly vertical descent in a tight mini-canyon. It then pushes on and unleashes its white veil down an elongated slide that crashes into a plunge pool above an overhanging mossy, dripping stone cathedral before the water gets turned downstream. Power and majesty exemplified in Pennsylvania's second-highest waterfall.

For your grand finale, take the Upper Dingmans Creek Trail using a gaggle of steps to climb then curve around a tributary of Dingmans Creek. Ascend more and reach the top of Dingmans Falls and an observation area. Here you can experience the crashing cascade from on high. Peer up Dingmans Creek from the observation area and you can admire yet another waterfall in a tight gorge on waterfall-rich Dingmans Creek.

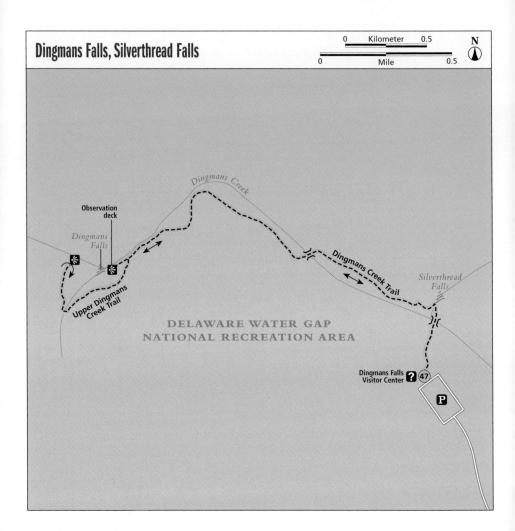

Miles and Directions

0.0 Follow the wide Dingmans Creek Trail away from the visitor center and enter woods thick with rhododendron. Cross a long bridge over Dingmans Creek.

0.1 Reach very unusual Silverthread Falls. This 80-foot spiller cuts a super-slim channel through a weakness in the surrounding rock, resulting in the skinniest chute fall you have ever seen, hence the name Silverthread. An excellent viewing spot can be had from the trail bridge spanning the low-flow stream of Silverthread Falls. Note the squared-off catch basin at the fall's base.

0.2 Cross back over to the left bank of Dingmans Creek. Head right, now on a pea gravel track.

0.3 The trail splits. Walk the low route to the observation deck and the base of Dingmans Falls. Backtrack, then join the Upper Dingmans Creek Trail, ascending curved steps and gaining more perspectives of Dingmans Falls.

0.5 Reach the top of the observation area just above the cusp of Dingmans Falls, giving an added angle to the experience. Backtrack to the trailhead.

1.0 Arrive back at the trailhead, completing the waterfall hike.

Dingmans Falls is a beautiful cataract that has been attracting visitors for generations.
RUSTY GLESSNER

You can see why Silverthread Falls got its name.
RUSTY GLESSNER

48 Lower Hornbecks Falls

This is an enjoyable trek from the moment you leave the trailhead until you reach Lower Hornbecks Falls, a mighty cascade with a mighty plunge pool. Visit a second, smaller fall before turning around. Set in a deeply wooded valley in the Delaware Water Gap National Recreation Area, the walk is nothing but you and nature.

Waterfall height: In order, 28 feet and 14 feet
Waterfall beauty: 4
Distance: 2.4-mile out-and-back
Difficulty: Easy to moderate
Hiking time: About 1½ hours
Trail surface: Natural
Other trail users: None
Canine compatibility: Leashed pets allowed

Land status: National recreation area
Fees and permits: None
Maps: Hornbecks Creek Trail; USGS Lake Maskenozha
Trail contact: Delaware Water Gap National Recreation Area, (570) 426-2452, www.nps .gov/dewa

Finding the trailhead: From the intersection of PA 739 and US 209 in Dingmans Ferry, take US 209 south for 2.7 miles and turn right into the signed trailhead for Hornbecks Creek (this right turn is 0.2 mile south of the US 209 intersection with Chestnut Hill Road). Follow the gravel trailhead access road a short distance to dead-end at the actual trailhead parking area. GPS: 41.188500, -74.886167

The Hike

Hornbecks Creek flows amid a gorgeous little valley cutting through the plateau of the Poconos down to the flats along the Delaware River. Luckily for us, the creek lies within the Delaware Water Gap National Recreation Area, thus keeping the setting wild, complete with a trail to Lower Hornbecks Falls, a brawny froth of white spilling into an amazingly large plunge pool. Upstream of there you can visit one more unnamed waterfall before the point where the Hornbecks Creek Trail ends.

The trail once continued up Hornbecks Creek to the falls on the upper part of the stream. These upper waterfalls are commonly referred to as the Indian Ladders. However, just because the trail is closed does not mean you cannot visit the Indian Ladders. It is simply a matter of picking up the Hornbecks Creek Trail from its upper trailhead on Emery Road, which is detailed in the Upper Hornbecks hike.

Having said that, do not walk the closed, hazardous former trail between Lower Hornbecks Falls and the Indian Ladders. The Park Service has tried to stabilize the trail without success. If you are at the Hornbecks Creek Trail off US 209, it is but a few miles drive to the upper trailhead where the Indian Ladders can be found.

Perhaps you will be satisfied with the hike to Lower Hornbecks Falls. The trek begins on a wide gravel track. Hornbecks Creek gurgles off to your right, having made most of its 600-plus-foot drop from the Pocono uplands to the Delaware River. Below here it runs under US 209 then meanders through fields for a bit before ending at the Delaware River about 0.5 mile below the trailhead.

From the late 1700s through the 1800s, the Hornbeck clan populated this area, giving the creek its name. There was even a tavern near what is now the trailhead, operated by Jacob Hornbeck. The area was filled with Deckers as well, and at different times what is now Hornbecks Creek was called Deckers Creek.

The trailhead is now just an open spot in the woods. From here, you enter the canyon of Hornbecks Creek, a place where wooded hillsides rise above streamside narrows where Solomon's seal, Dutchman's-breeches, and trillium carpet the floor under widespread sycamores and maples. The well-maintained path makes for easy walking.

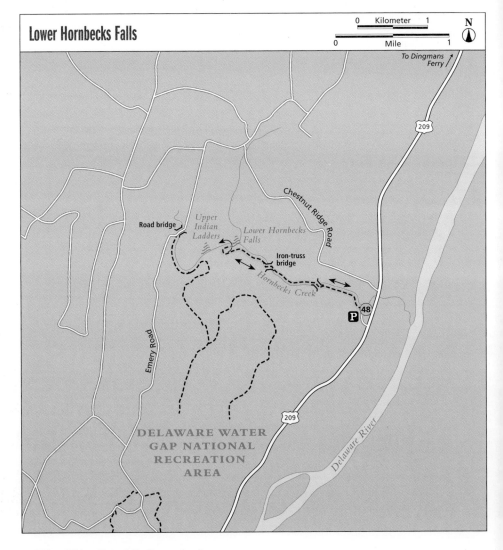

Lower Hornbecks Falls

The gorge has closed in by the time you bridge Hornbecks Creek the first time. You are now on the right-hand bank heading upstream. Look for huge jack-in-the-pulpits as well as stone fences from pre-park days when subsistence farmers tried to scrabble out a living in this hollow. The forest has recovered magnificently, however, once again proving nature will not allow a void.

The second bridge over Hornbecks Creek is noteworthy itself. The imposing iron and wood structure, completed in 2016, seems out of place in this forest. The path is more primitive beyond the second bridge and squeezes along the left-hand bank with a steep slope rising above. The appearance of yellow birch trees signifies the cooler environment of the upper, narrower canyon. These hardwoods with the signature peeling yellow-gold bark favor cool, moist conditions such as those found here along Hornbecks Creek. Ahead, beautiful stream scenes play out one after another.

You then come to Lower Hornbecks Falls, also known as the Lower Indian Ladders. First, take the right spur to the base of the falls and the plunge pool. Here a rocky

Unnamed falls above Lower Hornbecks Creek Falls

foreground gives way to a huge pool from which rise slick stone walls, except where Hornbecks Creek has carved a passage, whereupon the stream makes a swift slide and almost levels off before making a wider, steeper sheet of white, disappearing into the depths of the pool.

To view the falls from above, take the trail climbing up the left bank of the falls then reach a lesser cataract of about 15 feet in width, making a 14-foot drop into a very hard-to-reach plunge pool. Beyond here the trail has washed away. Do not keep going.

Miles and Directions

0.0 Leave the trailhead, passing around a wire gate, and join the doubletrack Hornbecks Creek Trail. Head northwest, entering the canyon of the stream.

0.4 Cross over to the right-hand bank on a trail bridge. Continue up the right-hand bank of Hornbecks Creek. Ahead, look for evidence of farming.

0.6 Walk a bluff above the creek.

0.8 Cross over to the left-hand bank on a long, elaborate iron-truss hiker bridge. Continue up the valley.

1.0 Split right at the spur to the base of Lower Hornbecks Falls, ending at the massive plunge pool. From there, backtrack a bit then climb on the trail up the left bank, first visiting an unnamed waterfall then walking to the top of Lower Hornbecks Falls.

1.2 After peering down on Lower Hornbecks Falls, backtrack to the trailhead.

2.4 Arrive back at the trailhead, completing the hike.

Another cascade continues its trajectory down lower Hornbecks Creek.
RUSTY GLESSNER

49 Upper Hornbecks Falls

Starting at the upper end of Hornbecks Creek, this short but exciting hike leads to multiple waterfalls, one after another after another, in a part of Hornbecks Creek that is also known as the Indian Ladders. The culmination of the trek is reached at the triangular-shaped cataract dropping some 40 incredible feet.

Waterfall height: 10 to 40 feet
Waterfall beauty: 5
Distance: 0.6-mile out-and-back
Difficulty: Easy
Hiking time: About ¾ hour
Trail surface: Natural
Other trail users: None
Canine compatibility: Leashed pets allowed

Land status: National recreation area
Fees and permits: None
Maps: Hornbecks Creek Trail; USGS Lake Maskenozha
Trail contact: Delaware Water Gap National Recreation Area, (570) 426-2452, www.nps .gov/dewa

Finding the trailhead: From the intersection of PA 739 and US 209 in Dingmans Ferry, take US 209 south for 2.6 miles and turn right onto Chestnut Hill Road (this right turn is a little before the US 209 road bridge over Hornbecks Creek). Head up Chestnut Hill Road for 1.5 miles, then turn left on Emery Road. Follow Emery Road for 1 mile, parking on the left after bridging Hornbecks Creek. The official trailhead is on the west side of Hornbecks Creek. GPS: 41.195428, -74.910070

The Hike

These falls, often called the Indian Ladders, are not only a worthy and fascinating set of cataracts to visit, but the name Indian Ladders is also on the top-10 all-time names for a Pennsylvania waterfall. The moniker conjures up an image of a series of falls coming one after another, step by step or rung by rung—and that is accurate when referring to the falls of Hornbecks Creek.

The commonly bandied about number of waterfalls on Hornbecks Creek is a dozen, stretching from the Pocono Plateau to the Delaware River. Having traversed the stream, I can say for certain there are at least a dozen falls. However, when getting into officially counting waterfalls, it can be difficult to determine when one waterfall ends and the next one begins, especially this upper section of Hornbecks Creek.

The white pour-overs come in rapid-fire succession, and when the water is up the gorge positively roars, going for a full quarter mile, starting with the uppermost spiller, a 20-foot slide that empties into a deep plunge pool before running into a stone wall and turning right. The creek then narrows and cuts a cleft in the adjacent evergreen forest with scattered fern pockets, frothing off hemmed-in shelves then gathering in small but deep pools, only to overflow and recklessly dive into the next

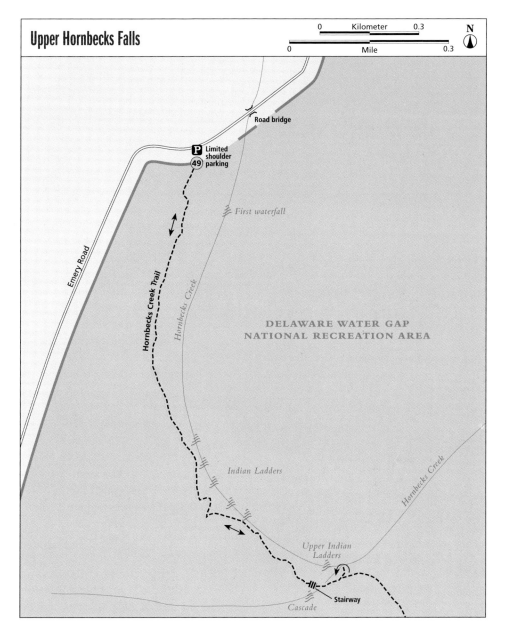

pool, where the water swirls then goes yet again—in stair-step fashion, or perhaps a ladder, scouring ever deeper into the land.

This incredible middle section makes the individual falls nearly indistinguishable from one another. However, you will know when you reach the bottom of these upper falls. This is where you take a wooden stairway to the base of a 40-foot pour-over. One of my favorite spillers in all of Pennsylvania, this 40-foot pillar of rock

Upper Indian Ladders, the 40-foot triangular falls on upper Hornbecks Creek, is one of the author's favorites.

and water makes a symmetrical stair-step descent, widening as it tumbles, ledge over ledge, changing course depending on how much water is moving down Hornbecks Creek. Beyond here, the trail continues to soon reach the connector trail linking to the Ridgeline Trail that is part of the Pocono Environmental Education Center Trail system, then ends.

Photographers can—and do—spend hours wandering up and down this stream segment. You will see plenty of user-created trails around the falls. In fact, a bootleg trail runs down the opposite bank of Hornbecks Creek all the way from Emery Road. Exercise caution not only for your personal safety but also for the valley itself. Excessive user-created paths can lead to erosion around the falls. Protect the resource.

Miles and Directions

0.0 Leave the roadside parking area and walk south on a natural-surface trail amid pines and blueberry bushes. You soon hear waterfalls off to your left—the uppermost Indian Ladders. Pass an old stone fence in the woods. Spurs lead to one waterfall after another.

0.2 The Hornbecks Creek Trail switchbacks. A series of cataracts spill to your left.

0.3 Stairs lead to the base of the lowermost of the upper falls of Hornbecks Creek. Look right as you walk down the stairs to see a tributary of Hornbecks Creek make its own cascade. After reaching the bottom of the stairs, you can hop around to enjoy a face-on view of this most magnificent of waterfalls—the 40-foot pyramid-like spiller impeccably framed in stone and greenery. Below here the path travels a short distance to meet the connector trail linking to the Pocono Environmental Education Center trail system. Beyond the intersection, the trail is closed due to washouts and unstable soils. Backtrack to the trailhead.

0.6 Arrive back at the trailhead, completing the hike.

A cascade near the 40-foot triangular falls tumbles down moss-covered "steps."

50 Tumbling Waters

This waterfall hike follows a nature trail looping through the Delaware Water Gap National Recreation Area, starting at the Pocono Environmental Education Center. Here you walk wooded uplands past ponds and along quiet wooded ridges before dropping to the stream of the Tumbling Waters, where a two-tiered waterfall fills an equally impressive plunge pool, while a longer, more inaccessible cataract spills just downstream. The hike then straddles a ridge, opening to an inspiring view of the Delaware Valley below. Stop by a lesser fall en route back to the trailhead.

Waterfall height: In order, 30 feet, 70 feet, 12 feet
Waterfall beauty: 4
Distance: 3.0-mile loop
Difficulty: Easy to moderate
Hiking time: About 1¾ hours
Trail surface: Natural
Other trail users: Groups from Pocono Environmental Education Center

Canine compatibility: Leashed pets allowed
Land status: National recreation area
Fees and permits: None
Maps: Tumbling Waters Trail Guide; USGS Lake Maskenozha
Trail contact: Pocono Environmental Education Center, (570) 828-2319, www.peec.org

Finding the trailhead: From the intersection of PA 739 and US 209 in Dingmans Ferry, take US 209 south for 4.8 miles to Brisco Mountain Road. Turn right and follow Brisco Mountain Road for 0.8 mile, then stay straight just a short distance on Emery Road (Brisco Mountain Road veers left) and come to the Pocono Environmental Education Center on your right. Park in the lot in front of the main building. GPS: 41.171217, -74.914633

The Hike

The Pocono Environmental Education Center (PEEC) is the starting point for this waterfall hike. The mission of the center "advances environmental education, sustainable living, and appreciation for nature through hands-on experience in a national park." The national park is Delaware Gap National Recreation Area, the scenic swath of Pennsylvania and New Jersey stretching across the falls, hills, and bluffs rising from the great Delaware River.

The PEEC chose a fine spot for its center, for it is near not only Tumbling Waters but also other area highlights to which trails were built after the center's founding over four decades ago. Before the PEEC was established, the grounds were home to Honeymoon Haven, a resort catering exclusively to newlyweds.

Starting in September of 1972, the resort was slowly transformed into the environmental center we see today. Through the years PEEC has engaged in different partnerships and utilized myriad revenue streams, seeing its visitation rise. Today the

The upper drop of Tumbling Waters

center hosts single-day and multiday meetings, camps, groups, and individual visitors, accompanying from 15 to 300 ecotourists at a time, and is open year-round. The main building near the parking area offers environmental education displays about the locale as well as a bookstore. Take time to explore the facility before or after your waterfall hike.

Make sure to grab the *Tumbling Waters Trail Guide* to take with you on the hike. It not only has a map but also shares interpretive information about the human and natural history of the trailside terrain.

Leaving the environmental education center, you first cross Emery Road then cross Brisco Mountain Road. Look for signs of previous habitation, as much of this area was farmed a century back. The Tumbling Waters Trail then skirts Pickerel Pond before joining a ridgeline. You meander southward, angling your way to the unnamed stream that is home to Tumbling Waters. You turn into the watershed only to curve back away from the stream in a deep evergreen forest.

Trailside view of the Delaware Valley

Cascade along unnamed stream near Brisco Mountain Road

Finally, a spur trail switchbacks down to the watercourse and a flat between the two parts of Tumbling Waters. The upper part of the waterfall is easy to reach and you walk up to its base, where a large plunge pool stills after its two-tiered 30-foot descent. The first part of the drop divides into parallel chutes of water, then briefly slows in a pool, followed by a second, wider curtain drop.

This is the part of Tumbling Waters enjoyed by all. However, there is a lower 70-foot drop that is frankly very difficult to reach, but you can glance at it easily from its top. Here the stream is narrowed by rock gates then dives off a stone lip and stays slender while caroming down a stony chute before flattening out at the bottom. Use caution if attempting to view this lower fall.

Although the loop hike leaves Tumbling Waters, the highlights are far from over. You will next climb along a ridge where views of the Delaware Valley, once slated to be flooded for a dam, will inspire. The wooded heights of New Jersey stand across the unseen river. Next you will find the ruins of a former hunting camp before reaching a stream running parallel to Brisco Mountain Road. This waterway features a cascade just below the trail. This low-flow spiller makes an angled faucet-like descent through a narrow chute before widening into a sheet of aqua.

After crossing Brisco Mountain Road, the Tumbling Waters Trail returns to the environmental education center, where it then meanders past some shorter nature trails before reaching one of the facility roads. Turn left and follow this road just a short distance, returning to the parking area. ˙

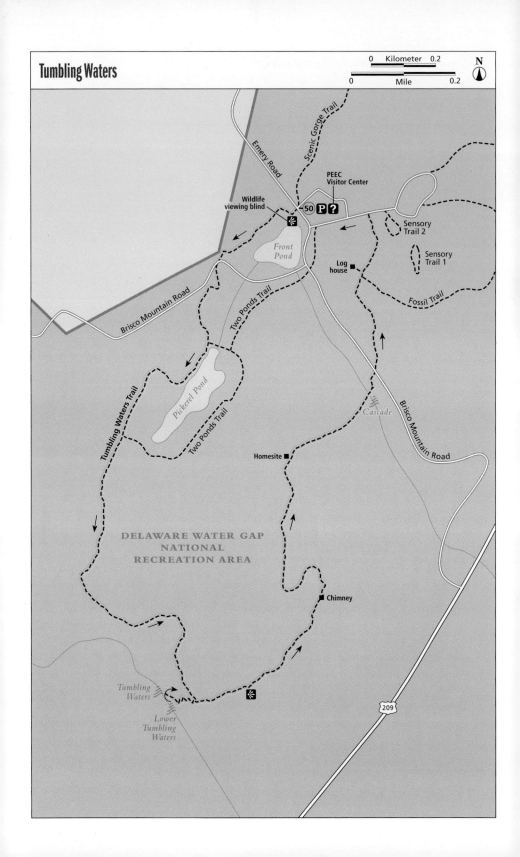

Tumbling Waters

0 Kilometer 0.2
0 Mile 0.2

N

Emery Road

Scenic Gorge Trail

PEEC
Visitor Center

Wildlife
viewing blind

50 P ?

Sensory
Trail 2

Front
Pond

Log
house

Sensory
Trail 1

Fossil Trail

Brisco Mountain Road

Two Ponds Trail

Tumbling Waters Trail

Pickerel Pond

Two Ponds Trail

Cascade

Brisco Mountain Road

Homesite

DELAWARE WATER GAP
NATIONAL
RECREATION AREA

Chimney

209

Tumbling
Waters

Lower
Tumbling
Waters

Miles and Directions

0.0 From the main PEEC parking area beside Emery Road, join the Tumbling Waters Trail southbound by crossing Emery Road. The orange-blazed trail runs in conjunction with the Two Ponds Trail. Stroll atop a boardwalk, then pass a wildlife-viewing blind near Front Pond. Continue through former farmland. Note the rock fence line from the agricultural days.

0.1 Bridge a little rocky creek, then keep along the stone fence line.

0.2 Cross Brisco Mountain Road, then resume trail hiking. Enter a copse of evergreens.

0.4 Come alongside Pickerel Pond, then turn away.

0.7 Meet the other end of the Two Ponds Trail. Stay southbound with the Tumbling Waters Trail.

1.0 Start descending off the ridgeline you have been following. It seems you are heading toward the creek of the Tumbling Waters falls, but instead the trail turns away and climbs a little hill.

1.3 Scoot alongside a steep bluff.

1.4 Reach the spur trail to Tumbling Waters. Split right and switchback downhill to level off in a flat. The upper part of Tumbling Waters is upstream. Reach the cataract's plunge pool, coming nearer to the two-stage 30-foot spiller. You can view the top of lower Tumbling Waters by walking downstream to the cusp of the falls as it narrows upon reaching a stone rampart then makes a caroming 70-foot dash, ultimately to level off. Reaching the base of this lower fall is tricky. Use extreme caution if attempting this.

1.6 Return to the main loop after visiting the falls. Climb along a dry, sparsely wooded, gravelly hillside.

1.7 Come to an open vista and contemplation bench. Gaze across the Delaware River valley into New Jersey. Continue along the ridgeline, gaining more views.

1.9 Pass the ruins of an old hunting cabin, its chimney standing tall. Turn away from the brow of the ridge and pick up an old farm road, curving south then back north again.

2.3 Pass a growing-over clearing of a pre-park homesite. Look left for the foundation of the home.

2.6 Reach an unnamed streamlet running parallel to Brisco Mountain Road. An angled 12-foot cascade flows to the right of the trail. Follow the trail left, then cross the creek, cross Brisco Mountain Road, and climb into pines, still northbound. Stay with the blazes in this maze of old roads.

2.8 Reach a junction. Here a short spur heads left to a log cabin, and the Fossil Trail goes right. Keep straight.

2.9 Emerge at the facility road. Turn left toward the visitor center.

3.0 Arrive back at the visitor center, completing the hike.

51 Bushkill Falls

This iconic Pennsylvania attraction is a must-do waterfall hike. Located at the southern end of the Poconos, this private park—in operation over a century—contains an incredible array of cataracts located along Little Bushkill Creek and Pond Run Creek. You will view waterfalls from 10 to 100 feet in myriad forms, all complementing one another. Despite that aquatic splendor, you may be more amazed at the land bridges and wooden walkways that lead you through the gorges of this natural tourist attraction.

Waterfall height: 10 to 100 feet
Waterfall beauty: 5+
Distance: 1.9-mile loop
Difficulty: Moderate, does have many stairs and elevation changes
Hiking time: About 1½ hours
Trail surface: Natural, wood, gravel
Other trail users: None

Canine compatibility: Leashed pets allowed
Land status: Private park, seasonally open to public
Fees and permits: Fee required
Maps: Bushkill Falls; USGS Bushkill
Trail contact: Bushkill Falls, (888) 287-4545, www.visitbushkillfalls.com

Finding the trailhead: From exit 309 on I-80 near Stroudsburg, take US 209 north, staying with it for 11.5 miles to Bushkill Falls Road. Turn left and follow Bushkill Falls Road for 1.7 miles to enter the park on your left. GPS: 41.117233, -75.007817

The Hike

To some people, Bushkill Falls may seem more of a tourist destination than an outdoor destination. Located in the Pocono Mountains adjacent to the waterfall-laden Delaware Water Gap National Recreation Area, Bushkill Falls has been a regular stop for Eastern Seaboard big-city residents to enjoy the natural attributes located in these highlands above the Delaware River. They have been coming here for a century.

Before you cast a jaded eye toward Bushkill Falls, ask yourself: If this parcel of land along Little Bushkill Creek were located within the nearby Delaware Water Gap National Recreation Area, would you think it is a beautiful part of a national park? For no matter whether the land is privately owned or held in the public trust, Bushkill Falls is one handsome part of Pennsylvania, and is home to some of its most striking waterfalls concentrated in one small area.

In operation since 1904, Bushkill Falls has a trail system that has to be seen to be believed. Starting out with a simple swinging bridge above the Main Falls, Charles Peters's attraction has expanded and now includes an incredible number of land bridges attached to the sides of gorges, wild walkways, and angled stairwells traversing the gorges here. The construction of these land bridges will amaze you as much as the waterfalls will.

The cataracts here rank every bit as high if not higher than any other waterfalls in the Poconos. Main Falls tumbles tall and majestic 100 suspenseful feet, while Lower Gorge Falls cuts its way through a narrow defile. Bridal Veil Falls flitters in a white screen from upon high. And there are others still.

It is not just the falling water or the trail construction that you will appreciate, for the natural attributes of the canyons through which Little Bushkill Creek and Pond Run Creek flow present geological wonderment upon which rise forests and flowers. Expect a lot and this park will deliver. After all, you are paying an admission fee.

Additionally, the park features an ice-cream parlor, a gift and clothing shop, a visitor center, and miniature golf as well as a few other touristy-type attractions. It also offers a picnic area in addition to a fishing and paddleboat lake. Therefore, swallow your pride, pay your money, and enjoy this iconic Pennsylvania waterfall destination.

Bridges like this take you through fascinating otherwise-inaccessible gorges.

Main Falls makes a torrential dive.

I recommend taking the Red Trail. It leads you past all the major waterfalls and is the longest walk in the park at 1.9 miles. You will encounter numerous trail intersections, but stay with the red blazes marked along the path and your clockwise loop will reap huge rewards. *Note:* The park is closed during winter season. Call ahead during the shoulder seasons before coming here.

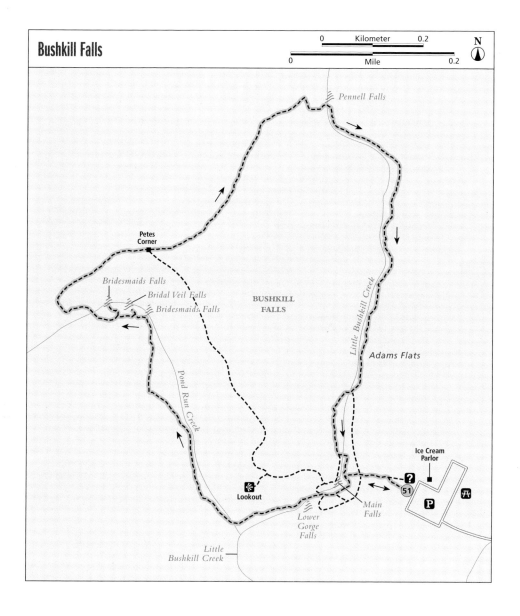

Bushkill Falls

0   Kilometer   0.2

0   Mile   0.2

N

Pennell Falls

Petes Corner

Bridesmaids Falls

Bridal Veil Falls

Bridesmaids Falls

BUSHKILL FALLS

Little Bushkill Creek

Adams Flats

Pond Run Creek

Ice Cream Parlor

Lookout

Main Falls

Lower Gorge Falls

Little Bushkill Creek

51

Miles and Directions

0.0   After paying your entrance fee, pass through a building then begin following the Red Trail. Descend toward Little Bushkill Creek. Ahead, come to an intersection just above Main Falls. Head left, looking for the red blazes. Circle around 100-foot Main Falls and the massive plunge pool below. When the falls are roaring, the mist resembles rain. Observation points are continuous, and spur trails connect to the Yellow Trail. Continue on a phenomenal wooden walkway along the side of the deep gorge.

0.1   A trail leads up to the lower end of the huge plunge pool of Main Falls. Check out Main Falls, then continue down the gorge, bridging Little Bushkill Creek. A dead-end bridge crosses atop Lower Gorge Falls.

0.3   Cross a bridge and turn up Pond Run Creek. The trail becomes natural surface. Ascend along the dancing waterway in deep woods. The path is rocky in places.

0.6   Reach the first Bridesmaids Falls. The 20-foot cataract dives over a ledge then splashes down an angled ledge. Ascend steep steps, then come to Bridal Veil Falls. This 22-foot spiller makes a wider curtain-like descent over rock. Enjoy the excellent walkway going to a fine photo point—expect to see scads of waterfall lovers taking selfies here. Climb to a point above Bridal Veil Falls, then take the spur to the upper Bridesmaid Falls. This cataract makes a sloped dive through a tight gorge then bangs against a wall before swirling in its plunge pool. Resume the ascent along Pond Run Creek.

0.9   Come to an intersection known as Petes Corner. Here a shortcut trail leads right, back to Main Falls, passing the Delaware Valley Lookout along the way. Keep straight here, toward Pennell Falls, although most visitors cut right.

1.0   Walk under a transmission line.

1.2   Cross the bridge near 10-foot Pennell Falls, flowing over a tilted rock shelf. Turn down Little Bushkill Creek. Enjoy some easy walking while passing through Adams Flats.

1.6   Cross a bridge and begin another segment with land bridges attached to the side of the gorge amid incredible scenery. A trail going left bypasses this section and heads for the visitor center.

1.8   Cross back over Little Bushkill Creek, still deep in the gorge. You are just above Main Falls. Here you can cut across the stream yet again to view Main Falls from the west side. The loop then turns away from Little Bushkill Creek. Backtrack, climbing toward the visitor center.

1.9   Arrive back at the visitor center, completing the inconceivable waterfall hike. Consider exploring the other entertainment, shopping, and food options here at Bushkill Falls.

Bridesmaid Falls exhibits a veil of white.

Waterfall Hikes of
Southeast Pennsylvania

The lower drop of Mill Creek Falls (hike 54)

52 High Falls at Ringing Rocks Park

The waterfall here is but one element of Ringing Rocks Park, a geological marvel situated in the Delaware Valley of eastern Pennsylvania. It is easy to visit not only the low-flow falls here but also the strange boulder field, where the bang of a hammer on these abnormal stones creates a bell-like sound.

Waterfall height: 15
Waterfall beauty: 3
Distance: 0.6-mile out-and-back
Difficulty: Easy
Hiking time: About ½ hour
Trail surface: Natural
Other trail users: None

Canine compatibility: Leashed pets allowed
Land status: County park
Fees and permits: None
Maps: Ringing Rocks County Park; USGS Riegelsville
Trail contact: Bucks County Parks and Recreation, (215) 757-0571, www.buckscounty.gov

Finding the trailhead: From the intersection of Delaware Road and Easton Road/PA 611 in Riegelsville, head south on PA 611 for 2.9 miles, then turn left onto PA 32 south. Follow PA 32 south for 2.1 miles, then turn right onto Narrows Hill Road and follow it for 0.4 mile. Turn left on Ringing Rocks Road, then turn left into Ringing Rocks County Park after 0.9 mile. GPS: 40.560420, -75.128616

The Hike

Hiking at Ringing Rocks County Park in far eastern Pennsylvania's Delaware Valley, just across from the New Jersey border, may be the strangest hiking experience you will ever have. Normally, when preparing yourself at a trailhead, you will often see people loading day packs with snacks, water bottles, rain jackets, medical kits, and the like, and while hiking you may see people holding trekking poles or an old-fashioned wooden stick in their hands. However, rarely do you see people—and I am talking more hikers than not at Ringing Rocks County Park—loading hammers into their packs at the trailhead or carrying hammers in their hand while walking down the trail. It is strange, I tell you—strange!

Nevertheless, there is a reason, and the name of the park probably gives you a hint. Within the park bounds, a 7-acre expanse of rock known as the Bridgeton Boulder Field contains thousands of unusual rounded rocks that upon whacking with a hammer yield a ringing sound not unlike a bell. So very strange—I cannot help but wonder who was the first person to hit these rocks with a hammer, thus popularizing this peculiar phenomenon.

Furthermore, when the park is crowded, you will hear this ringing and banging shortly after leaving the trailhead and working your way to High Falls—a more

Waterfall photographer to right of High Falls gives the cataract perspective.

typical feature to be seen at a park. En route to the falls it is almost impossible not to stop at the 10-foot-deep boulder field to watch—or participate in—the rock ringing.

This is not the only place in the world this phenomenon occurs. In fact, there are two other places in the Keystone State where ringing rocks can be found—Ringing Rocks Park in Lower Pottsgrove Township and Stony Garden in State Game Lands No. 157 near Quakertown. There is a Ringing Rocks in Montana, but beyond there you have to venture to Australia, England, Scotland, Namibia, or Mexico to experience such a phenomenon. So this is a big deal, and difficult for scientists to explain.

However, this is a waterfall guide. Therefore, we ring the rocks and march on toward High Falls. The trail is well used and beaten down beyond the Ringing Rocks. This is no surprise since the park and trail system is quite small, so one can visit both destinations in under a mile of hiking.

Meandering onward, the trail aims for High Falls Run, which drops 400 feet over its course between here and the Delaware River below, flowing through the hamlet of Narrowsville just before it enters the Delaware. High Falls Run, when flowing, slides over a wide stone slab above High Falls and makes for a fun place to explore. Here you can access the top of not particularly high High Falls as it narrows to spill over a stone cusp into a boulder-strewn rock garden. By simply dropping to the base of the falls and doing a little hopping around, waterfall enthusiasts can gain excellent

The mysterious Ringing Rocks curiously produce a ringing tone when struck by a hammer.

face-on perspectives of High Falls. You will see that the falls almost always flows exclusively on the right side of its angled ledge.

Unless you want to see the Ringing Rocks only, do not come here from midsummer through late fall. High Falls will likely be dry. However, when it is flowing you can get a double dose of outdoor fun with the Ringing Rocks and High Falls. Just remember to bring the hammer.

Miles and Directions

0.0 From the trailhead, walk west away from the parking area. The trail soon splits. Stay right toward High Falls in hardwood forest.

0.1 The Bridgeton Boulder Field opens to your left. The 7-acre swath of rounded rock may be inhabited by hammer-wielding outdoor enthusiasts banging their tools, resulting in ringing reverberations. Continue beyond the boulder field, resuming thick woods rich with tulip trees.

0.3 Reach High Falls. You can walk the streamside flats above the falls as well as drop to the base of the angled ledge. Backtrack to the trailhead.

0.6 Arrive back at the trailhead, completing the walk.

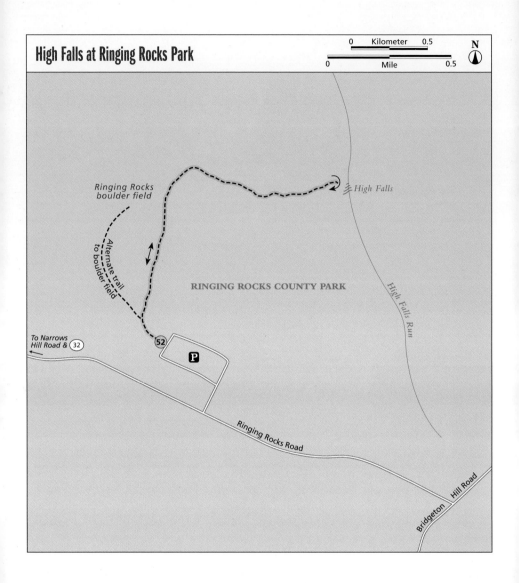

High Falls at Ringing Rocks Park

0   Kilometer   0.5

0   Mile   0.5

N

Ringing Rocks boulder field

Alternate trail to boulder field

High Falls

RINGING ROCKS COUNTY PARK

High Falls Run

52

To Narrows Hill Road & 32

P

Ringing Rocks Road

Bridgeton Hill Road

53 Sweet Arrow Lake Falls

Make an easy trek to a pretty pour-over at a happening county park. This cataract—the outflow of dammed Upper Swatera Creek—is the centerpiece of an attractive little scene where the released stream drops off a ledge then curves through a water play area before flowing on to Upper Swatera Creek. The walk to the falls is short, so consider adding other trails to your waterfall walk, or enjoy other features including picnicking, paddling, fishing, birding, or even disc golf.

Waterfall height: 14 feet
Waterfall beauty: 3-4
Distance: 0.4-mile out-and-back
Difficulty: Easy
Hiking time: About ½ hour
Trail surface: Asphalt, a little natural
Other trail users: None

Canine compatibility: Leashed pets allowed
Land status: Schuylkill County park
Fees and permits: None
Maps: Schuylkill County; USGS Swatera Hill
Trail contact: Schuylkill County Parks and Recreation, (570) 527-2505, www.sweetarrow lakepark.com

Finding the trailhead: From exit 104 on I-81 just north of Ravine, head right on Molleystown Road to quickly turn right onto PA 125 south. Follow PA 125 for 2.2 miles to turn left onto Sweet Arrow Lake Road and follow it 1.4 miles to turn right onto Waterfall Road. Follow Waterfall Road 0.5 mile to turn left into a large parking area at Sweet Arrow Lake County Park. The Waterfall Trail starts at the north end of this parking area. GPS: 40.568936, -76.367149

The Hike

Okay, I'll admit it, Sweet Arrow Lake Falls is not entirely natural. Back in the 1800s, Upper Swatera Creek was dammed to ensure the Union Canal a reliable water source. Though ostensibly created for business purposes, it wasn't long before locals from nearby Pine Grove began boating and fishing 60-acre Sweet Arrow Lake, as well as picnicking and playing along its shores. Then in 1862, a flood burst the dam but it was rebuilt. In the 1920s, what became PPL reconstructed the dam for power generation. This may have been when the outflow of the impoundment, where Upper Swatera Creek was once again freed from its watery bonds, was altered a bit, forming the current cataract set in a mini-gorge. A close-up look at the pour-over reveals telltale straight-line blasted sections where rock meets water and tumbles 14 feet into a deep pool. Nevertheless, the scene is a pleasant one, and worth a walk, especially when you consider that Sweet Arrow Lake and 123 adjacent acres were purchased in 2001, ultimately to become Sweet Arrow Lake County Park.

Today, trails course through the preserve. Picnicking, fishing, and paddling on the no-gas-motors lake are popular. And so is going to the falls. The dedicated Waterfall Trail leads you straight to the scenic spiller, ensconced in a hemlock-shaded mini-gorge. One of the more rewarding aspects of visiting Sweet Arrow Lake Falls is the ability to admire it from numerous angles, including from above, for a metal hiker span runs overhead the wall of whitewater. Admire it from the trail bridge, then cross the bridge and look at the cataract head-on from a little picnic area. After that recross the bridge and look at it from the fall's plunge pool, deep where the cataract makes the straight nosedive then shallows to a rocky segment bordered by a small beach, where kids and adults gravitate to splash in the waters of newly freed Upper Swatera Creek.

This trail bridge delivers an unusual view of Sweet Arrow Lake Falls.

Other hiking trails take you along the south shore of Sweet Arrow Lake and well into preserved wetlands at the head of the impoundment. Consider making a day of it at this fun little county park with a waterfall you can savor from multiple vantages.

Miles and Directions

0.0 Leave the parking area off Waterfall Road, joining the Waterfall Trail, heading northeast on an asphalt path. The dam of Sweet Arrow Lake looms to your left. Enter pine and hemlock woods.

0.2 Come to a trail intersection just before the bridge over Upper Swatera Creek. Here, the Wood Duck Trail goes left. We stay straight, bridging Upper Swatera Creek just above Sweet Arrow Lake Falls. After the bridge, turn right onto the Berger Dam Trail for a straight-on view of the falls. After that cross the bridge again, then drop to the beach and water play area below the falls. Finally, rejoin the Waterfall Trail back toward the trailhead.

0.4 Arrive back at the trailhead, completing the waterfall walk.

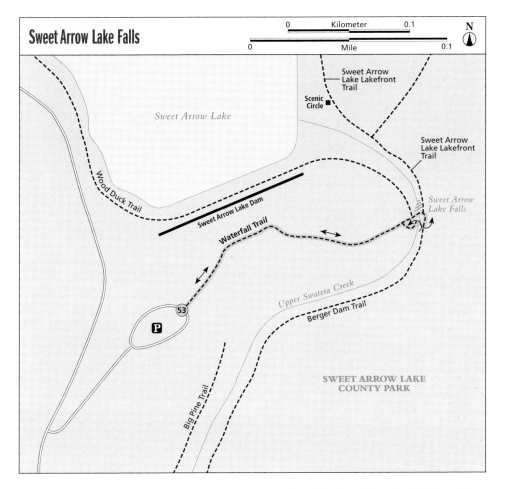

54 Mill Creek Falls of York County

This historic waterfall hike in the lower Susquehanna River valley not only leads to a fine cataract but also takes you along the former Susquehanna & Tidewater Canal, where you find ruins of a sawmill, limekiln, and Lock 12. Start by viewing ruins, then come along the old canal, cruising among spring wildflowers to reach Mill Creek. A short trek up that stream leads to 18-foot Mills Creek Falls, tumbling toward its mother stream, the Susquehanna River.

Waterfall height: 18 feet
Waterfall beauty: 3–4
Distance: 1.4-mile out-and-back
Difficulty: Easy
Hiking time: About 1 hour
Trail surface: Natural, a little concrete
Other trail users: None

Canine compatibility: Leashed pets allowed
Land status: PPL Utilities land
Fees and permits: None
Maps: Mason-Dixon Trail Lock 12-Holtwood Dam–Osprey Nest; USGS Holtwood
Trail contact: Mason-Dixon Trail System, https://masondixontrail.wixsite.com/mdts

Finding the trailhead: From exit 4 on I-83 just north of the Maryland line, take PA 851 east for 10.5 miles to the hamlet of New Park. Veer left onto New Park Road and stay with it for 3.7 miles, then turn right onto Bridgeton Road and follow it for 5.4 miles to PA 74. Turn right and stay with PA 74 for 2.1 miles, then turn left onto PA 372 and follow it east for 2.2 miles to turn left onto River Road just before bridging the Susquehanna River. Follow River Road just a short distance, then turn right into the Lock 12 Historical Area. The trail starts in the lower lot. GPS: 39.813424, -76.329014

The Hike

Before railroads came to dominate American shipping, rivers were the primary way to move agricultural and industrial products. Of course, rivers had their challenges—too much water, too little water, roaring rapids, freezing over, and being open to the winds. Canals seemed to be the answer. Water levels could be regulated, flows could be controlled, and reliable animal power could replace manpower and the vagaries of wind power. Canals were typically built in river valleys, as the rivers could help supply water and riverside flats were somewhat friendly to canal digging and construction.

Thus was built the 45-mile Susquehanna & Tidewater Canal, completed in 1840. The four-year project linked Wrightsville, Pennsylvania, to Chesapeake Bay down Maryland way. The canal featured twenty-nine locks to compensate for the 233 feet of elevation change between Wrightsville and Chesapeake Bay. Along with a few emerging railroads, the Susquehanna & Tidewater Canal linked shipping from the Great Lakes to the cities of the Eastern Seaboard.

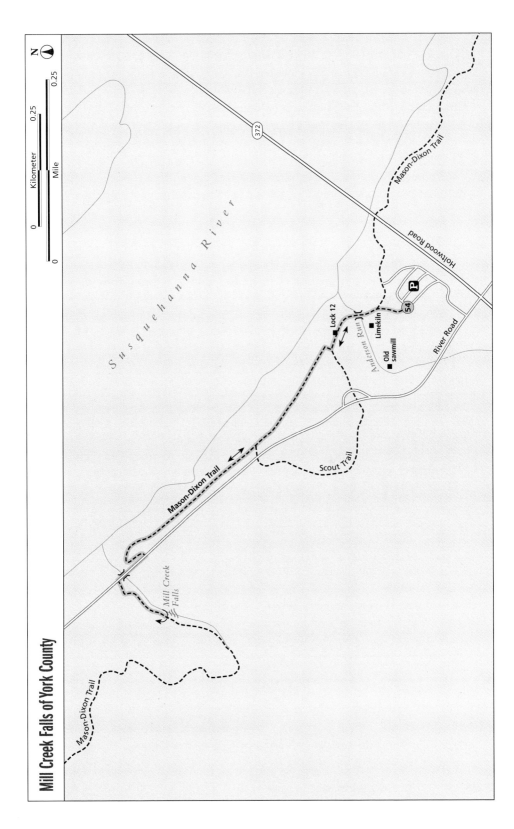

Mill Creek Falls of York County

For years it carried coal, pulled on small (by today's standards) barges by mules. The story of this canal ends in 1894, when the last load of coal was delivered to Baltimore via the Susquehanna & Tidewater. Railroad transportation was simply more efficient, leading to the demise of canals throughout Pennsylvania and beyond.

Today, some parts of the old canal have survived to now become historical relics, such as Lock 12. The PPL property has now reverted to nature, and the long-distance, sky-blue-blazed Mason-Dixon Trail runs some of its 200-mile course through this part of the Susquehanna Valley.

The hike leads from the Lock 12 parking area down past a picnic and play area beyond old Anderson's sawmill and the circular ovens of a limekiln before bridging Anderson Run and reaching the intact walls of Lock 12 after joining the Mason-Dixon Trail. The hike takes you along the lock, and you then bridge the old canal and head northwest in wildflower-rich riparian woods with the Susquehanna River to your right and the rising valley to your left. The Mason-Dixon Trail leads to Mill Creek, past more ruins, then up Mill Creek to Mill Creek Falls, an 18-foot dashing spray of white making a few warm-up tumbles before a primary ledge drop into a shallow, fast shoal that continues dipping toward the Susquehanna River. On your return trip give the ruins and relics a second look, appreciating this historic slice of the Keystone State.

Miles and Directions

0.0 Leave the lower parking area, descending a concrete walkway through a picnic and play area. Reach the Mason-Dixon Trail and head left, crossing Anderson Run on a trail bridge.

0.1 Come to Lock 12. Walk along the lock, then reach a bridge. Here, the Scout Trail heads left. We head right, crossing the bridge over the old canal and then turning left upstream in riparian woodland, where Dutchman's-breeches grow by the thousands in spring.

0.3 Pass the other end of the Scout Trail. Stay straight with the Mason-Dixon Trail.

0.6 Turn up the Mill Creek watershed, passing small cascades. Rise beyond mill ruins, then join River Road to span Mill Creek then turn left, up Mill Creek, still on the Mason-Dixon Trail.

0.7 Mill Creek Falls comes into view from the elevated trail. Drop to the cataract's base and enjoy the lower ledge drop as well as the upper tiers of the waterfall. Backtrack, reexploring old ruins.

1.4 Arrive back at the trailhead, completing the waterfall hike.

Mill Creek Falls dances down to meet the Susquehanna River.

During spring, hikers will see Dutchman's-breeches by the thousands en route to Mill Creek Falls.

Hike Index

About the Author

Johnny Molloy is a writer and adventurer based in Johnson City, Tennessee. He has been exploring and writing about waterfalls and the wilderness since the 1990s. Johnny has explored the splendor of Pennsylvania to hike, camp, paddle, fish, photograph, and chase waterfalls from the Ohio border to the New Jersey state line. His outdoor passion started on a backpacking trip in Great Smoky Mountains National Park while attending the University of Tennessee. That first foray unleashed a love of the outdoors that has led him to spending most of his time hiking, backpacking, canoe camping, and tent camping for the past decades.

Friends enjoyed Johnny's outdoor adventure stories; one even suggested he write a book. He pursued his friend's idea and soon parlayed his love of the outdoors into an occupation. The results of his efforts are over eighty-five guides. His writings include waterfall guidebooks, hiking guidebooks, camping guidebooks, paddling guidebooks, comprehensive guidebooks about specific areas, and true outdoor adventure books covering all or parts of twenty-eight states. Molloy also writes for varied magazines and websites. He continues writing and traveling extensively throughout the United States, endeavoring in a variety of outdoor pursuits. His non-outdoor interests include serving God as a Gideon and University of Tennessee sports. For the latest on Johnny, please visit www.johnnymolloy.com.

THE TEN ESSENTIALS OF HIKING

American Hiking Society recommends you pack the "Ten Essentials" every time you head out for a hike. Whether you plan to be gone for a couple of hours or several months, make sure to pack these items. Become familiar with these items and know how to use them. Learn more at **AmericanHiking.org/hiking-resources**

1. Appropriate Footwear

6. Safety Items (light, fire, and a whistle)

2. Navigation

7. First Aid Kit

3. Water (and a way to purify it)

8. Knife or Multi-Tool

4. Food

9. Sun Protection

5. Rain Gear & Dry-Fast Layers

10. Shelter